America's Constitutional Soul

The Johns Hopkins Series in Constitutional Thought
Sotirios Barber and Jeffrey Tulis, Series Editors

America's Constitutional Soul

Harvey C. Mansfield, Jr.

The Johns Hopkins University Press
Baltimore and London

The Johns Hopkins University Press
701 West 40th Street
Baltimore, Maryland 21211
The Johns Hopkins Press Ltd., London

∞

The paper used in this book meets the minimum requirements of American National
Standard for Information Sciences—Permanence of Paper for Printed Library Materials,
ANSI Z39.48-1984.

Library of Congress Cataloging-in-Publication Data

Mansfield, Harvey Claflin, 1932–
    America's constitutional soul / Harvey C. Mansfield, Jr.
      p.   cm. — (The Johns Hopkins series in constitutional thought)
    Includes bibliographical references and index.
    ISBN 0-8018-4114-3 (alk. paper)
    1. United States—Constitutional history.   2. United States—Politics and government.
3. Conservatism—United States.   I. Title.   II. Series.
JK21.M26   1991
320.5'2'0973—dc20   90–19210

Page 237 constitutes a continuation of the copyright page.

For Samuel H. Beer

Contents

Preface

The chapters of this book are essays written independently of one another during the last ten years to set forth a constitutional view of American politics. Though the topics are different and the occasions diverse, the essays have a common aim that justifies their collection here. The constitutional viewpoint as I see it is a formal one, and it is endangered today by the galloping informality or increasing democratism of our politics.

Form or *formality* is not the first thought one might have when considering our Constitution, and I admit that the point I am making verges on the theoretical. But our political scientists, law professors, and even some of our politicians seem to have lost all sense of what living under a constitution means. This was not the case in 1787 when our Constitution was made. Since then, however, various unwholesome doctrines have arisen, somehow both incendiary and stupefying, that aggravate the tendency of any regime, including democracy, to take itself to an extreme. To give them all one name, let's say *postmodern*, meaning disillusioned with reason, enlightenment, progress, and liberal constitutions. The postmoderns have caused us to lose our pride in the American Constitution, the most glorious product of modern political science and still its best justification. We are induced to forget that constitutional democracy is better democracy—both safer and nobler—and that it is better because it has an order, or structure, or form.

Postmoderns do not as a rule directly recommend more democracy, claiming it to be good even in unlimited amount; rather, they attack every obstacle standing in the way of popular will. This is the galloping informality I object to. My objection has to be theoretical to counter the present danger, which has the character of willful disillusionment with a government that works. But I do not speak here for the sake of theory or *sub specie aeternitatis*. In the Introduction I undertake a defense of the formal in politics through a not so unfriendly or disgusted review of my profession. But I cannot say I am quite satisfied with it, and I have a few suggestions that, if accepted, will guarantee perfection.

The book begins with political commentary on the elections that have made the Reagan revolution. Readers gifted with prescience will already suspect that I favor that change, and all will discover that I am a frank, I trust not a blind, partisan. To tell the truth, I have pretty much given up on liberals as political allies—not, of course, as personal friends or worthy foes. The reason is quite simply that liberals have given up on liberalism, including liberal constitutionalism. They have fallen into bad company, the postmoderns I mentioned who, with their fancy foreign ideas, should have been suspect to liberals and rejected by them. In the preface of a previous book, *The Spirit of Liberalism*, I claimed to be a friend of liberalism, an annoying friend. I am still available on that basis but now I appeal more directly to conservatives, who remain on the whole open to the constitutional argument. The election essays are republished with minor modifications but retaining the original tenses, so that the reader can see as I did (including the rise and fall of my hope for party realignment). In each case I tried to show how the main issue in the election raises a general, constitutional question about American politics.

Part Two takes up *pride*, a particularly political quality ill understood in social science today. Social scientists of all kinds prefer to suppress or sublimate pride with the delusive concept of *interest*. But a matter of pride is at first precisely a consideration that is not in your interest. The connection between constitution and pride is through the formal: the formal, whether a trifling item of dress or an important instance of political conduct, shows what we would sacrifice our comfort to wear and our leisure to defend. Policies such as affirmative action that overlook the factor of pride in constitutional rights, assuming that a benefit however gained is a boon, will miscarry; and political thinking that tries to simplify this complicated topic will mislead.

Parts Three and Four need no explanation. On constitutional origins, I remind everyone of the primacy of the religious issue, to which our liberal constitutionalism was first addressed; I try to establish what was new in the American conception of the separation of powers; and I make a point about the nature of government by consent. In Part Four my theme comes to the fore in five chapters that present the need to defend the forms of the Constitution. I do not sound a call to alarm, because first one must be convinced of the need. One must see what the forms are and why they matter. Forms matter: let that suffice for a preface.

Acknowledgements

This book had its origin in the Eugene McDermott lectures I gave at the University of Dallas in 1984 under the title "Liberal Constitutionalism." Part One consists of articles I wrote for the British journal *Government and Opposition* on American elections in the 1980s, in each of which I tried to raise a constitutional issue. Chapter 4 was the 1984 Leonard Schapiro lecture at the London School of Economics. My thanks go to Professor Ghiţa Ionescu and Mrs. Rosalind Jones for the warm favor and friendship shown to their occasional American correspondent. Chapter 8 was written for one of the many conferences to which my friend Robert A. Goldwin has invited me. To watch him preside is an education in politics and diplomacy more valuable than the talk. A similar association with Henri Cavanna, genial director of the Fondation Internationale des Sciences Humaines, led to the writing of chapters 12 and 13. Chapter 9 was given as the Arthur M. Wilson lecture at Dartmouth College in 1985.

I am grateful to the Lynde and Harry Bradley Foundation and the John M. Olin Foundation, Inc., which have generously supported the Program for Constitutional Government in the Center for American Political Studies at Harvard. My associates in the program, William Kristol and R. Shep Melnick, planted and nourished many of my thoughts. Soterios A. Barber and Jeffrey Tulis, editors of the Johns Hopkins Series in Constitutional Thought, have given me encouragement and sage advice. Eli Feen assembled the manuscript with his characteristic care and intelligence.

America's Constitutional Soul

1
Introduction: Political Science and the Constitution

When it comes to American politics, I am an amateur. I love America at its best, or even at its most characteristic: "only in America." Perhaps this kind of love ought to qualify me as a professional, because it requires one to learn what those two Americas are. But in practice, professionals— elected politicians, journalists, and professors of American politics—look down on amateurs. All would look askance at someone who thinks *amateur* means "lover" instead of "bumbler."

Nonetheless, though an amateur, I have listened to the professionals from an early age (my concern here is with the professional academics), and having become a political scientist of a different sort myself, I have watched things happen for more than forty years.

In that time I have seen two revolutions in political science, the behavioral revolution in the fifties, led by Robert A. Dahl's *A Preface to Democratic Theory* (1956), and the postbehavioral revolution of the late sixties exemplified in Theodore Lowi's *The End of Liberalism* (1969). In what follows I shall concentrate on these two revolutions, and not attempt to draw up a catalog of notable figures and varieties of opinion. The two revolutions were actual events; I am not speaking of ideal types or heuristic constructions. But I shall not cover all positions possible to take or actually taken by the professionals in American politics, and I mention only a few names. Thus I leave it to my colleagues to decide for themselves in the privacy of their consciences whether they have done justice to the American Constitution. There the worst sentence they can receive (as Edmund Burke once said) is a private whipping.

Each of these revolutions was designed to overthrow a reigning method of study that was regarded as stuffy and imprecise. Each wanted to replace what was seen as formalism with its own new realism. The behavioralists objected to putting the focus on institutions as their predecessors had done. To study institutions is to accept the possibility that formal collectivities can determine how politicians act; such study requires one to believe that the purpose of the institution, for example, legislation in Congress, might actually be the motive of those involved in it. It is much more realistic and precise, the behavioralists said, to put aside that presumption, indeed any presumption as to motive, and turn the focus on actual behavior, which they understood as distinct from all the professions of politicians and their academic spokesmen.

The postbehavioralists, in turn, accused the behavioralists of scientistic formalism. In constructing their value-free explanations the behavioralists had turned their backs on the reality of values in politics. They did so in a vain attempt to attain a certain scientific detachment from the object of their inquiry. But in effect they merely blinded themselves to the presence of values, a presence they could understand only in terms of *interests*. Interests are wants that anyone would have in a certain situation, as opposed to idiosyncratic excesses of chance individuals. With that understanding, or misunderstanding, they made solid what is merely contingent and thus gave unwarranted justification to the status quo. According to the postbehavioralists, scientific *detachment* is impossible; what poses as detachment is really a scientific *attitude*, reflecting a value and a dubious one too. The behavioralists not only misdescribe what they see in politics but also fail to understand themselves. Consciously or not, they conceal their values behind the formal mask of their science.

Each of the revolutions I have witnessed has been by and large successful. Apparently the appeal to realism in political science has considerable, perhaps cumulative, force. Soon after revolting the behavioralists captured control of most of the major departments of political science in American universities, most of the journals, and most high offices in the American Political Science Association. There were grumbling and occasional protest from the institutionalists, but little outright resistance. And again in the late sixties, the postbehavioralists had their way with the new orthodoxy, which hardly defended itself against the accusation of involvement in the American system and complicity in its work of political oppression. Some prominent behavioralists confessed their sins and joined the protest of their rebellious students, with the result that now, in the early nineties, the line between behavioralism and postbehavioralism has been obscured to the advantage of the latter. Behavioralists no longer disdain "normative" political science as they used to when they were young and virile; and politically, the whole political science profession has been pulled to the Left by postbehavioralism.

Perhaps with insight, or perhaps because of my incompetence in mathematics, I was never tempted by behavioralism. Therefore I never felt the need for postbehavioralism. Both kinds of revolutionaries, though fighting on the side of realism, seemed to take pride in a wordiness that ill suited their claims to focus on behavior and action. The behavioralists introduced scientific jargon to the profession and thereby, not long after, to the political world. Instead of clarifying the language of politics, this mighty contribution has inflated the pretensions of outside commentators while demeaning the work of practitioners. For example, consider how the word *elite*, used to describe politicians, ignores what they do and gives them a taint of undeserved privilege. And the postbehavioralists, rightly rejecting the obscurantism of their opponents, have filled the air with hoopla over values and precious talk about the self. As an example of such puffery, consider further how the behavioral description of elites has been succeeded by the postbehavioral denunciation of elitists: what were factors in a scientific system have become characters in a political psychodrama. Neither *elite* nor *elitist* is close to the reality of *politician*, a person who accepts one's elevation over others as a matter of course, or of necessity, but wonders what to do with one's position and how to stay there.

It seemed to me, therefore, that the pursuit of realism has its own formalism, revealed in a peculiar style of talk that is at some distance from the language of politicians, although politicians in our day quickly pick up vogue expressions from universities. I began to think that the resort to formalization by those seeking to penetrate the formalities is no accident, that there is something necessary to formal expression in the study of American, or any, politics. Both behavioralists and postbehavioralists tried to find what is real by looking under the appearances or the formalities, taking for granted an opposition between the formal and the real. The formal, both parties supposed, does not represent anything real but merely covers it up; the point, then, is to unmask the formal. Could it be that this general strategy is mistaken? That the formal is, if not the whole of reality, a part—even the greater part?

In America, the forms and formalities of politics are stated in a written document that has the force and dignity of law—indeed, of fundamental law. Perhaps the common mistake of the realists is to focus on the extraconstitutional, rather than on the Constitution; or more accurately, to consider the extraconstitutional *as opposed to*, rather than *as a part of*, the constitutional. An argument had to be made on behalf of the Constitution—not only for its wisdom but even more for its explanatory power in the study of American politics. To provide the constitutional argument is the common purpose of the essays in this book.

To restore the constitutional, it is not enough to return to the "institutional" political scientists, much as I esteem them and prefer them to their successors. For one thing, the institutionalists did not put up much of a fight against the behavioralists. They objected, and most of them refused to change their ways; but the objections usually took the form of grumbling in private or oblique allusions in print. One had the feeling—this was a point cultivated by the behavioralists—that they were merely set in their ways rather than possessed of a reasoned justification for a focus on institutions. Indeed, I do not know of any reasoned defense of the institutionalist point of view. No institutionalist responded at length in print to Robert Dahl's provocative book. What opposition there was to the behavioralists came from political theorists, not from the specialists in American politics who were most directly affected by the behavioral revolution. The theorists directed their fire on the moral obtuseness of behavioralism as well as, of course, on its relegation of the classics of political theory to an antiquated, irrelevant past. Theorists did not make the point that the political science of American politics was going to deteriorate. In any case, their debates made little sense to the institutionalists, and theoretical defenders who were fighting seemingly unnecessary battles were not much appreciated. In sum, the institutionalists had almost nothing to say for themselves, a fact their students noticed. Some of them joined the other side; others compromised as if there were no issue in play; some others held to—but the trouble was that there was not any faith, only a practice.

The deeper reason for the easy defeat of institutional political science was that it agreed with the antiformalism of the behavioralists (and the postbehavioralists too, when they came along). The name *institutionalists* was applied to them after the behavioral revolution, when something was needed to designate their stubborn reluctance to leave their home base in Congress, the executive, or the judiciary to venture forth on the high sea of "behavior." They had no definition, or even any definite ideas, of *institution* to cling to. When, for example, a generalized notion of *decision making* made its appearance in political science, denying the distinction among legislating, executing, and judging—thus threatening the noun *institution* through an attack on its supporting verbs—no instinct warned them to protest this deliberate destruction. Their desire for self-preservation was not equipped with a sense of danger, and, discounting public proclamations of revolution, they underestimated the ambition of the behavioralists. They thought they could rely on their own knowledge and good sense. They believed that the toleration they showed to the behavioralists would be reciprocated.

Although most of the institutions to which the institutionalists were attached were constitutional, they did not see them as inspired by the Constitution. Although they knew far more than most political scientists today, they were not, as a rule, students of the making of the Constitution. They did not see the period of the making of the Constitution as a constituting or founding of the institutions they knew so well; indeed, the idea of *founding* was not familiar to them. In the books they wrote and in the courses they taught, they did not begin from the Constitution except to make a quick departure: "that's not the way things are done now."

Of course, specialists in constitutional law such as Herman Pritchett and Robert McCloskey studied the origins of judicial review in the founding period, and they were constitutionalists in a lively sense. But of all parts of political science, constitutional law suffered most from the behavioral revolution. The study of cases implied that argument and justification were important, perhaps a cause of "behavior"; and the focus on landmarks such as *Marbury v. Madison* suggested that singular instances of deliberate decision could be crucial. Both these elements of traditional constitutional law were regarded with hostility by behavioralism, which favors the nonverbal and seeks to quantify. For a time, constitutional law was hardly studied in graduate schools or published in political science journals. But if the behavioral revolution was most overwhelming in this sector, it was also the least productive. To quantify the working of the judiciary proved difficult or impossible. "Jurimetrics" died a quick death, and "judicial behavior" has been unable to free itself from the constraint of certain authoritative cases. And this least successful application of behavioralism was the most vulnerable to the postbehavioral revolution, which has restored constitutional law with a vengeance—but also with open disrespect for the Constitution.

Most institutionalists were, and remain, political Progressives. Although they were often perceptive and critical observers, they had a partisan stance that came immediately from Franklin Roosevelt's New Deal and more remotely from Theodore Roosevelt's and Woodrow Wilson's progressivism. The progressive source of opinion is diverse and not easily characterized; it spilled over partisan distinctions and nourished and influenced many whom it did not unite. One central tendency common to Progressives and New Dealers, however, is dissatisfaction with the working of the Constitution.

Woodrow Wilson, perhaps the most powerful intellect in the movement, was the first American president to criticize the Constitution. Theodore Roosevelt, though proclaiming himself "a steward of the people" eager to exploit the silences of the Constitution and to infuse it with an alien spirit of populism, nonetheless retained an appreciation of constitutional forms and was sensitive to the constitutional difficulty he had created. Wilson went further. His objection was not that the Constitution was being perverted or that it worked badly because citizens and politicians were not living up to their duties under the Constitution. The Constitution itself was at fault in its original design; it was a Newtonian mechanism intended to work by action and counteraction, not meant to get anywhere, not meant to make progress. Though the Constitution did not need to be discarded, it required a new spirit of populist leadership to reanimate and redirect its obsolete structures. The formal constitutional structures, in this view, operate negatively to prevent action by government. The end of the Constitution—for which its forms are designed—is to produce an equilibrium among the separated powers, not to move the whole government toward the solution of problems, in the direction of progress. Left to itself, the Constitution brings stalemate or deadlock. One easily recognizes the Wilsonian inspiration behind James MacGregor Burns's *Deadlock of Democracy* (1963). Burns is a New Dealer, a biographer of Franklin Roosevelt, and a prominent institutionalist in political science.

Accompanying the progressive politicians were progressive historians, J. Allen Smith and Charles Beard (cited in note 2 of chapter 13) at their head, who offered the first debunking of the American founders in American historiography. They cut the founders down to size, arguing that the Constitution was the product of, and protection for, the founders' own selfish interests. Smith and Beard implied that there was no distinction between the politics of constitution making and ordinary politics, that no "founding" had taken place that is entitled to special respect. Their researches have not held up, their methods have been found to be lacking in science, and Beard's economic interpretation of the Constitution has been superseded by a more fashionable concern for ideology. The tone is not so critical now, but that is because the debunking has been accomplished. Not only the aura but also the idea of founding have been lost. Gordon Wood's influential book *The Creation of the American Republic, 1776–1787* (published in 1969) treats the Constitution as the work of an oligarchy, a product of the elitism of the "worthy," he says disapprovingly.

One should mention, besides the historians, the legal realists Oliver Wendell Holmes, Roscoe Pound, and Benjamin Cardozo, who helped fashion the notion of the *living Constitution*. The living Constitution is not one constituted as a whole and developing in accordance with its beginning but an artifice capable of many possibilities not determined by its founding that are disclosed as the Constitution lurches along, or "lives." And behind the politicians, the historians, and the legal theorists was the philosophy of pragmatism, above all opposed to anything smacking of formalism.

Pragmatism seeks a science of the emergent, the evolving, the developing as opposed to fixed conceptions defined by formal boundaries. It looks for the play of adjustment and compromise rather than statements of principle that may prove to be boastful or deceptive. Pragmatism is result-oriented in everything except with regard to itself; for any human contrivance may fail the pragmatic test but (it is thought) the test never fails. Thus progress as conceived by Progressives was not so much the motion of some fixed thing toward a better state as an evolution in which the institution changes by adjusting to its reception. The comparison necessary to a firm sense that progress has occurred becomes difficult because little or nothing remains of the original by which to judge its improvement. The Progressives surely regarded the democratization of the Constitution as an advance, but in their pragmatism they lost clear sight of the Constitution, which should have been more democratic in their view, and the comprehensive vision they denied to the founders had also to be withheld from reformers. The historical view of institutions adjusted to their context is strictly inconsistent with the progressive view that wants to criticize contexts, but the American pragmatists managed to retain their reforming optimism despite their kinship with German historicism. Indeed they thought that being in tune with the times made their progressivism more realistic, hence gave them greater reason for optimism. In fact, however, their distrust of formal institutions made it difficult for them to identify and measure progress, and thus to give credit for it either to politicians or the people. Was the American Constitution fated to be democratized, or was there any merit in the change?

Herbert Croly's *The Promise of American Life*, a progressive standard published in 1909, is no longer read, but it shows what informed the constitutional thinking of the earlier institutionalists. The Constitution, Croly asserts, is "on the whole an admirable system of law and an efficient organ of government" (p. 351). But with this praise he means to say that it is not in need of radical amendment now; he does not endorse, or attempt at length to understand, the principles of the Constitution. Instead, he claims that the attitude of the Federalists, representing the interest of well-to-do citizens in stability and property, was "distrust of the democratic principle"—by which he means their antagonism to it. Yet despite being tainted in its fundamental provisions, which cannot be modified, the Constitution is adaptable by amendment and interpretations, and capable of being transformed through specific changes. To sum up: although Croly thinks that the Constitution is fundamentally wrong, it should not be overthrown because it need not; and it need not be overthrown because it is adaptable and its adaptability is unrelated to its principle. Croly is no revolutionary, for the institutions against which one might revolt do not have the power to prevent change that will occur by adaptation.

Croly's picture of the Constitution is not so different from the one to be found in the founding document of the behavioralists—the only book to attempt a comprehensive comparison of behavioralist theory with pre-behavioralist political science—Robert A. Dahl's *A Preface to Democratic Theory* (1956). Dahl, too, believes that the Constitution is fundamentally undemocratic, thus wrong; but his dislike does not reach the level of opposition, much less revolution, since he agrees that the formal provisions of the Constitution do not have much effect. He goes further than Croly in his concern for the extraconstitutional over the constitutional and in failing to give the founders credit even for making an adaptable constitution. Croly's political distrust of the founders' Constitution becomes Dahl's methodological suspicion of constitutions as such.

Thus the contrast between the institutionalists and the behavioralists in regard to the Constitution is far from complete.[1] In fact, Dahl compares his political science with Madison's—not Woodrow Wilson's, which was based on his own critique of Madison, not so different from Dahl's. To the extent, then, that institutional political scientists were Progressives or New Dealers—and most of them were—their concern for the Constitution that orders and animates institutions was compromised. The institutionalists were not in need of behavioralism to call their attention to the importance of the extraconstitutional. They had discovered and studied parties and pressure groups (a more lively and expressive name than "interest groups"), institutions not mentioned in the Constitution. If the institutionalists had been forced at the point of a gun to define *institution*, they would probably have tried to make their definition as formless as possible: an institution is a practice that emerges and grows without a principle to guide it that is necessary to its existence; it is "instituted" without a mindful beginning and proceeds toward a plurality of possible ends; it has a history rather than an essence. This would already be a behavioral definition. The behavioral and the historical have a kinship hidden beneath the scientific formalism that seems to keep them distinct.

Institutional political science needs to be made more aware of its constitutional basis. Institutionalists do have an inchoate sense of what a constitution means in their practice of adopting and defending the institution they study. Montesquieu spoke of the tendency in Britain, the country of his rational constitution, for citizens to advance their partisan causes behind the institutions of the constitution—the legislature or the executive—that were available to be captured and used. Naturally, citizens would change parties from one branch to the other as it became

convenient, just as in America Democrats and Republicans have exchanged their institutional loyalties between the presidency and Congress
from Franklin Roosevelt to Ronald Reagan. But institutional political
scientists, loyal to the subject of their study, maintain their integrity by
remaining a defender of the president or of Congress despite a change in
the party holding the institution. The possibility of such loyalty should
help political scientists realize that an institution is a form with varying
content, for example, Congress with various members and tendencies
over the years, whose worth does not depend on any single immediate
result. It should enable them to sense, further, that a form can be a cause
of behavior, not always a mask behind which the real action takes place.
Institutional loyalty implies a certain elevation above the immediate context as opposed to a *pragmatic* attitude that wants to exploit the institution as the means to an external end. But even the pragmatist, as I said,
is not pragmatic about pragmatism; and the Progressives may have had an
abstract love for progressive institutions such as primaries and referenda
that would outlast their use for progressive ends. (Or would Progressives
learn a lesson from the tax revolts of our time?)

If it is possible, then, to be an institutionalist, why is it not possible to
be a constitutionalist? Why is it not *necessary*? If one sees in oneself a
certain elevation above the bare, immediate result, one should extend the
recognition to others, more gifted, who were in a situation in which it was
necessary to look at the whole. When the institutionalist reflects on the
staying power of institutions, he must admit the possibility that they were
formed for a purpose. The purpose may indeed have been an immediate
response to provocation, as happens frequently when legislators get the
urge to pass a law; and afterward the institution acquires a "life of its
own." But what happens by accident can happen by intent: perhaps some
wise superlegislators—call them founders—anticipate the need for a popular legislature to blow off steam by passing unwise measures. The possibility of constitutional design must be seriously investigated and not
quickly dismissed or referred to another desk at which someone does
political theory.

It is not common sense but something quite different—pragmatism—
that systematically denigrates the importance of whatever is formal in
politics and in life generally. Common sense knows that when people
"dress up" or otherwise behave formally they conceal certain things. They
do not publicly perform ablutions or other activities that are always done
in private even though they are very necessary. But of course on formal
occasions people do not even behave as they normally do when others see
them. They cover over defects they are normally content to let appear;
they try to look their best.

Despite accusations prevalent in the late sixties, there is nothing fake or phony in this behavior. The very lack of ease and stiltedness in those unused to formal occasions, as well as the polish in those who are accustomed, testify that formal behavior is meant to be obvious and recognizable as such. When we are formal, we are not confidence men trying to conceal where we come from and who we are. Quite to the contrary, we are trying to show who we are by actions that declare what we think is important. We dress up when we are attending church, going out on the town, seeing someone important, or passing a milestone in life. The things we conceal are concealed so as to reveal the things we desire to reveal. The formal is fundamentally a self-revelation, only secondarily a self-concealment; and the latter is instrumental to the former. The formal is a fact of human life, something to be explained, not explained away. If it is pragmatic to face facts, it is pragmatic to accept not only the existence but the sovereign importance of formal activities that people take trouble, nonpragmatically, to carry out. When we "do it right," we usually mean ceremonially, not efficiently. Indeed efficiency disappears into ceremony; an efficient wedding is either a correct one or none at all.

How, then, is the formal a fact of politics? In America the formal political principle is that all men are created equal. This is stated in the Declaration of Independence, one of our two founding documents (a document being paper reserved for formalities). The other document, the Constitution, is inspired by the principle while also introducing important formal qualifications to it necessary to make it serve a political purpose. For the equality of all men might seem at first (as in the state of nature in the philosophy of Hobbes and Locke) to foreclose the possibility of any political ordering enabling some to govern others. The principle of equality was announced so as to make clear that however widely Americans had held it, it was now formally adopted as their ruling principle. Revolutionaries, while busy changing things that matter the most to them, usually take the time to make it plain to all in some formal declaration that a new regime is in power. If they do not, it is because they are too weak to do so, or because they merely intend a change in personnel (but that change, too, is announced).

A pragmatist might respond, however: if revolutionaries want to waste their time in formalities, what is that to us living after the day of battle, when boastful cries seem out of place and no longer inspire action? The objection would apply also to the solemnities of constitution making which do not anticipate the jostle and friction in the actual working of institutions. In any case, the pragmatist might continue, Americans do not live up to the principle of equality, which in many aspects of our lives is a mere formality.

It is of course true that Americans are not all equal and that one would go very wrong to describe their politics as if they all lived in the same way. But the reason is not that formal principles are meaningless. It is partly that full equality is not intended and partly that it is impossible. The actual equality of living in the same way is precluded by the American belief in individual rights, which yield a society characterized by pluralism and diversity. These are two vogue words Americans use to dress up their inequalities, since one cannot have difference without inequality. Their use illustrates the power of the principle of equality, which consists in silencing contrary, competing principles. Inequalities cannot be simply suppressed if they are part of the truth about human beings, but they can be subordinated to the main truth according to Americans, which is equality. So we suppose that pluralism is the consequence of indulging equal rights rather than a forthright admission of the inevitability of inequality.

In this way of handling a truth uncomfortable to us we show that we do not mean full or actual equality as our principle. Our formal principle is one self-consciously adopted as such, intended to maintain a discrepancy between formal and actual equality. A *right* is a formal notion with varying context according to the choice of its holder. Equal rights, therefore, cannot but be a formal equality. Americans live up to their principle when they maintain equal rights as opposed to actual equality, and of course they do not always do so. But when they do not, they suffer the sort of shame and discomfort that was evident in the controversy over slavery in America even before it came to civil war.

Most important, in America one cannot confront the principle of equality in public. No one in politics, or even in the universities, can argue on behalf of inequality and expect to be more than barely tolerated, much less heard. In the sense that they will not listen to any other principle, Americans live by the principle of equality. In that sense they "live up to" it—a revealing phrase that makes a further point. The formal, while making manifest who actually rules and by what principle, states the rulers' aim or intention. The formal principle shows the rulers' behavior in the light of their intention; it is a standard to live up to, enabling the rulers and also outside observers to judge a society by the light it holds to itself. A political science, therefore, that looks to the form looks to the end, an *end* not in the Machiavellian sense of outcome but in the sense of intention. The ruling power in a society is not a mere accumulation of behaviors in which it has successfully contested inferior powers, as if it had no aim or any aim. That power, rather, is headed in a certain direction; it is a power *for some purpose*, not an abstract superiority. The form coincides with, or is identical to, the end in the sense that it is going there, but not in the sense that it has arrived. In our example, America's formal principle of equality indicates the direction it wants to go, not that it has succeeded.

Thus, the form of a society is both the same and not the same as its end. That it is the same refutes the behavioralist belief that the informal, extraconstitutional powers behind the scenes are greater than the formal power. That it is not the same enables us to see how, contrary to behavioralism, the formal power can be a cause. For if the formal power cannot guarantee the result it wants, it can indicate the direction toward which it wants to go and thus become the cause of going if not getting there.

That is the sense in which the office of the presidency—a form—can be the cause of a president's behavior. Being in the office does not ensure that a president will act, as we say, "presidentially"; some presidents have been quite disappointing. But why were we disappointed? Because we had some better notion of the office derived in part from an understanding of the Constitution and in part from the formation of the office by the best presidents. The formal cause is an end that attracts, as distinguished from a motive that pushes. It is therefore somewhat different from what we call an *interest*. It would be the interest of a president to defend the powers and prerogatives of the presidency; this is a pushing motive that would operate almost unfailingly on any president, even a mediocre one. All presidents since 1973, for example, have refused or avoided compliance with the War Powers Act, which to them seems to curtail the president's emergency power. But is it in a president's "interest" to be a great president? Here the element of aspiration enters and seems to call for a name nobler than *interest*—perhaps *virtue*.[2] Whereas interest requires no uncommon exertion or imagination but comes automatically, as it were, with one's situation, virtue in the full sense is rare, risky, and difficult, and is at most prompted or suggested by the situation, not dependably assured. A political science that knows how to recognize a formal cause is open to the possibility of virtue; otherwise it is not. Behavioralism knows only the pushing causes that work unfailingly, or almost so, or with a calculable probability. Insisting on prediction, it sees only the predictable.

Of course, one must not despise the predictable. The American founders, as we shall see in chapter 10, were well aware of the distinction between virtue and interest but deliberately obscured it. With good reason they distrusted the formal principle of republicanism, which is hostile to strong government; and they wished to introduce a new republicanism having a better appreciation for the predictable, behavioral consequences of the principles of all previous republics. So they fashioned a government of separated powers that would work with part interest, part virtue—and with the distinction between them covered up. At one point in *The Federalist* Alexander Hamilton implies that it is to the interest of a president to set risky and lofty goals for himself. He means that the office of the presidency encourages virtue, but he wants to call that virtue "interest" so as to keep it within the bounds of the republican principle and not suggest the idea of aristocracy or monarchy.

Such subtlety is beyond the ken of the behavioralists, and it is lost on the postbehavioralists. The latter accept the behavioralist view that the American regime is a system of interests arranged predictably to support the wealthy, but they deny any necessity to the system. They laugh at the ridiculous claim of the behavioralists to have discovered the nature of politics when in fact they have been seduced by a bad idea and are sleepwalking under the spell of the American Dream. Thus the postbehavioralists have the merit of reintroducing ideas as causes of political behavior. *Interests* are not really material—hence nonideological as they may appear to be; they derive from an idea, which in turn derives from a value.

What is a value? A *value* is a verbal noun named for its source in valuing, a mysterious activity that takes place at a level below rationality. A value comes dressed up in reason, or "rationalized," but its inner truth cannot be judged by reason because it is prior to reason. In this view (which has gained adherents on the Supreme Court) the American Constitution expresses "constitutional values" that are the cause—the pushing cause—of its provisions and principles. So the postbehavioralists turn out to agree with the behavioralists in reducing the formal principle to informal, private causes behind it. They merely substitute *values* for *interests*. If the merit of the postbehavioralists is to have rediscovered the importance of ideas, their demerit is to misinterpret ideas as values. Although they wish to recover some sense of the public or community in political science, they fail because values are intrinsically private and idiosyncratic. Values do not make claims on the attention of other human beings by appealing to some common ground. Values merely assert the feelings of the valuer, and it is up to others to bow or get out of the way. When the principle of a society is taken to be its values, the formal is once again reduced to the interests behind it. What is a value but an overstated interest distorted by affectation?

In this brief defense of the importance of the formal in political science I do not claim to have settled or even raised all the relevant issues. I have been addressing not the methodologists in the profession but rather practicing political scientists for whom methodologists are both bullies and parasites. Methodologists can always be dealt with by calling in toughs of a higher order. But perhaps practicing political scientists could learn to defend themselves without depending on political philosophers to bail them out when in trouble.

Political scientists should recognize that political science has always been essential to American political life, and they should develop greater respect for the consequences of what they think. The new republicanism of the Constitution—a theme of this volume—was made possible by American improvements in political science. So says Publius, author of *The Federalist*. Changes were made in both republicanism and constitutionalism as previously understood so that they could be brought together for mutual aid in a new union of ideas and institutions.

Previous republicanism had maintained that republics needed to demand more of their peoples than other regimes, hence required virtue. To get virtue, it was necessary for republics to be small, strict, and homogeneous. The American founders gave that opinion a cold bath in reality. They saw that if their republic was to fare better than previous republics, it would have to be imperial in size, diverse in population, and commercial rather than martial. In modeling the government, the American republic would have to appeal to interest as well as virtue so as to be open to ambition. These changes had their origin in the liberal constitutionalism of Locke and Montesquieu. But those thinkers were not republicans and however democratic their political foundations may have been, their operative political principle was not the equality of all men. On the one hand, the American founders showed how constitutionalism could become popular, and on the other, they showed how republicanism could be made viable.

The achievement was recognized at the time, and even boasted of in *The Federalist*; but since the Progressives, it had been lost to sight. Ever anxious over the influence of the rich, the Progressives began to think of Publius as spokesman for powerful and sinister interests rather than as an author with a subtle and complicated analysis of interests. *The Federalist* fell out of favor and came to be despised as mere party propaganda—and for the antipopular party too. But in 1958, Martin Diamond wrote an article in the *American Political Science Review* entitled "Democracy and *The Federalist*" that challenged the Progressives' presumption, showed with the necessary distinctions how *The Federalist* was indeed democratic, and rescued the work from neglect. Diamond pointed out that, to appreciate the argument of *The Federalist*, one must treat it as a whole and to begin with, therefore, take seriously its pseudonymous author Publius as an evident sign from three of the founders that in writing the papers they intended a community of thought.

Diamond was joined by Herbert Storing, Harry Jaffa, Ralph Lerner, Marvin Meyers, and others in the ambiance of Leo Strauss at the time, who attempted to apply the notion of founding from the classical political science of Plato and Aristotle to the "founding fathers." The classical notion describes in the best case a comprehensive work of deliberation, not beyond partisanship but beyond ordinary, shortsighted partisan advantage. It is in the light of the best case that one should assess lesser creations—most or all actual regimes—looking from the standpoint of what they might be so as to render justice to their best motives rather than squinting from underneath to spy and disclose what is ordinary, banal, deluded, or base. This current of thought has gathered momentum and spread its influence in recent decades, but it has not yet had its full impact on institutional political scientists, to whom I recommend it.

The institutional political science of our day, with its studies of constituted groups and accidental eddies of interaction in politics, is part of, and heir to, a grand movement in modern political science dating from Hobbes and Locke of which it is barely aware. That movement is both less and more than a comprehensive founding of the classical kind. It is less because it wants to establish a limited government that does not attempt to rule over economic and cultural life directly through laws on what can be said and done (though of course minimal and indirect regulation is necessary). Such political science can be called *liberal* because it is more concerned with liberty than with virtue, though it wants both. And it can be considered *institutional* because it believes it can achieve through institutions—in government either a sovereign power or separated powers—what previously was thought to be attainable only by inculcating virtue. Institutional political science is realistic since it does not try to "change human nature" but takes men as they are found, or even a little worse, preoccupied with self-preservation and self-interest; and then it uses incentives (as we say today) to channel those interests through institutions toward wholesome, or at any rate harmless, goals.

Yet with the realism of the new political science comes an ambition far beyond that of classical political science. Although the new program was for limited government, the new political scientists originally hoped by this means to put an end to revolutionary partisanship, which had been caused, according to the liberal analysis, by putting too much faith in virtue. The modern constitution, or system of institutions, would first moderate (if not altogether deny) the claim of virtue to rule and then balance the interests of society through representation so that none could feel so despised as to be disposed toward revolution. Though less comprehensive than a classical founding, the modern constitution is in principle permanent, having made allowance for changes arising from non-revolutionary parties and provision for constitutional amendment. Now since modern political science believes it has found a remedy for political disease, it would be unnecessary and wrong to continue the calm, standoffish unconcern of classical political science toward active political life. A more capable political science should be more forward with advice, more ready to accept responsibility. The American Constitution was the product of a political science confident of its competence to introduce a new era of human liberty.

Since then confidence has fallen off, but not always because of better understanding. For the founders, a fair prospect for America's experiment in republican government depended on a distinction between democracy and republic to the advantage of the latter, clearly made in *Federalist* 10. It is true that they distrusted democracy, but not because they loved aristocracy. They distrusted democracy for the same reason that they rejected aristocracy—because they distrusted human nature. "Men are not angels." To make popular government work well, they thought it necessary to prevent a representative, constitutional republic from descending to the extremes of democracy, in which the people under the influence of demagogues make all decisions actively and immediately. Such degeneration, called "majority faction" by Publius, is very likely in a republic because it is easy to confuse the people's will with their judgment.

What prevents the confusion, and thus maintains republics as opposed to democracies (we say, *pure* democracies) is a certain constitutional space between the people and their government allowing the government a certain, limited independence so that it can develop a certain character and responsibility of its own. Constitutional space is provided by *institutions* (including federalism, which gives literal space a constitutional dimension), and institutions are forms giving a characteristic dignity, or plain stubbornness, to whomever their incumbents may be. As forms, institutions stand as obstacles to the immediate gratification of popular will, while at the same time facilitating and effecting the ultimate governance of the people. Only with a certain distance from the people does a government serve it well. The founders believed that the main business of a political scientist is to set up and defend the institutions defining constitutional space (this is my term).

Our political scientists, behavioral and postbehavioral, seem to believe to the contrary, that political science should knock down institutions and close any distance between people and government. They want more democracy, and yet more—up to a limit they do not know how to define; and the realism of their attack on constitutional formalities (from which I began this introduction) is designed to get it. One result is that political scientists no longer know how to identify demagogues. The behavioralist says that a demagogue is merely a statesman misliked and denies that it is possible to "operationalize" the distinction. The postbehavioralist, disdaining methodology, sings in unison with the demagogue. But the demagogue is the death of democracy, and a political science that cannot identify a Huey Long or Joseph McCarthy needs to operationalize its operationalism. For the difference between demagogue and statesman is clearer and more important than a methodology, and the methodology should be judged by its capacity to distinguish them, not the reverse.

The more informality there is, the less time you have to wait for what you want—unless you want something reasonable. Political scientists have become rampant democratizers because they have lost faith in reason. But, lacking faith in reason, they ought to lose confidence in political science, in themselves. Yet they do not; they continue to behave as if they had a profession. And what is a profession but a formal institution? All I ask for is a little self-knowledge.

Part I

The Constitutional Meaning
of Reagan's Electoral Victories

2

The 1980 Election: Toward Constitutional Democracy?

The presidential election just held* appears to have been a momentous event. It was the greatest repudiation of an incumbent president and party in America since that of Hoover and the Republicans in 1931. Predicted by no one—not by political scientist, pollster, or politician—this was as much a surprise to joyful Republicans as to luckless Democrats. The voters had not discussed the matter much, except in deprecatory terms borrowed from the media, and on the morning after they too looked around among themselves with wonder and satisfaction.

It could hardly be believed, as Carter's pollster asserted, that everyone turned to Reagan on the last day when the hostages held in Iran failed to appear. Something so considerable must have been meditated, or at least prepared; and the misfortune for Carter does not explain why the Democratic senators, who were not involved with Iran, were voted out. Perhaps the large number of "undecideds" were Reagan voters, too embarrassed to confess their decision to callers they suspected were unsympathetic. Or perhaps—a wishful fantasy of mine—the voters deliberately did not disclose their intention to the pollsters since they knew that sovereignty stays alive only with an occasional surprise. The voters may have sensed that they can be exploited if they can be predicted.

Some Rejected Explanations

In the difficult task of interpreting this result, certain negatives are clear. This was not merely a repudiation of Jimmy Carter's presidency. The

*Chapter 2 was first published as "The American Election: Towards Constitutional Democracy," *Government and Opposition* (1981): 3–18.

voters installed a Republican Senate, as noted, together with thirty-three additional Republicans in the House of Representatives; and they did this to a Democratic Congress they had kept throughout the Nixon years, including Nixon's landslide victory in 1972, a 24-point margin compared to Reagan's 10. And that Congress had not been notably subservient to Carter. To do so, working-class, union, Catholic, and Southern Democrats deserted in droves.

Nor was this an election staged by the media between two shallow candidates representing nothing serious. That was what the independent candidate John Anderson believed, but it was he, not Carter and Reagan, whose campaign was created rather than reported by the media. Carter is no rhetorician. He cannot orate, and he is so incapable of persuasion that he cannot convince himself, much less others, of anything. With this inability goes an insensitivity to how he looks to others, which he has never overcome despite all his media consultants. He did not see that his careful weighing of difficult decisions, when not conveyed with confident argument, came across as vacillation. His campaign speeches consisted of unconnected statements addressed to the wholesome fears of the diverse sections of the Democratic coalition. He did not realize that these statements added up to nothing and that they made him look nasty. He was much disliked by the reporters.

The media were hostile to Reagan because of his opinions. He was frightened out of candor by slips early in his campaign that were unduly magnified, and he resorted to making things seem easy. His hopefulness, good nature, and libertarian views ("getting government off the people's backs") inclined him away from stressing exertion, strain, and sacrifice—words that came naturally to Carter even when he had nothing to suggest. Reagan himself gave the impression of firmness without asking for it in his fellow citizens, and he told Americans that their affairs were in a mess, but not in a crisis. The dissatisfaction with all three candidates that was widely reported during the campaign—"none of the above"—appears in retrospect to have been dissatisfaction with Carter and his party. If the Democrats had seemed satisfactory, only a grumbling minority would have remained to compare Reagan's qualities to Goldwater's, Nixon's and Ford's, probably to Reagan's advantage.

The campaign was conducted under difficult conditions imposed by the technology and habits of modern media. Whereas a presidential candidate used to offer set speeches on different topics, this campaign was focused on the evening television news and the one or two minutes of "exposure" that each major candidate could expect on the show. Even these moments were not left at the candidate's disposal but introduced and analyzed by newsmen who were not to be taken in by mere words and considered it their responsibility not to let the candidates have their say. As a result, Reagan's "one-liners" and Carter's blunt assertions were almost required of them. Carter was a more effective candidate than president, but a very poor president ill served by his virtues: by his intelligence, which made him linger and revise; by his quickness, which made him evasive; and by his courage, which made him unafraid to give up on his initiatives. Reagan was an excellent campaigner, as good a speaker as one can be without eloquence. He has been consistently underestimated by those who seek refuge from simple truths in self-deceiving complexities, and the question concerning him is not whether he is slow, stiff, stupid, wild, and hard, but whether he has the sternness of character needed under trial. In the campaign he had no trouble rounding off the sharp edges of his opinions. But he did not reveal what he would choose when choice hurts and how he would get the people to agree.

Also to be rejected as insufficient are interpretations that confine the desire for change in the electorate to economic or foreign policy. Though Carter's incompetence in both was no secret, again the Democratic Congress did not have to be blamed. There is evidence in polls that the public accepts the intractability of inflation and unemployment, and that it does not think America can have its way in the world by bluster. But it was not just the money and not just the power; it was a matter of virtue in work and thrift and in defending one's honor. Reagan promised not merely better times, but more specifically that workers and savers would be rewarded, and that America's leaders would stop feeling guilty and start supporting its friends. Economic and foreign policy were the two salient issues in a larger whole.

The Repudiation of the Values of the Sixties

What seemed to happen in the election of 1980 was a general repudiation of the values of the 1960s. To those who espouse them they are: the Third World, human rights, liberation, freedom of choice, equal rights for women, freedom for irreligion, rights of defendants, gay rights, consumerism, school desegregation, affirmative action, free expression, and welfare rights. To those who oppose them, they are, respectively: lack of patriotism, abandoning one's friends, lack of self-restraint, easy abortion, interchangeability of the sexes, atheism in schools, increased rights for criminals, respectability for homosexuals, contempt for producers, forced busing, reverse discrimination, license to pornographers, and living off others. Although one might wish to pick and choose among these items, they seem to make a package. Together they are the values of self-expression, a strange combination of idealism and hedonism characteristic of our day and recognizable by all who live in free countries, not only by Americans.

Self-expression in the 1960s was rightly called "radical." It has a political consequence that sharply distinguishes it from liberalism, both from mundane liberalism that builds upon self-preservation and the right to life and from the higher liberalism that looks to human rationality. As opposed to these liberal opinions, which insist on fear of others or respect for them, there is nothing in self-expression that requires or encourages one self to seek the consent of others when expressing itself. Self-expression is not concerned with problems of government; among human rights, the right to consent to government, which was the protection of all other rights, according to the Declaration of Independence, gets no attention. Those who are "into" self-expression do not care whether they gain their point by persuading a majority.

It is no accident that most of the policies associated with these values have been begun by parts of the government not directly dependent on an elected majority. Above all, the judiciary through both the Warren and the Burger Courts has initiated a series of major policies and sustained them, without apology, against majority opinion and the protests of elected representatives. The judiciary has acted, it claims, only in response to urgent calls for justice from the Constitution, which coincidentally has been developing toward the values of self-expression at a pace far exceeding the ability of a majority to keep up with it. It is also no accident, therefore, that the opponents of these values have been called the "Silent Majority" (in Nixon's time) and lately have called themselves the "Moral Majority." The "Moral Majority"—to be sure, a self-serving name adopted by fundamentalist preacher Jerry Falwell—supplied some of the cutting edge, the "Silent Majority" most of the weight, of the Republican victory in the November election. This majority seems not only to have disapproved of the values of the 1960s but also to have felt that government was out of control because it was beyond the reach of the majority. It turned on Jimmy Carter with anger because in 1976 he had appeared to share its feeling but during his term as president he had forgotten the majority and given himself over to bumblers and sophisticates. This was an election in which the majority went beyond the assertion of its opinion to the reassertion of its right to rule.

It might seem quite superfluous for the majority to reassert its right to rule in a country that since the sixties has been enjoying or suffering a movement of opinion called a resurgence of "populism." For the values of self-expression described above are presented as popular values; if not held by the people, they advance the cause of the people. Why would it be necessary for democrats (or Democrats) to repudiate the Carter administration, which was devoted to making government as good as the people and in particular to the expunging of every element or practice in government and society that could be labeled "elitism"? To see why it was reasonable and necessary for democracy to assert itself against populism, one must understand what this populism is, how it became established, and how it has governed. That a new populism could have gained hold of American politics is a measure of the decline in the understanding and practice of *constitutional* democracy that has taken place. Lest the account I have given be taken for too optimistic a view of Reagan's victory, we must remind ourselves that a silent or moral majority is not necessarily a constitutional one.

The turnout at the election was 52.4 percent of potential voters, compared to 54.3 percent in 1976, 55.7 percent in 1972, 60.9 percent in 1968, and 61.8 percent in 1964. These percentages are difficult to compare with percentages in elections in other free countries because they compare the number of actual voters with the census of adults.[1] The percentage of registered voters (registration being easy but voluntary in the United States) actually voting, with allowances for mortality and mobility, might be 85–90 percent. Nonetheless, these figures continue a trend in recent years of diminishing turnout at presidential elections and, at the same time, of greater participation in the presidential primaries. If the candidates in 1980 were widely regarded as mediocre, it could not be denied that they were the popular choice of a method of selecting presidential candidates that since 1968 has become ever more popular. While seventeen states held primaries in 1968, twenty-three held them in 1972, twenty-nine in 1976, and thirty-seven in 1980. Why are more voting in the primaries (though not at a higher rate) and fewer voting in the final election? The answer is to be found in the decline of political parties which has been well documented by American political scientists.[2] But that decline has been promoted, if not begun, by the group of educated populists who seized control of the Democratic party after 1968. To see what that group has done, we must make a brief review of the function of parties in elections in America.

Critical Elections and the Constitution

Elections were guaranteed in the American Constitution as the formal occasions for popular choice, more formal in America because written down in one document held to be above ordinary law. In elections, democracy makes a deliberate choice because it is a formal one: it calls to account, sets a tone, perhaps gives a mandate, and installs a government. Partly for its own entertainment, partly to give exercise to its leading citizens, it also holds a race. Although the Constitution guarantees elections and prescribes a method of electing the president in an electoral college of which the founders were particularly proud—Hamilton called it "if not perfect, at least excellent" (*The Federalist*, no. 68)—the Constitution quite properly does not prescribe how a majority must be collected. To do so would be to tell the people *what* to choose in the guise of telling them *how* to choose, for they would have had to vote for a government party or parties if they had had to vote through one to fill the constitutional offices. Instead, the founders left the forming of majorities to private initiative. They seem to have preferred temporary coalitions of interests and opinions so as to secure moderation in the majority (Madison's argument in *Federalist* 10). But early on, the politicians established parties, to which the people (that is, the Jeffersonians) at first consented enthusiastically as a temporary measure, and later reluctantly, when parties became a regular necessity. By the time of Martin Van Buren, and partly because of his arguments,[3] parties were part of what one might call the "public constitution" of the United States, no longer derided and deplored but accepted as a respectable addition to the written constitution, in fulfillment of its requirements though not required by it.

Moreover, a pattern can be found in the way in which parties have been used to gather majorities in elections. As political scientists such as V. O. Key, Harry V. Jaffa, and W. D. Burnham have shown, certain *critical elections* in American history—those in 1800, 1832, 1860, 1896, and 1932—established majority and minority parties which lasted until the next critical election, when a new majority was formed. The ordinary, noncritical elections in-between were fought on the issues of the critical elections, issues that recall and revive the spirit of the American Revolution in an effort to remind Americans who they are and what they are about. Americans have not had a party of order and a party of progress, as John Stuart Mill expected in a liberal society, with a majority for one or the other according to whether it was time for appetite or digestion. British party history since the advent of universal manhood suffrage roughly satisfies Mill's expectation, with the advantage in tenure to the Conservatives and in accomplishment to the Liberal and Labor parties.

In America, however, there has been one clear majority party over a number of elections owing its primacy to a great victory in one critical election whose principles it repeats and whose partners it rallies in following elections. The majority party, each in its turn, has stood for progress differently defined; and the minority party has either had to go along with the majority (liberal Republicans, in recent years) or oppose it in-effectually (Goldwater Republicans). It is as if the American people had decided not to make a big choice but once in two or three generations. This pattern would serve to distinguish choice from whim in the behavior of the electorate while retaining the advantages of both. Many critical choices imply a flighty, unserious people of doubtful character that decides as lightly as a king; but if critical choices are adhered to for periods of decades, they dignify both themselves and the noncritical choices. At the same time, noncritical choices made through habitual party loyalties after critical elections can be exercised as easily as whims. If a democratic electorate had adopted "the theory of critical elections" as the maxim of its behavior—a fanciful possibility—it would have chosen well.

In the 1970s, however, American politics appears to have undergone a critical change without a critical election. Since the last critical election in 1932 (or 1936) establishing the Democrats as the majority party, the New Deal has had a life full of incident and accomplishment. By the 1960s, signs of decrepitude were apparent in New Deal programs and cracks had appeared in the New Deal coalition; it was time for another critical election, a new majority, and a party realignment. This expected event has perhaps now occurred, but it did not come so soon as it might have. Nixon (not to mention Eisenhower) may have had the opportunity in his own victories to overthrow the Democratic party, but he was not able to do so. Although fewer voters now identify themselves as Democrats, still fewer call themselves Republicans; and the trend of both has been downward. Nonetheless, a critical change had occurred between 1968 and 1980: the *liberal* in the American sense, that amiable fellow the New Deal liberal, once dominant but never dominating, almost disappeared from view.

How Populism Replaced Liberalism

The liberal disappeared not by being defeated in an election; rather, he was replaced within the majority party by a new political type, less agreeable in his habits and more unruly in his desires, who has also gained imitators among conservatives and the Republican party. The new political type is also called "liberal," having taken over the name and approximately the same place in the spectrum moderately to the Left. Thus, one finds him neither in a new party nor with a new name. Many New Deal liberals, now often called "moderates," are unaware of their own eclipse, and while vaguely uneasy with what the younger generation is coming to, have felt obliged to keep up with the times and have been taken into camp by the new liberals. The more knowing of the old liberals have been branded "neo-conservatives" for their struggle to repudiate the new liberals.

The most open event by means of which the new liberals can be identified is the coup d'état—Richard Neustadt's expression—by which they took possession of the Democratic party from 1969 to 1972. The 1968 Democratic convention in Chicago, marked by rioting in the streets of radicals against the police and by dissent within itself between defenders and opponents of the war in Vietnam, nominated Hubert Humphrey, the last liberal politician of presidential caliber in American politics. When Humphrey was defeated and Nixon took on responsibility for the war, the Democrats decided to "open up" their party with reforms. The McGovern-Fraser Commission of the national party laid down "guidelines" for state parties which soon became rules requiring them to facilitate participation, establish quotas or "affirmative action" for "disadvantaged groups," and use proportional representation of Democratic voters' preferences in sending delegates to caucus or convention. In effect, these new rules applied strong pressure on Democratic state governors and legislators to legislate presidential primaries, and the consequence of the increase in primaries has been a party convention with little to do but ratify the choice of voters in the primaries. The McGovern-Fraser reforms themselves were never put to the voters or to Democratic voters or even to Democratic conventions—except those in 1972 and thereafter that were chosen under the reformed rules. Moreover, the resounding defeat of the unelectable McGovern in 1972 was not taken for a popular judgment on the method used to nominate him. Carter's defeat has led to some second thoughts but not brought about a reversal of that method.

The Republicans, meanwhile, fearing to appear less democratic, were soon forced to imitate the Democratic reforms. Even though Reagan might have been the Republican choice under a deliberative party convention in the old style, he was in fact selected by the new populistic method of primaries, for which his actor's training rather than his years of party service was the better preparation. If the McGovern-Fraser reforms are not reformed and the present trend continues, party conventions will lose their force and party nominations their value. In time, all candidates might follow the example of John Anderson in 1980 and use the parties for their own convenience. Anyone who watched the 1980 party conventions saw two organizations that at times appeared to be no more than convenient receptacles for interest groups. The Democrats in particular were used by the National Education Association (the biggest teachers' union with 9 percent of the delegates at the convention) and the feminists, who succeeded in attaching a provision to the platform denying assistance to any Democrat opposed to the Equal Rights Amendment. Clearly, if the parties are used only for convenience, they will soon lose even convenience.

Who are the new liberals who have inspired and profited from these changes, and how have they governed? Their outlook is populist, their class is professional. Until recently, "educated populism" would have been a contradiction in terms in American politics, but these populists are intellectual descendants of the expensively educated radicals of the 1960s who demanded "participatory democracy." This slogan, originating in the universities and carried into the streets, has found its way into respectability and decorum since it has been adopted by the growing class of professionals who claim to speak for the disadvantaged as well as for themselves.

In *participatory democracy*, to participate means not to contribute to a common good but to express oneself; to "demonstrate"—not one's reasons but one's feelings; and then to call upon government to give effect to these feelings by passing new laws and regulations. Such legislation is typically designed to "open up" society and make it as democratic as government; environmental regulation, for example, has the purpose not only of cleaning the air and the water but also of making private industry democratically accountable. While the formal institutions of government are weakened, the power, influence, and extent of government are greatly strengthened so as to democratize society. In the Democratic party reform discussed above, only a greatly strengthened national party could have so reduced the function of the party convention. But since government is strengthened through an attack on its own forms, people's loyalties to the institutions of government are undermined, and then, as government is used to reform society, their private loyalties are also eroded. Thus Americans not only witness but promote a strange development of more government together with more cynicism about government.

Participatory democracy as Americans have seen it work in the 1970s is a reckless expansion of government to effect a reckless reduction of government. Its end is "power to the people," to quote another radical slogan of the 1960s; and its means is "to make government as good as the people," one of Jimmy Carter's 1976 campaign slogans. Making government as good as the people in order to make it subservient to the people requires making it as powerful as the people. What is omitted in this interesting circle is the task of gathering a majority, which used to be performed by the parties. Instead of the coalition politics typical of its past, America, as has been widely remarked, is developing "single-issue" politics. The single-issue groups, such as movements for and against abortion, or women's rights, typically argue in moral terms against "special," that is, selfish interests; and they claim that their concern should be enacted into a law for the whole. But they do not feel obliged to show how their issue can be matched with other issues to construct a program and a majority coalition by which to govern the country.

Instead, as issues become policies and are enacted into legislation, the issue groups turn into interest groups and as the legislation produces its intended or unintended effects, interest groups divide and proliferate around those effects clamoring for more or less budget and more or less regulation. Lobbyists, never absent in Washington and never bashful when present, have increased enormously in the 1970s. They hobnob with a correspondingly increased number of executives in the government who have specialized in the relevant policy. The result is what Hugh Heclo has called "issue networks" of knowledgeable policy professionals sharing technical expertise rather than belief, committed to advocacy rather than persuasion, and skilled in analysis rather than bargaining.[4] In sum, moralism and professionalism, far from confronting each other, cooperate, and the radicalism of the 1960s, without losing much of its fervor or any of its self-assurance, settles into the careers of the 1970s and 1980s. These are the careers of the "New Class" as Irving Kristol has dubbed it—the educated professionals who live for the people and do not object to high taxes. They are the ones whom Reagan and the Republicans defeated in the November election, for they had already defeated the New Deal liberals.

Whether the victory of Reagan and the Republicans is a "critical election" that will govern American politics for its time cannot be seen in 1982 (see chapters 3 and 4 for further discussion). It has the makings of a critical election: a party rather than a personal victory over an incumbent, exhaustion and confusion in the defeated, a recognizable shape of new policies. But if this election is to be a critical one, it must restore the possibility of a critical election by reviving the parties. If party loyalties are to be changed, they must first be recreated. How might this be done? It has been customary among political scientists, and the argument on parties I have given has followed this custom, to show that the working of the Constitution depends on extraconstitutional institutions such as parties. It is necessary now to show conversely that the working of extraconstitutional institutions depends on the Constitution, that semiformal institutions depend on formal ones.

Rights and Forms in the Constitution

Americans have always been known for taking pride in their Constitution. Although many foreigners (not Tocqueville, however) have wondered at an attachment that seems excessive, the best American statesmen have encouraged it. Lincoln once recommended in an early speech that his fellow citizens should develop a "political religion" of rational reverence for their laws and Constitution.[5] Historians have remarked on the propensity of Americans to dispute political issues in terms of constitutional questions. But despite the heavy celebration of the Constitution at its bicentennial, less and less is heard of it in political discourse. It is not studied in the law schools, where most American politicans learn their profession and sometimes their trade too. The law schools teach them to revere neither the law nor the Constitution, but rather a legalistic political theory (of which more later) pretending that the latest interpretations of certain parts of the Bill of Rights are "human rights." To avow one's respect for the Constitution would be ridiculous and politically backward.

For some time now, avowed respect for the Constitution has been the mark of a conservative—of the vintage of Robert Taft or perhaps Barry Goldwater. When Goldwater ran for president in 1964, he denounced the degradation of the Constitution under Democratic rule. Nixon in his presidency promised (but failed) to appoint "strict constructionists" to the Supreme Court. This was a sign that the debate was not over different interpretations of the Constitution but whether to take the Constitution seriously or not. In 1980, however, the Republican platform did not discuss the Constitution, and Reagan made nothing of it in his campaign. He promised to appoint justices (including a woman) with a conservative philosophy and did not mention the Constitution. Apparently he is close in this matter to the populists of the New Right. They have attempted to stock the Constitution with conservative amendments in order to counter the liberal amendments that activist justices have inserted in the guise of interpretations; Reagan would try to "conservatize" the judiciary rather than confine it to its constitutional task. One hardly need say that the surest evidence of decline in respect for the Constitution is the number of amendments being proposed. After it is openly acknowledged that the Constitution and the judiciary that interprets it are being used for partisan advantage, it will not be long before the Constitution fails to provide even this, because its use depends on its seeming to be above partisan advantage.

Originally the Constitution was a liberal idea in the great sense of *liberal*—an idea of liberty defined by the rights of man. This is the sense in which it is comprehended by both liberals and conservatives of the present day, but not by radicals or by their populist cousins. To understand our differences, then, it is necessary to recall that sense. A liberty defined by the rights of man makes a fundamental distinction between rights and the exercise of rights whereby the government protects rights and does not interfere with their exercise. For to have a right means to have the free exercise of it. Certain exercises of rights could destroy the rights of others, and thus might be legitimately prevented or curtailed. But in general, a society based on rights must be ready to tolerate their free exercise, and that society is healthy according to its own principle to the extent that it maintains toleration and is pleased with the result.

The American Constitution does two things to protect the distinction between rights and their exercise. It establishes a government to secure rights, and it provides rights against the government to limit its scope. Both the government and the rights against it are forms or formalities of which the content is not specified. The power of the president, for example, is not his personal property—nor is it the majority's—to use for the purpose of self-expression, and the right of free speech does not specify what will be said. The power of forms or formalities to prevail over content is necessary to the distinction between rights and their exercise. Liberty as we have known it is protected by its forms.

These observations have come increasingly to be questioned in American politics. From both Left and Right have come demands that the exercise of people's rights be examined by the government and changed if found wanting. From the Left, "the quality of life" has been held up as a legal standard; from the Right, "morality," with little or no regard for what government cannot persistently do in a liberal society. The government's attack on de facto segregation, for example, presupposes that government is capable of going beyond law and form to root out every act of segregation. The attempt to go beyond equality of opportunity, by way of affirmative action, to equality of result is another example. To do such things requires a stronger government than either liberals or conservatives have been willing to accept. It turns partisan debate from disputing over which rights need more protection to clamoring against the behavior and opinions of one's fellow citizens. Little or no attempt is made to find an impartial solution in the institution of a right that is necessarily formal, but rather the excuse for interference is given in the complaint that any unequal exercise of a right destroys the right for others.

The aberration from liberalism in the great sense should be recognized as causing fundamental damage to liberal Constitutionalism (though it hardly ever is) and should be traced to the values of self-expression described above. Those values derive from a pernicious doctrine of the self, with its origin in Nietzsche, which has infected liberal societies throughout the West. According to this doctrine, the need for self-expression arises from the alleged lack of a defined self (or "sense of identity"). Lacking definition, the self must assert itself, and in its self-assertion (the truer name for self-expression) there is no reason to respect the assertive-ness of others. Others would deserve respect only if they had rights, but rights attach only to selves that can be defined as individuals. By the doctrine of self, a self has no fixity even in potentiality, thus no rights. The self becomes what it is only by its activity of assertion; so its "right" is as much or little as it can exercise. The self overrides the distinction between rights and their exercise. As we have seen, one's self may therefore feel entitled to call on the government to aid in its self-assertion without feeling moral concern for persuading a majority.

These notions are current and familiar, but they have entered American politics in the 1970s through many new claims for compensation (noted again by Hugh Heclo). Such claims seek compensation for past injustices done not only by human beings (against women and blacks) but also by chance and nature (against the handicapped and the old). Groups advancing these compensatory claims are not satisfied to have asserted their rights so that they can make a fresh start. They want everything made whole and restored to them, as if they had had everything at the beginning. An explanation of how people might be entitled to this com-prehensive compensation happens to exist in John Rawls's *A Theory of Justice*, published in 1971 and by far the most influential work of political theory in America in the 1970s.

Rawls's theory appears to be liberal because it begins from an *original position* in which persons have rights; this position resembles the *state of nature* in which, according to Hobbes and Locke, the rights of man must be discerned. Rawls's original position, however, abstracts not merely from the artificial distinction of society, but also from all qualities and accidents that make for human differences. In this situation persons are taught by Rawls's theory to discount the advantages of their individual qualities before they know what those qualities are. They must consider human qualities not as individual but as constituting a social pool, from which the disadvantaged, or those who regard themselves as disadvant-aged, have a right to draw. No one has a natural right to his inherited qualities, that is, to his individuality, any more than to the external goods he may have inherited. No one deserves what he gets from the exercise of his capacities (which are not really his own), and society is not merely permitted but enjoined to inspect the rights and to claim what is needed for compensation. This inspection would have to apply to rights of speech as well as property.

Because of Rawls's desire to have it both ways on the questions divid-ing the liberalism from radicalism, his theory is more complicated but not more significant than this account of it. By blurring the difference be-tween liberals and radicals, it has had the effect of leading liberals unaware into radicalism. It is surely the most widely used justification, especially in the law schools, for overriding the constitutional distinction between rights and their exercise. Crowds of young lawyers appear before the judiciary and the executive branch to press claims in advance and in defiance of what the people have voted.

No right is more critical than the right to vote, because all other rights depend on it for protection, though not for justification. No other right illustrates so well the distinction between right and exercise as the right to vote, because it is obvious that a government that can examine and overturn the exercise of the right has annulled it. At the same time that the practice of elections has been extended in primaries and in the increasing use of referendums, the meaning of an election has been under attack in America. We have seen a populism that pays scant attention to the choice of the people in cahoots with a legalism that has little regard for the law and the Constitution.

If Reagan is to establish his election as a critical election, he must restore the efficacy of formal, constitutional choice. His own leadership, if it is to leave a lasting mark, will depend on his party's fortune; his party's fortune, on the strength of the parties; the strength of the parties, on respect for the Constitution; and respect for the Constitution, on understanding the Constitution. Reagan would be well advised to find his conservativism in the Constitution rather than to adopt a conservative populism. If he does the latter, he is likely to discover that the radical means of populism will overcome and outlast the conservative ends. He has before him the example of American liberals, who believed that they could make common cause with the radicals. The liberals have lost to the conservatives in 1980 because they had surrendered to the radicals in the 1960s and 1970s. In the connection between the public disappearance of the liberal and the decline of constitutionalism there is food for thought for both liberals and conservatives.

3

The 1982 Congressional Election: Reagan's Recalcitrant Economy

In the congressional election of 1982 Ronald Reagan asked the American people to "stay the course," and they responded with a definite negative that is nonetheless difficult to interpret.* The results were bad for the Republicans: a twenty-six-seat loss in the House of Representatives, creating a ninety-nine-seat Democratic majority and ending the de facto Reagan majority there; and a loss of seven state governors together with many state representatives. The Republicans held their margin of eight in the Senate.

That these results could have been worse was small consolation for the Republicans, because they could have been worse so easily. A shift of 43,000 votes could have defeated five Republican senators and lost the Senate. To keep the Senate, Republicans relied on liberals or moderates in their ranks who had noticably and frequently failed to support the president. In almost all contests, Republicans who expected to win easily had trouble; Democrats who expected to have trouble won easily.

On the Democratic side, the results were a vindication of the negative, stand-pat strategy of Speaker Tip O'Neill. He spent the last two years waiting for Democrats to come home, while making it clear that they still had a home; and home they came. Moreover, the turnout of faithful Democrats seeking revenge for the debacle of 1980 and not now having to vote for Jimmy Carter was unusually high. The success of O'Neill's strategy depended on his confidence that Reagan's election in 1980 was not the sort of *critical election* realigning party divisions and establishing a new party majority that some commentators, including this one (in chapter 2), thought it might have been. By intent of the Constitution

*Chapter 3 was first published as "The American Congressional Election," *Government and Opposition* 18(1983): 144–56.

midterm elections are short-term judgments, and perhaps, with another turn of the business cycle, Republicans will resume their advance in 1984. (In fact they did not, though the economy improved.) But it cannot be said in 1982 that the trend is in their direction, though, perhaps, there is reason to suppose from the present strength of Republican ideas that they may learn how to gain electoral advantage from them. In 1982, the Democrats surely remain the majority party, except that being the majority party no longer means what it used to. As I worried in the preceding chapter, it remains a question whether Americans, with less and less attachment to formal political institutions of any kind, are capable of a critical election establishing a long-term majority.

That doubt is what makes the election difficult to interpret. The people declared their will, but not so willfully as in 1980, when they delivered a mighty surprise. To be sure, most of the polls somewhat underestimated what was to be a Democratic success, and it was a source of quiet, if ineffectual, satisfaction to some that the apparatus of science was no advantage over political experience or cagey observation in predicting the result. But after the election has been predicted, it must be interpreted, lest it appear to be mere willfulness. To do so, the people allow their interpreters to think out loud by contrast to the courtiers who used to murmur their speculations as to what the king's frown could mean. Winston Churchill noted, even before he himself became an object of popular ingratitude, that willfulness and whimsicality were once accepted without protest in royalty by courtiers just as they are now taken for granted in the people by democratic politicians. For the honor of democracy, however, one must try to find more meaning in an election than in the arbitrariness of one king, multiplied by the number of the electorate.

We will assume, then, that the American people, after giving Reagan a landslide victory in 1980, did not decide to change the course in 1982. They decided on an adjustment of the course, and delivered their decision rather brusquely, leaving it to Reagan and O'Neill to make the adjustment, not in the delicate manner of economists skillfully fine-tuning the economy, but by conflict and compromise from the secure bastions afforded them by the American Constitution. If this is not the correct interpretation of the election, it is the only practicable one. The Democrats have no alternative course to propose at the moment, and though Reagan suffered a defeat, he was not repudiated.

Reagan's course has been defined as a revival of the economy by withdrawal of government intervention. How far the withdrawal should proceed is unclear and open to debate, but that is the debate in American politics in 1982. The "Reagan revolution" consists in having made that question the leading, indeed the inevitable, topic of debate. Reviving the economy, it is agreed, would require slowing or stopping inflation, improving productivity, and reducing unemployment. By August 1981, after eight months in office, Reagan had achieved significant cuts in taxes and in the federal budget in a remarkable string of victories in Congress. The cuts were significant not because they were felt immediately—the tax cut in particular, spread over three years, was mere compensation for "bracket creep" caused by inflation and almost canceled by a previously scheduled social security tax increase—but because it was thought that these cuts gave promise of more.

In fact, however, August 1981 proved to be the high point of Reagan's first two years. In that month Reagan won a victory on taxes, defeated and punished a strike by the air traffic controllers, and, while asleep, downed two marauding Libyan planes. From then on, things began to go sour. The stock market went down, interest rates went up, and it became necessary to admit that the economy was in a recession. A narrow but sweet victory over Speaker O'Neill was to come in May 1982, but only modest cuts in "social programs" (welfare) were accomplished. "Entitlements" in social security and medical insurance have continued their alarming growth, but small cuts in the latter were not accepted and cuts in social security were not even proposed publicly. Progress in reducing government regulation of business has also been modest. And Reagan was forced to accede to the tax increase called "revenue enhancement" which Republican Senator Robert Dole initiated. After that came the election. In sum, although the Republicans have the initiative and set the terms of debate, and although such change as occurs is likely to be in the direction they favor, they have not made themselves the majority party and do not seem to be gaining a majority. Why not? Two difficulties have become obvious: the recalcitrance of the economy and the incoherence of Republican conservatism.

The Recalcitrant Economy

In 1976, when Jimmy Carter and Gerald Ford were contending for the presidency, Carter scored significantly when he asked Americans to ask themselves: are you better off? In 1980, Reagan used that same question against Carter with still greater effect. In 1982, Democrats used it against him. "Are you better off?" is a question that first tempts, then haunts politicians in liberal democracies. They cannot leave it unasked and they cannot prevent its being asked. Reagan's response to it was that Americans are on the way to being better off, but they must "stay the course." "Stay the course" was an appeal to the patience, in the rather restricted sense of willingness to wait for better things, and all the polls showed, and still show, this willingness to exist in the minds of Americans. It was an appeal, in a rather restricted sense, to virtue. When politicians in a liberal democracy cannot point to wealth, they ask for virtue—as the means to wealth. So when you hear of virtue, or rather self-restraint, in such a society, you can be sure that times are bad.

Times are not that bad, Reagan attempted to say. His administration had in truth achieved the signal accomplishment of reducing the worst and the most stubborn inflation that Americans had seen, from 18 percent when he took office to 5.1 percent. This inflation was what Theodore White, in his fine book *America in Search of Itself* (1982), calls the "Great Inflation," because it seemed to have changed not merely the terms of economic exchange in America but the habits of life—and much for the worse. Such an inflation forces one to live for the moment, to spend and borrow, and if anything is left, one does not save it in the sense of putting it by but lends it out for short terms at usurious rates (in money market funds). That way of life is not only bad for business but also bad for life. But of course in the process of reducing inflation Reagan's administration raised unemployment from 7.4 percent when he took office to 10.4 percent in November 1982. And of unemployment it can also be said, especially in view of generous unemployment compensation, that the effect is worse on the habits of life than on income. Not to have a job seems to signify society's lack of esteem for the contribution one can make, and for the unemployed it is unnecessary to blame impersonal economic forces when some person is available and liable.

Reagan had trouble getting credit for reducing inflation but could not avoid being blamed for unemployment. In his buoyant hopefulness he had promised that everything would get better, and he was not unjustly held to that unreasonable standard. That he had merely settled everyone's first concern, inflation, was not enough, and the cost—in that no cost had been stated—was too high. Besides, since prices were still rising, the reduction of inflation was not so apparent as are the numbers of those who are thrown out of work. People do not speak worriedly of inflation as they used to, but they forget to congratulate Reagan for its reduction. It is a mistake to solve the problem you were elected to solve; then people no longer need you and they turn to others who promise something new. Franklin Roosevelt, whom Reagan admires, did not make this mistake. He did not make Americans so wealthy that they failed to respond to his condemnation of the "economic royalists" who held them down.

Reagan's enemy, by contrast, is the government he now heads, which he wants to get off our backs. Whereas the Democrats can attack the few and the rich, he cannot afford to attack the many and the poor, even though they elected the government that sits on our backs. Whereas

Roosevelt could blame the troubles of the economy in his charge on Republicans, Reagan cannot so readily accuse Democrats, in Congress and especially in the electorate, of foiling his good intentions and well-laid plans. Part (or most) of what is meant by saying that Reagan has not yet found a dependable majority to support him is that he has not yet found a vicious minority for the majority to blame. So it blames him. It is to Reagan's credit that he does not devote his life to the search for vicious minorities, as did Richard Nixon, but he does seem to need some equivalent and counterpart to Roosevelt's economic royalists to help unite his majority and to keep it united in dislike of some minority despite adverse economic conditions. Virtue is a fine thing, but for reasons about which Machiavelli is our teacher it combines more securely with dislike of one's enemies than with gratitude to one's friends. Thus it was not consistent for Reagan to ask, "Are you better off?" in 1980 and then to appeal for patience in 1982. It is, perhaps, an inconsistency forced upon him by political necessity in liberal democracies today, but it is confusing to the people he governs. If being better off is the end, then withdrawal of the government from the economy is a means that must be judged by its success in achieving the end; and who is to say when patience should reach its limit, especially since little or nothing was said at first about the necessity for patience? Or is liberation of the economy from government intervention the end, or an end, regardless of whether it makes us better off?

In keeping with the latter possibility, we note that Reagan's policies, particularly his concentration on inflation (with the aid of the Federal Reserve Board), have tended to promote certain kinds of behavior and certain characters and to demote others. Borrowers and spenders thrive on inflation; workers and savers benefit from steady prices. This consequence is independent of any calculation of how much borrowing and how much saving makes us better off. One could assert plausibly that it is better to live by one's own efforts as worker and saver than to live beyond one's means and off others, even when the latter route seems more profitable. Is not the purpose of withdrawing government from the economy to liberate the people so that they can lead productive lives, rather than merely to enrich them in lives of dependency? The Reagan revolution has in fact initiated a moral change—a shift in power, favor, and reward from the unproductive to the productive. That, again, is why the rise in unemployment was such a reproach to the Reagan administration: it is not that more people are suffering and need compassion or deserve more income, as the Democrats say, but that those who desire work cannot find it. Reagan in fact promotes what used to be called, in the Nixon days, the "work ethic," but he has not relied on it. Instead, he put faith in supply-side economics, which because of his faith is now called Reaganomics.

Supply-side economics was supposed to make us better off and better at the same time. It would "get the economy going" and "put America back to work" because withdrawal of the government from the economy, particularly the tax cut, would release pent-up desires to produce. No restraint or patience would be necessary because the government, while reducing its share in the economy, would improve its revenue with a reduced share in greater activity. Necessary government spending could be maintained, and the deficit would diminish or vanish.

There is no need to say what went wrong (even if I could!). Something went wrong because something always does go wrong. Then it became necessary to invent a slogan, "stay the course," and to make a necessity of virtue. Modern economics from its inception in the seventeenth century and in its present working consists essentially in providing a substitute for virtue. It promises to make everyone better off, and it promises, sometimes expressly, always implicitly, that becoming morally better either will result automatically (socialism) or does not matter (capitalism). At its inception modern economics had to defend itself against the traditional moralists, who based their doctrine on the folk wisdom that men should not put their faith in good times. Bad times are bound to follow, and those who have relied on prosperity will come to grief. Men should put their faith, therefore, in something that does not depend on the chance of good or bad times, in virtue and in what secures virtue. To understand what modern economics as a whole is driving at, as distinct from its technical successes and its intramural disputes, one would have to reenter this original dispute. But we can gain some appreciation of the Reagan administration's troubles with a recalcitrant economy by means of a few reflections on the relationship between modern economics and modern constitutionalism.

Constitutionalism and the Free Market

Modern economics takes hold of the alternation between good and bad times, which is obvious to all and was thought to be irremediable, and transforms it into the *business cycle*. To speak of a business cycle means to assume responsibility for natural dearth and to reinterpret it in terms of the course of the economy, as caused by predictable human actions or reactions (crises of overproduction, of slack demand, etc.). With this reinterpretation economics assumes responsibility for making people better off ("improving their lot," the lot that would have been theirs from nature or by chance), since knowledge of the business cycle will enable us to dampen the fluctuations of the cycle or at least to ensure that the trend of fluctuations is upward. Preceding and paving the way for the impressive claim by modern economics to extend the bounds of human knowledge and power were a change in morality, to transform virtue into liberty and to understand both in terms of rights, and a change in political science, to construct a constitutional government to secure those rights. The three movements of economics, morality, and politics have converged in the ideals and practices of modern liberal democracies, but not without trouble. One difficulty—the same one we have discerned in Reagan's first two years—has been the conflict, as liberal democracies judge themselves, between a measure of performance and a standard of rights. Are such societies to be judged by how much better off we are or by how well our rights are protected?

Even more essential to modern economics than the business cycle is the very notion of the *economy* as a market of exchange separate or separable from outside influence, particularly from political determination. But the free market was not only a discovery of modern economics; it was also a necessary convenience for modern morality and modern political science. In modern morality the free market permitted virtue to be redirected toward liberty since it left a sphere of private action unsupervised by authority and rewarded a spirit of independence unguided by habit. In modern political science, the free market is a double help. On the one hand, it justifies the claim of modern constitutionalism that a state limited to protecting our rights will free us to make ourselves better off as well as better. On the other hand, the free market, in which government does not intervene, relieves government of responsibility for the distribution of goods among rich and poor and for the ups and downs of the business cycle. As a result of this happy conception, now unfortunately lost to view even in imagination, free governments get credit for the general enrichment of their peoples and avoid the blame for the harm done to particular individuals or classes and to everyone in hard times.

To have a free economy implies, or used to be thought to imply, that the government should not be held to a standard of economic performance. What happens in the economy is the fault of the market, that is, no one's fault. To have such an economy might be regarded as a democratic decision to put the economy out of reach of democratic decision. But such a decision would never be made if it were considered a choice; democratic peoples would deny themselves their power of choice in economic matters only if they were convinced they must do so because economic matters must be understood by science. Economics as a science is necessary to the freedom of the free economy. There can be no free economy without economists who are ready to supply the laws of such an economy, preferably "natural laws" that operate regardless of human choice. For to be an economist it is not enough to have opinions, however well grounded; one must own a curve.

It is nothing new to say that economics is in disarray today, but the trouble may go deeper than is generally perceived: it is becoming questionable whether such a person as an economist exists. The doubt has arisen from developments within the science of economics itself. Since Keynes, economics has assumed responsibility not for the economy as an autonomous system that will bring benefits if left alone, but for an economy that will deliver unbroken prosperity and full employment to all classes at all times through a combination of autonomous laws and appropriate government intervention. The greatly expanded pretension of economics to be a "policy science" has been successful in raising economics in public esteem and thus in raising economists to prominence as public figures. Such success was achieved not by the economists' own doing but by the politicians of the New Deal and its successors who found Keynesian economics first useful, then essential to their programs. As public figures economists increasingly became political figures (coincidentally, at the same time as their value theory, in long-delayed recognition of Nietzsche, began to cast doubt on the value of economic goods). Then since the late sixties we have witnessed the Great Crash and Depression of Keynesian economics. The Great Crash is the nearly simultaneous failure of the programs of government intervention that were to make up for deficiencies in the untended economy, and the Depression that followed and is still upon us comes from the lingering expectations that Keynesian economics aroused but could not satisfy.

Supply-side economics is a return to supply as an independent factor, that is, to the initiative of the "private sector" (a revealing Keynesianism), as opposed to concentrating on the manipulation of demand that is characteristic of Keynesian economics. But supply-side economics promised the Keynesian promises nonetheless. It precisely did not return to the long-term view that pre-Keynesian economics insisted on; its principal recommendation for a tax cut was at the opposite extreme from a call for patience. In any case the Keynesian promises have been mechanized in the flow of economic statistics by which the government tells us, every month or every week, whether we are better off. These indicators run parallel to the monthly polls by which we are informed whether we *feel* better off. Government is held to a standard of performance that no human institution can attain and that thereby obscures, with false precision, the responsibilities of which it is capable. The true extent of these responsibilities becomes clearer when one begins to discern the choices that have been made, and the choices come to light when one sees the virtues that are being promoted.

In discussions with economists one should always try to find out, regardless of the analysis and conclusions, how they recommend people to behave—for example, as borrowers or savers. If one model of behavior seems better than others, then one should choose the model closest morally to virtue, so that one can be ready with that compensation and consolation for the inevitable collapse of the analysis and conclusions. By looking for the moral bottom line of an economic model one can convert economic behavior into an end in itself. Thus economics can be kept, paradoxically, to the function of a means rather than an end. Economists, who to their credit if not their credibility frequently disclaim the desire for power if not money, can be returned toward their premodern functions as contemplators of the inevitable and counselors of virtue.

The Incoherence of Republican Conservatism

Keynesian economics, then, has made government responsible for the business cycle, but the interventions by government that it has recommended or accepted have not succeeded in controlling the business cycle. On the contrary, those interventions have themselves become uncontrollable factors in government budgets. Yet if the interventions are more and more generally regarded as not having worked, the spirit of interventionism remains alive in the standard of performance to which government is held. The responsibility remains although the means of exercising it have been discredited. Supply-side economics is an attempt, so far not notably successful, to exercise the Keynesian responsibility in a non-Keynesian or pre-Keynesian way. But if we are to rely on the market, we must be satisfied with what it gives us. We may have certain objectives; we may take advantage of opportunities; but we cannot demand certain results. For example, we could not demand a certain level of employment, because to do so is to change the nature of employment. A job is not a job unless you have a boss and unless you can lose the job. When the government guarantees a job, it becomes something like a professorship; the economy descends to the productivity of a university, and society becomes as ill-natured as an academic community that is not supported by a buoyant economy.

If these remarks are taken as a call for a return to laissez-faire economics, or to any particular economics, then my point has been missed. The reservations I have expressed are to economics as such, and only especially to the greater pretensions of Keynesian economics. They are perhaps expanded expressions of the sound, prudent skepticism of economics that one can find in politicians of both parties and particularly in certain conservative Republicans, such as Senator Dole, who have acquired a reputation for responsibility as opposed to ideology.

Whereas the Democrats are the more popular party, the Republicans are more responsible. *Responsible* in this sense means responsible not for things one has caused but for things one has not caused. The spending for social programs (welfare) and entitlements (social security, government pensions, and medical care), which conservative Republicans have consistently warned would go out of control, has in fact done so and is, nevertheless, their responsibility. These Republicans were appalled at the blithe demagoguery of Democrats who, in full knowledge that changes must be made in social security, accused the Republicans during the election campaign of wanting to change it. These Republicans were leery of supply-side economics and now openly reject it. They prefer monetarism, not because it works better, but because it establishes a self-regulating mechanism that would permit government to withdraw from intervention in the economy. They worry about the size and the growth of the deficit, and they want a balanced budget except that they want to achieve it by prudent management instead of by a constitutional amendment. They distrust this nostrum and others like it, though they may vote for some items on the list of conservative constitutional amendments because they think them unimportant. Someone in Washington, not a conservative, offered to combine the school prayer and balanced budget amendments in an amendment requiring American schoolchildren to pray every day for a balanced budget.

Responsible Republicans laugh at this but do not think it is funny. In their sober, Burkean prudence, they distrust the ideological Republicans who abound on the national scene. These include the supply-siders, libertarians, moralists from Protestant fundamentalism, and unelected politicians of the New Right who want to take over the country by direct mail (they get their support from contributions solicited by mail). One should also mention denizens of conservative think tanks and the neo-conservatives—some of them prudent, some ideological, all of them zealous exposers and undoers of liberal mistakes.

The debate in American politics today, one can say with little exaggeration, is within the Republican party between those with ideas and the prudent distrusters of ideas. It is still true, as Senator Daniel Patrick Moynihan said two years ago, that the Republican party is the party of ideas. The Democrats still bubble with conceits and jokes, but they are so lacking in fresh ideas that they have taken up worrying about inflation and the deficit as do the prudent Republicans. They defeated the conservative constitutional amendments in the Senate by invoking quite without apology the filibuster privilege, which they used to denounce as undemocratic when it was used against them. They have voiced some of the demands of the labor unions for protectionism, and they have toyed with a *dirigiste* policy of government investment in private industry. But for the most part, and with considerable success, they have left the initiative to the Republicans and settled into respectability as the party of the status quo that can manage the country more sensibly and more fairly than Republicans with their crazy ideas. Let us Democrats (they say), who made the mistakes, be responsible for them now.

This prudence being suspect, but prudence in general being preferable to ideas, one might be content that President Reagan adjust his course in consultation with the responsible Republicans, as indeed he did with his bill for "revenue enhancement." But the responsible Republicans are used to taking over problems created by others; hence they are somewhat lacking in a sense of direction and their electoral appeal is in doubt, not in their own case but for a Republican majority. Reagan had then to look to combine the responsible Republicans with Republicans who have ideas for solving problems and gaining adherents. It would be imprudent and impatient to abandon supply-side economics just before it might bear fruit, and when its appeal to wage earners might become clear. That appeal must not be made too crassly, because, as asserted above, the monetary benefits of any economics are fitful and undependable. Besides, supply-side economics is vulnerable to the complaint that it makes the rich richer. It would be better to emphasize that income tax cuts reward earners and producers, and that productivity, as George Gilder noted in his *Wealth and Poverty* (1981), has its aspect of virtue. Reagan's hopefulness can be justified if it is grounded on how people ought to live when the government is off their backs, rather than merely on how they will feel with extra money in their pockets.

What America needs is a certain constitutional space between people and government to allow the government to regain control of its affairs, thereby enabling the people to regain control of its government. When government is held responsible for prosperity always and to all, it is not merely tempted but required to buy what has to be produced. It loses control of its spending and people become dependent on the welfare and entitlements that were supposed to secure their freedom. The connection between a free constitution and a free market was originally the discovery of liberalism. It is now the task of conservatism to restore that connection, with prudent regard for new circumstances and with diminished faith in economics. What Reagan could do to restore it was uncertain. His farsighted proposal for "New Federalism," in which the states would assume responsibility for welfare, was doomed in the near term by the 1982 election. But the federal deficit remained, and Reagan tried to use it to force a revealing choice between tax cuts and spending. The choice may not go Reagan's way, as the 1982 election may portend, but the recovery of choice from the gush of uncontrollable spending is a recapture of self-government.

4

The 1984 Election: Entitlements versus Opportunity

It is no exception to the contingency of human things that events can occur as expected: this happens so as to lull us for the next surprise.* "A good election for poll takers," said one headline, of Ronald Reagan's lopsided victory. His 18-percentage-point margin was exactly predicted by Gallup and roughly approximated by others in a 10- to 25-point range of misses. Once again it was confirmed that science can give mathematical expression to our expectations in politics. But the expected result was also a welcome sign that the American polity was healthy enough to reelect a president in whom few—rather his supporters than his opponents—could have been disappointed. A people's ability to express gratitude to its leaders is more than a measure of political stability; it is one end of political stability and when exercised is the most ennobling act of popular sovereignty.

A triumph for President Reagan was not, however, a triumph for the Republican party, and therefore was not entirely a triumph for President Reagan. Republicans suffered a net loss of two seats in the Senate and gained only fourteen in the House of Representatives, a result comparable to the elections of 1956 and 1972, when popular Republican presidents (Eisenhower and Nixon) won easy victories for a second term but did not improve the status of their party from minority to majority. It is the habit of Americans to maintain over long periods majority and minority parties, a two-party system that does not alternate victories but keeps a dominant majority and a long-suffering minority in national politics (relieved by local dominance of the national minority in many places). Many had wondered whether a party realignment would reverse the majority and

*Chapter 4 was first published as "The American Election: Entitlements versus Opportunity," *Government and Opposition* 20. (1985):3–17.

minority parties at a stroke, as happened in the so-called critical elections of 1800, 1860, and 1932.

Obviously a party realignment of this kind did not take place. Instead, incremental changes favorable to the Republicans portended a future realignment, together with the continued, perhaps intensified, division for now between a Republican presidency and a Democratic House of Representatives. I shall first discuss the changes and then consider the stability of incumbents when they do not deserve gratitude.

A Personal Victory?

It has been said that the election came out as one would expect with a personally popular president in time of prosperity: thus no realignment and no mandate for Reagan's policies. The people voted out of self-interest mixed with a small measure of gratitude, since the most attentive self-interest looks to the immediate future rather than the present or past. This explanation tells why the incumbent won, but not why the incumbent was Reagan nor how the Democrats might dislodge him apart from waiting for recession. It also does not say whether prosperity was luck or success, or what it consists in: a job, a slightly higher income, or a feeling that things in general are going well. In this skeptical vein Speaker O'Neill, the Democratic leader in the House of Representatives, claimed not unreasonably, if somewhat inconsistently, that the president had no mandate but that the Democratic House had been reelected to serve as watchdog. He meant that the forces in conflict had not been changed, so that Reagan had no new justification for advance, and he no duty to retreat.

That the result was merely a personal victory for Reagan, or an incumbent's victory in prosperity, however, cannot be maintained. Even in the House the Republicans won nineteen of twenty-eight open seats, doing well when incumbency was not a factor. And the Democrats may have held their total net loss to fourteen by raising their expenditures in closely contested races to an average slightly exceeding that of the Republicans. This money came from PACs (political action committees), some of them unions but most of them business groups, impressed with the power of incumbency, who confirm once again Machiavelli's view that money goes to power, not power to money. The total popular vote for the House was almost exactly equal, as compared to a slender margin of 51.4 percent for the Democrats in 1980. But because of gerrymandering the Democrats got 253 House seats for their half, the Republicans only 182 for theirs. Moreover, in elections to state legislatures Republicans continued to make gains from their low point in 1974 when they controlled only seventeen of ninety-eight state legislative chambers (Nebraska has a unicameral legislature whose members are officially nonpartisan); in 1984 they controlled thirty-two after a new gain of four. The most impressive change was in the South, where conservative voters are increasingly turning Republican on the state level. Control of state legislatures is important in national politics because they (with much clumsy interference from the courts) reapportion congressional districts every ten years.

Yet the House remains Democratic, and the Republicans will not find the Senate easy to hold in 1986. It is in the presidency that realignment seems already to have occurred. The Republicans have such an advantage in presidential elections from the West and the South that they have only to fight on even terms in the Midwest, while conceding the Northeast, to win easily. They have won four out of five elections since 1968, three of them by margins designated with the semiofficial metaphor *landslide* (hardly flattering to democratic choice); and the Democrats have won only once, narrowly, with a Southerner. Complementing this decisive fact is evidence from exit polls that the Democrats are losing more of their traditional strength in the South and among blue-collar workers, and that the youth vote (ages 18–24) went Republican for the first time, voting for Reagan 48 to 41 percent and calling themselves Republicans over Democrats 40 to 34 percent. This group is said to lead the trend. First-time voters of whatever age went for Reagan by 60 to 39 percent; new registrations helped Republicans more than Democrats.

Moreover, Republicans have the new ideas, the ruling ideas and the dominant strategy. Gary Hart ran for the Democratic nomination with the slogan "new ideas," but in fact his proposals for military and tax reform were modulations of Republican issues, and in attempting to put a distance between the Democrats and blacks and unions, he was struggling to do what Republicans have done easily. The ruling ideas in American politics in 1984 are Republican: the reduction of government regulation and social programs, strong defense, Reaganomics favoring savers and investors, and hopeful partriotism.

The Democrats, once the progressive party, have no progressive measure in view that they wish to promote; so they defend the progressive measures they once enacted, now known as "entitlements," and now regarded as progressive only in their uncontrolled cost. Their main issue in the campaign was the budget deficit, an issue handed them by Reagan that they eagerly and foolishly clasped to heart as if it were not the concern they had ridiculed for many years. For the dominant strategy since 1981 in American politics has been Reagan's. His decision to cut taxes before cutting spending, indeed while increasing military spending,

put Democrats on the defensive by forcing them to choose between cutting their own programs or raising taxes to pay for them. *Progress* as
Progressives have defined it is out of the question; it has been replaced by
opportunity, which does not call for new expense and promises a better
life with less government. The Republicans, once known as reactionaries,
are no longer so called: they do not demand a return to the past and they
do not merely react to others. Reagan did not accomplish this reversal
with his 1981 tax cut, but he made the new situation clear to all in that
impressive stroke, so that he and his party could profit from it. His
strategy was so simple—both obvious and easy—that its effectiveness and
his prudence continue to be underestimated. It was not merely Reagan's
luck that his opponent began his campaign with a proud, self-congratu-
latory promise to raise taxes.

The Party of the Sad

The campaign was vapid and lackluster. It was sustained by a succession
of media events such as the "age issue," each of several days' duration, in
which the attention of voters seemed not to penetrate to the substance,
such as whether Reagan is too old to be president again, but remained on
the media surface as people wondered how the age issue would affect the
campaign. Wondering about the campaign is not the same as holding a
campaign, however. The media news, with its boring self-preoccupation
and its constant worrying over news management and the lack-of-issues
issue, helped to prevent actual news from occurring. Keen reporters allowed many seconds of exposure to the two candidates on the nightly
television news as material for their own reflections on that day's latest
twist. Reagan had a surpassing advantage over Walter Mondale in the
knack of conveying his message with a few words, a shrug, and a smile
through the doltish, moralistic truculence of the reporters. His campaign
was designed to the last detail to use this advantage, as was Mondale's to
minimize it; for in the media everything is calculated with a view to
chance superiority in the use of the media. The media that are supposed
to convey the campaign to the people almost become both the campaign,
by determining its character, and the people, by representing their reactions.

This is not to say that either Reagan or Mondale did well in the two
debates. Mondale won the first one because Reagan did less well than
expected, and Reagan won the second by meeting the new, lower standard set by his first performance. Neither candidate came within sight of
the command that urbanity and wit afford to men of the first rank in such
a situation, yet neither managed to achieve in the debates the power and

dignity of simple sincerity, which is nature's compensating resource for second-raters. The campaign was not governed through the media, but nothing was omitted in the attempt to do so, whether in the media or by the candidates. One does not know whether to be more impressed by the limitations on human calculation or by the strength of the human desire to calculate.

Reagan did not run as a Republican, joining his record and his program to the revival of the Republican party; rather, he presented himself as a former Democrat, still a man of the people but one who, like many others now, had seen the error of his party's ways. He evoked the memory of Roosevelt, Truman, and Kennedy, presidents of a size and style no longer seen today—among Democrats. Mondale, in his gracious concession speech on election night, said he was thinking of "the poor, the un-employed, the elderly, the handicapped, the helpless, and the sad." The sad! And indeed the Democrats at their convention had stopped playing their old standard, "Happy Days Are Here Again" (celebrating the end of Prohibition in 1933), only to have it picked up by the Republicans at their convention. Mondale's concern for the sad was for those who had noth-ing to be sad about; it was the same group that had suffered malaise during the Carter administration (in his most notorious speech, Carter spoke of a "malaise" in the American people) and alienation in the 1960s. Reagan harked back to the cheerfulness of earlier Democratic presidents, and skillfully imputed to them in their graves a renewed joy at the defeat of their programs and their party. His audiences were supplied with American flags for all, and they cheered for Reagan as Americans had cheered for their Olympic winners earlier in the summer, with pardonable excess arising from relief of the demand for self-doubt.

Reagan, as is his wont, did not ask for any sacrifice, or propose any noble goal. In particular, he made sure not to be outpromised by the Democrats in maintaining social security payments. He referred to the Reagan revolution, whose purpose is to get the government off our backs, but never called it a revolution, lest it seem to require effort. "Leadership that works" was his slogan, and when he said "works" he did not mean the kind of work from which one sweats either for himself or the people. His kind of idealism makes idealism easy, even *seem* easy, since the mes-sage is not merely that good will is enough—a message that is the false ease of liberal idealism—but that good *humor* will suffice. If only govern-ment will cease its incompetent interference, individuals will take over their own responsibilities with a smile. While the Democrats, usually the happy party, tried to screw their faces into frowns at the deficit, Reagan did not worry and did not ask Americans to worry. But his insouciance was denied by his quickness to reassure the elderly regarding social security. Similarly, in foreign policy he had one easy success in Grenada to boast of, and an undamaging defeat in Lebanon from which he was quick enough to get out. The extrication from defeat in a way is more impressive than the management of success.

He showed he had learned the lesson of Vietnam, that the American people want quick victory or a quick way out; and he has said nothing about the need for patience and perseverance in foreign policy. He has allowed people to think that an arms buildup will lead without difficulty to arms control, and he has not spoken of the stubborn qualities of vigilance that a free people needs to keep itself on guard.[1] Although he has rightly stressed the evil of communism, he has not stressed its menace. The trouble in all this easy hopefulness is that it encourages the American people to believe they can have it both ways: both government payments and release from government regulation in domestic policy, both reduced commitment and heightened security in foreign policy—and therefore, they can elect both Democrats and Republicans. Reagan's failure to demand anything of the American people may have improved his own chances for reelection, but by reducing the size of the task, it softened the argument for voting for his party. Why give up the apparent benefits of the Democrats' established programs if the new policies require no sacrifice? Why then replace Democrats with Republicans?

Reagan's decision to run his campaign on his record rather than his program was meant to take full advantage of his incumbency, but it also handed a like advantage to the Democrats in Congress. The temptation to adopt this tactic must have been strong. Among the chances of the human events we call "elections" few opportunities to defeat one's opponent can have seemed so certain as Reagan's to defeat Mondale by running on his record. Reagan's record, though satisfying to most, and impressive to all, was by no means unassailable—but it was almost unassailable by the Democrats. In domestic policy they had been left with the deficit issue, as explained above. In foreign policy they faced a nation at peace not only with others but with itself, glad to be rid of the Iranian humiliation which it remembered and blamed on the last Democratic administration. Reagan's defeat in Lebanon, which he prevented from becoming a humiliation, could be successfully exploited only from the Right, by criticizing the military inefficiency that was shown. An attack from the Left would have seemed to emphasize that weakness and would have reminded voters of American weakness under the Democrats.

Again, it should not be believed that, because Reagan campaigned on his record, he was merely riding on his personality and the country's prosperity as opposed to the issues in a program. Performance is an issue as much as promises are issues, and Reagan's record was judged favorably not simply because it worked or because Americans liked him, but because he persuaded them to judge him by his new standard. With his winning ways he got them to accept his interpretation of his record, and to understand prosperity as opportunity. Nonetheless his "mandate," in the sense of what he can reasonably claim to have put across in the campaign, was confined to an endorsement of what he had done in his first term and a repudiation of what Mondale might have done in his.

The Ferraro Factor

After suffering with outsider candidates such as George McGovern and Jimmy Carter, who depended on populist forces hostile to the traditional interests of the party, the Democrats nominated the insider Mondale, former senator, vice-president under Carter, and candidate of the AFL-CIO, which had supported him, contrary to its usual practice, in the primaries. But though the insider played to win and kept shifting his appeal toward the center, he proved to have no substance except that lent by the outsiders, the McGovern wing of the party. This lack was strikingly revealed in his choice of Geraldine Ferraro as running mate. Mondale decided to make his choice for vice-president before the Democratic convention, after his own nomination was assured. He held a series of well-publicized meetings, by invitation to his home in Minnesota, with vice-presidential possibilities, meetings designed in the mode of the insider to recognize and reassure the various parts of the traditional Democratic majority. But doing this publicly created pressure on him to decide, so as to show he was not indecisive, as had been alleged, and it allowed outsider groups, particularly the National Organization for Women, to lobby for their candidates. Soon Mondale was forced to decide, and, since he had made a point of a new way of deciding, he could not easily conclude with an obvious, traditional choice such as a Southerner. So he picked the first woman ever to be on the presidential ticket of a major party.

She had been recommended by Speaker O'Neill, insider par excellence, and as an Italian, Catholic New Yorker, in a blue-collar constituency (though she herself was, it turned out, very well off), she balanced the ticket in time-honored fashion. But as a woman, the candidate of NOW, she represented the outsiders from the 1960s. Above all else, she was an "affirmative action" choice who would never have been considered if she had not been a woman. A three-term congresswoman with unwavering allegiance to the Speaker, she had never been mentioned as a presidential candidate; and the vice-president is someone who might become president. Despite difficulties arising from her own and her husband's finances, she proved to be a formidable character. Not all women liked her; some of them recoiled from her demonstration of the aggressive qualities necessary in a woman to succeed in politics. But as a means of recovering the Democratic majority, she was a failure because she was an immediate reminder of a policy, affirmative action, that has been rending that majority apart. Once, in denying (incompletely) that she was over-shadowing Mondale, she reminded her audience that whenever they saw her as candidate, "immediately they harken back to the person who made that possible, which is Walter Mondale." And so it was all for nought: according to one exit poll, New York Italian-American, Catholic women went for Reagan, 54 to 46 percent.

Thus Mondale let the South go to the Republicans without holding the Democrats' traditional strength among blue-collar workers. His only profit in this move was the Jewish vote, which went 32 percent for Reagan in 1984, as against 39 percent in 1980. Jews were antagonized by Reagan's wooing of Christian conservatives, by whom he helped himself win the South, and they swallowed both their fear of Jesse Jackson and their dislike of affirmative action quotas to support Mondale. Blacks went 90 percent for Mondale, and provided one-fourth of his vote. They had been mobilized for the election by Jesse Jackson's candidacy for the Democratic nomination, to which they rallied in near unanimity despite Jackson's far-left politics and his attraction to tyrants such as Qaddafi and Castro. Mondale gladly accepted blacks' votes while taking his foreign policy toward the center and speaking frequently of a strong America. At the end he did his best to raise fears for the American people's "entitlements," with mixed results as we have seen. He did himself no good against Reagan, but he probably helped the cause of the Democrats in Congress.

The Presidential and the Congressional Parties

If we step back from the result of the election and the campaign, we must revise our first impression because the gratitude displayed by the American people to its leaders was not so much ennobling as indiscriminate. Although a democratic election may provide an opportunity for, even a duty of, gratitude, such as the rejected opportunity of the British election of 1945, it is more typically an assertion of choice in which the health of a democratic constitution may be judged more by the robustness of the voters than by their deference to doctors. This election suggests that the American people, by returning both the Republican president and the Democratic House, were trying to have it both ways rather than make a choice. Discussing the British Constitution in its period of separated powers, Montesquieu spoke of the two parties (he meant the court and country parties) that gather around the two visible powers, legislative and executive.

In America now, the two parties are legislative and executive, and obviously many people belong to both. This condition is not necessarily deplorable, as in America it is considered that passage of the executive's program in the legislature is a task to be achieved, and not, as in Britain, a normal consequence of a party majority in the House of Commons. In America the task has usually been made easier, though not easy, by the existence of one clear majority party in both the legislature and the executive owing its primacy to a great victory in one critical election, a victory whose principles it repeats and whose partners it rallies in following elections. The question, then, of the American people's ability to choose comes down to its ability to live under the last critical election or make a new one. From presidential elections in the 1970s and 1980s it is clear that Americans cannot continue in the choice they made in 1932 for a Democratic majority, but from the congressional results it is apparent that they have not yet chosen to be Republicans. Perhaps we are headed for a realignment without a critical election, a "rolling realignment." In the meantime the resistance to this realignment seems to be mainly deplorable.

At present the American constitutional structure of separated powers nourishes a party of progress in the presidency and a party of order in the Congress. But the *progress* is incoherent and the order is largely corrupt. And the fault, I believe, lies not in the Constitution, but in a general departure from the Constitution of which Republicans are unaware and Democrats uncaring.

Consider first the Democrats, the party of order entrenched in Congress. There it lives by the devices of constituency service, nonpartisan in themselves, yet instrumental to the getting of not favors or rights, but "entitlements," under the broad welfare state legislation for which this party was responsible. At present, its legislative initiatives in domestic policy consist of generally successful attempts to expand this legislation marginally and to make it more costly. Congress cannot pass a budget under its own Budget Reform Act (1974), and it appropriates money under emergency procedures now become routine, while allowing the deficit to grow and blaming the president (who seems irritatingly unconcerned). A multitude of subcommittees encourages media display by their chairmen with the immediate object of gaining respect for their own assiduity and rectitude. Their further goal, the formal cause of the party of order, is incumbency. The emoluments of incumbency, for example, a large and growing staff, are less important than the professional dedication to the needs of the people such emoluments support. Incumbency for the sake of entitlements: that is the Democratic party today.

Entitlements versus Opportunity

A liberal constitution, in its most general principle exists to protect the rights of the people and to advance the public good. How did these rights come to be redefined as entitlements and the public good understood as the collection of entitlements? In the narrow sense an *entitlement* is a budget item that cannot be touched because the law awards it without reference to the number who claim it or to the cost. But the term has escaped into political philosophy and settled into American political practice. There it challenges the distinction, essential to liberal constitutionalism, between the rights the government exists to protect and the exercise of those rights by private individuals, or between state and society. For an entitlement is a right whose exercise is guaranteed to a certain degree by the government—a right that is therefore exercised to that degree by the government. An equal right to seek a job, for example, becomes an entitlement to a job or rather to the proceeds of a job, which the government performs as it were instead of the worker. In this way government spreads into society, looking for more private activities to equalize and, with decreasing reluctance, to exercise itself instead of, yet on behalf of, those it wishes to benefit. Thus it grows unchecked by the liberal understanding that constitutional government must be limited in scope and in methods, because the defenders of liberalism, the followers of Locke and Mill, have surrendered to the criticisms made by Marx and Nietzsche of the essential liberal distinction. The main obstacle to the growth of entitlements has been popular suspicion and opposition, applauded by a few conservatives, which have been more faithful to liberalism than have liberal intellectuals.

The manifest, utter failure of the social programs establishing entitlements has been ably summarized in Charles Murray's book *Losing Ground: American and Social Policy, 1950–1980* (1984). He shows that the progress achieved in the 1950s by the poor and by blacks in consequence of equalizing opportunity was slowed, and even reversed, because of Democratic legislation in the 1960s that turned rights into entitlements. "Popular wisdom"—in truth, liberal opinion—opposing this legislation on the grounds that it would make its beneficiaries dependents of the government has been proven correct, and the sophisticated dismissal of this objection proven wrong. But the political and constitutional consequences of welfare dependency have not been followed out, and the society of entitlements that makes dependents of all has not been seen in its full extent.

Not only the poor but others as well become dependent on their entitlements—blacks on affirmative action, workers on social security, farmers on subsidies, the middle class on student loans, and the rich on tax shelters. Indeed, the present tax code (in 1984) epitomizes the situation in its high rate, from which its many loopholes seem to offer relief but in fact lead to more dependency. A people so fragmented by its dependencies has difficulty in seeing itself as a whole and thus in making a choice as a people. Its various dependent groups can hardly be gathered in an active majority because self-restraint in any particular group for the sake of such a majority would make no apparent difference in the sum of entitlements and would bring no discernible benefit to it or to any other group.

Dependency thus reaches beyond private lives into politics, as each group votes to protect its own entitlements. These are the "special interests" for which the Democrats have become known. Under Franklin Roosevelt and Harry Truman, Republicans were accused of being the party of special interests, meaning those who take more than their share. It was the job of government, according to the Democrats, to regulate such interests and to put an end to their domination. Now, however, Democrats are accused of representing special interests of a new sort: those created by attempts to regulate the old special interests. Such interests are "special" not because they seek out new profit for themselves, which is characteristic of private groups in liberal society, but because they want to secure the advantages government is protecting for them. No group in America is now more victimized by this sort of dependency than are blacks by the policy of affirmative action. Their pattern of voting, not to mention the rhetoric of their leaders, shows that they regard themselves as dependent on government for their well-being, indeed even for their freedom. Whereas blacks have almost no representation in the presidential party, they are (as their leaders claim) the soul of the congressional party because in the policy of affirmative action they have what all other elements of that party seek to have. But precisely in this position blacks call attention to themselves as *the* special interest and thereby suffer from a new ill will that is not racism but is sometimes mixed or confused with racism.

In foreign policy the Democratic party encourages the belief that the American people have an entitlement to peace. For the right, proclaimed in the Declaration of Independence, of a people to assume a "separate and equal station" among the powers of the earth is understood no longer as

a right of self-defense and of self-development but instead as an entitlement to peace and prosperity that government has the duty to guarantee.
Since this task has not been accomplished by the United Nations, it falls
to the U.S. government; and since the president can take only preliminary
or temporary measures, Congress must pass a law; and since that law can
reach offenders only within America, the main enemy of peace comes to
seem the lawlessness of one's own country. The War Powers Resolution
of 1973 has thus been the cornerstone of the congressional party's foreign
policy, the war powers controlled therein being those belonging to the
U.S. military. "Human rights" in their entitlement understanding are
rights the U.S. government has a duty to guarantee anywhere, regardless
of the feelings or actions of the peoples involved; so it is not surprising
that, among these rights, the right of consent by which a people exercises
its other rights on its own is almost never mentioned. The nuclear freeze,
a kind of law proposed on behalf of humanity, is another item in the
extension of legal entitlements into international relations. It has been
promoted by Democratic intellectuals who also accuse Ronald Reagan of
simplistic thinking in foreign affairs.

If all this sounds like the talk of yet another ill-tempered critic of the
welfare state, let it be remarked at least that my principal objection is to
its political and constitutional effects, to which other critics, especially the
Republicans, are not sufficiently attentive. Despite the difficulty mentioned above of gathering a majority against entitlements, the Republicans have done so, though as yet only in the presidential party. That
majority has a rather abstract character, since it is not yet clear whether
its elements are willing to surrender their separate entitlements by electing a Republican Congress; so far they have passed up three opportunities
to do so in 1980, 1982, and 1984. The passage of a flat tax in the next
Congress would be an encouraging sign (see chapter 5), because it would
require an alienation of every group's favorite loopholes in exchange for
a better and more equal general incentive. At the moment, however, the
desire of Americans to check their Republican president with a Democratic House cannot be interpreted as suggesting the virtue of moderation.

The Republicans have become the party of progress understood as
opportunity, a word used constantly in Reagan's campaign. Opportunity
is more naturally suited to, and better symbolized by, the president, who
has the power and duty to act on his own and has arrived at the office by
a route that could almost never be described as an entitlement. America
is a land of opportunity because anyone can become president (and anyone sometimes has): the single example of the top political office, or a few
examples of successful businessmen, scientists, or inventors suffuse the

less attractive opportunities, which are open to the many, with a glow of success. Of course some opportunities can be called such only with sarcasm. But even those Americans who have little take satisfaction in the opportunity to have had more, and for their children to have more. Yet despite the central role of politics in making opportunity a viable democratic principle, most Republicans have seen opportunity in terms of incentive, as economic. The Democrats assert that this libertarian view is selfish, to which Republicans can reply that theirs is also the party of traditional or conservative values, of patriotism, family, and religion. Republicans, then, have two objections to the society of entitlements: one, arising from libertarianism, that it stifles incentives, another centered in the Moral Majority, that it is morally corrupt. Both are true, in my opinion, but the Republican problem is to reconcile them.

Libertarianism seeks to take the government off our backs and promises to put nothing in its place, neither conscience nor responsibility. It can be quickly described as the belief that a system of self-government does not require any self in the system to govern himself. It speaks of incentives but does not say toward what, except in the meaningless or all too easily understood phrase maximization of utility. It does not appreciate that individuality cannot be assumed but must be achieved, that an isolated individual is less (or more) than human, and that human beings come to the dignity of individuality by taking on the responsibilities of family and citizenship.

The *Moral Majority*, on the other hand, is concerned above all with the souls of Americans, but it has difficulty in finding a universal definition of the healthy individual soul suitable for a free, secular society. Whereas the libertarians try to minimize every influence of the state in society, the Moral Majority seems to want to abolish the distinction between state and society. It confuses persuasion with conversion, and it asks for public school prayer with arguments that would justify far more mixing of church and state. Or it clumsily adopts the language of rights used by its opponents, for example the "rights of the unborn" in the abortion debate. These are two glancing blows at the society of entitlements that do not strike its head and its heart. Its head is full of clever theories that have been substituted for liberal constitutionalism, and its heart is sick with the dependency and irresponsibility of the entitled. What we need is comprehensive reflection on the nature, and the ways and means, of self-government. This reflection can begin from the wisdom in the Constitution and its practices.

5

The 1988 Election: Another Reagan Triumph

The election of George Bush to the presidency in 1988 was a triumph for Ronald Reagan.* The margin of victory was substantial (54 percent to Bush over 46 percent to Michael Dukakis in the popular vote), though not of Reaganesque proportions. But then the master might not wish his apprentice to do as well as himself. Reagan has not only brought peace and prosperity in his own terms while in office, but has also succeeded in leaving a legacy. And the legacy is not only in the political changes he instituted but partly in the person of his immediate successor, the first vice-president to succeed as president by election since Martin Van Buren in 1837.

Yet if an unusually orderly succession marked Reagan's triumph, the limit of his success was also well defined by an institution. That institution is a reelected Congress teeming with Democratic opponents who are displeased with the character of Bush's campaign, ready to pounce upon presidential mistakes, and eager to insist on retention of the spending programs they had supported while running for reelection. Not many of them had to "run." Over 98 percent of incumbent members up for re-election to the House of Representatives were reelected, and most of those not reelected had been caught in a scandal. In the Senate, in which turnover is more frequent, only four incumbents were defeated in thirty-three elections. The Democrats gained three seats in the House and one in the Senate, despite Bush's easy win.

In sum, although the Republicans have their fifth victory in the last six presidential elections, there has been no party realignment. The long-term trend favoring Republicans since Reagan's first election in 1980 has stalled at 34 percent of the voters calling themselves Republicans and 37

*Chapter 5 was first published as "The American Election: Another Reagan Triumph." *Government and Opposition* 24 (1989):28–38.

percent Democrats, figures hardly encouraging for either party. Americans are accustomed to having a majority party that dominates both legislative and executive branches of the federal government, and most states, for decades. And when the people have put an end to one such majority, as in 1860 or 1932, they have installed a new one. But not now: "it's a whole new ball game." Republicans win the presidency with ease and cannot win Congress; Democrats do poorly in the presidential contest and cannot lose Congress. The situation has lasted long enough—particularly in view of successful Democratic resistance in congressional elections to the popularity of Reagan—to require explanation as something other than a transition between majority parties.

The explanation I favor can be found in chapter 4 on the 1984 presidential election, in which a distinction between the entitlements defended by the Democrats and the opportunity promoted by Republicans is developed. The party of order (the Democrats) presides over social programs that are understood not as rights to be protected by government and exercised by private individuals but as government services to which they are entitled without any action on their part. Under the American constitutional scheme, the party of order is situated in the legislature, in which upward adjustments in social programs may be effected and complaints may be registered against uncaring bureaucracy. The party of progress (the Republicans) appeals to dislike of the stagnation and dependency caused by automatic entitlements, and its home is in the presidency, the center of political initiative in the American system. Americans have not yet chosen—they have not yet been compelled to choose—between these parties. Essentially they want high entitlements and low taxes as long as it seems possible to have both. Which they will choose in a crisis they have not clearly said, perhaps because they do not really know.

That pattern of choice—or non-choice—was already evident in 1984, was strengthened by the Democratic recapture of the Senate in 1986, and has been confirmed by the most recent results. But to see the pattern in its *energeia*, let us turn from the election results to the preceding electoral campaign, and then to future prospects for governing the country. For the pattern of electoral choice, along with the nature of the campaign, has called into question whether the newly elected president has a mandate to govern. What is a mandate, in the current political situation in America?

The Reagan Legacy

The campaign took its shape from the Reagan legacy. In accepting the presidential nomination, Dukakis declared that the "Reagan era is over."

But in fact his campaign was responding to the new political situation, unfavorable to Democrats, that Reagan established.

What did Reagan do? He raised defense spending and cut taxes, thus creating a considerable budget deficit. The defense buildup was accompanied by a generally—by no means uniformly—successful foreign policy, which produced two results Democrats had to applaud. They had said the increased defense spending would heat up the arms race, and they had criticized the Reagan administration for supporting right-wing dictators. In fact—no doubt partly by good luck—the defense buildup was succeeded by an arms control treaty with the Soviet Union, the first actually to reduce the number of nuclear missiles. And the dictators have fallen upon evil days, especially in Latin America where the United States had been blamed most for their persistence. Moreover, if the Democrats could not bring themselves to approve it, they had to admit a certain revived pride in America's place in the world.

Here was a difficult point of attack. Was domestic policy a more inviting target? Reagan's tax cut in 1981 was followed by the remarkable tax reform of 1986, a bipartisan effort from which the Republicans may have received greater benefit. The tax cut was supposed to pay for itself, according to supply-side economics, by encouraging more productivity from a lower rate. But the extra revenue that indeed resulted from this source was far from matching increased spending on entitlements. The tax reform, supposedly revenue-neutral, established a conservative principle by greatly weakening the progressivity of tax rates. On entering office, Reagan had reasserted the pre–New Deal view of taxes as for revenue only, not to redistribute income. Liberals had favored the tax reform because it closed loopholes, and because they hoped that, when the time was right, they could raise the rates that had been lowered in compensation for the loss of exemptions and deductions.

The time was not right in 1988, however. In 1984, the Democratic presidential candidate Walter Mondale had made a bold promise to raise taxes, but the memory of his disastrous failure was still green. On the Republican side, the failure to cut middle-class entitlements was just as pronounced. Early in the Reagan administration the least hint of a modest paring was roundly denounced by Democrats and was punished by the voters in the congressional election of 1982. Thus the high deficit was incurred—deliberately risked by Reagan, should Congress not cut entitlement spending, and deliberately accepted by Democrats in preference to a cut in that spending.

One could say, without hostility to Reagan, that his political legacy is summed up in the deficit. Determined to build defense and cut taxes, he conceded that he could not keep his word to balance the budget as long as the American people continued to return a Democratic majority to Congress. He would await the trial of low taxes versus high entitlements and not surrender in advance, having secured a position in which the benefits of low taxes are as actual and sensible as those of high entitlements. The American people can then choose fairly, when they see they must, with close knowledge of the benefits they decide to forgo. Such a choice, Reagan could say, is more informed and responsible than the one his critics want him to make on behalf of the people; the latter alternative would make the people pay for the entitlements without having felt the full cost. Responsible democratic government should induce responsibility in the people one might conclude. But can we afford to suffer the crisis necessary to compel the American people to choose?

The L-Word

The presidential campaign was based on the Reagan legacy. Hence it seemed unpromising for the Democrats, who had to run against peace and prosperity, and on terms defined by Reagan. But recent events had gone their way, and they were convinced they could win. The Iran-Contra affair had caught Reagan in a manifest reversal of his policy against compromising with terrorists, and the exposure of secret dealings contrary to his will by his subordinates made people think he had been asleep. The Democrats were also emboldened by their success in foiling Reagan in the two most important issues of 1988, the appointment of Robert Bork to the Supreme Court and military support for the Contras in Nicaragua.

The Democrats decided they could win by concealing who they were. Having chosen Michael Dukakis in the primaries less contentiously than expected, they used their nominating convention in July 1988 to establish the theme of "competence, not ideology" announced by their candidate. Nominating conventions used actually to nominate a candidate; now they merely register the result of the primaries and set the tone for the campaign.

In the Democratic convention none of the extreme groups that had been so prominent at the previous convention in 1984 was on view; this time the party did not advertise its receptivity to "special interests" by presenting a collection of oddballs to television viewers. The feminists, gays, and pacifists—along with others on the Left—conceded their voice to Jesse Jackson and kept quiet themselves. Jackson is the first black to have come so far toward the presidency, but during the primaries he showed himself too far to the Left to be considered a serious candidate. Nonetheless, he was praised for his moderation, and at the convention he did not insist on any of his policy differences with Dukakis. The Democratic platform adopted there was comfortably vague, lacking the specific pledges that interest groups usually demand. Dukakis gave an able speech, asserting his own competence by contrast to the slipshod Reagan administration and claiming to be capable of "tough choices." Tough choices require hardness of spirit rather than traditional Democractic compassion, though in fact Dukakis did not intend to cut entitlement programs.

Until the Republican convention met in late August, George Bush seemed almost invisible. He had scored an even easier victory in the primaries than Dukakis. He allowed his opponent to gain a 17-point lead in the polls, and Democrats began to smell victory. But at the convention he gave his best speech ever, showing himself (with the aid of an excellent speech writer) in command and beginning to dispel his reputation as a wimp. Taking aim at the substratum of principle beneath policy, he asserted *values* as opposed to Dukakis's *choices*. Values determine choices, he seemed to say; so *ideology*, in Dukakis's slogan, directs competence. The election, therefore, is about ideology, and only secondarily about competence. Bush's campaign set about to "define" Dukakis, meaning to define him as a liberal—the dreaded L-word.[1]

The effort, skillfully managed by an experienced staff, was brilliantly successful. Soon after the Republican convention, a great shift in sentiment occurred, and from having been a woeful underdog, Bush emerged as the confident favorite. *His* values were those of the American mainstream; only his opponent's values needed to be defined. The ensuing, much-accused negative campaigning in speeches and especially in television advertising permitted Bush to appear as the forceful champion of American values, less and less a wimp. His attacks did not descend to name-calling, and by historical standards in America were rather pallid. They could be excused partly by Dukakis's attempt at concealment and also by the precedent set the year before by the Democrats' negative campaign against Bork.

A focus on values directed attention away from the reasoned deliberation that might turn values into policies. Similarly, Dukakis's boast of his ability to make tough choices did not disclose much of what he would actually choose. The superficial profundity of the one candidate was matched by the superficial resoluteness of the other, and both preferred to evoke an image rather than argue a point. Reason is feeble enough in human affairs, above all in politics, so that we do gratuitous harm when we make virtues of promoting the values that supposedly precede reason and of displaying the toughness that applies it. But the work of reason, even in simplified form, does not play well on television. Television seeks "sound bites" and "visuals." Even though most journalists favored Dukakis, the Bush campaign produced better one-line statements and more colorful pictures of flag-waving supporters.

It is possible to give a less Heideggerean interpretation of the celebration of irrational values and choices. Perhaps in speaking of values, Bush meant to appeal to common sense; and in defining Dukakis negatively, he was arguing in time-honored fashion, justified by Aristotle, from character rather than in enthymemes. In attacking Dukakis as the "liberal governor from Massachusetts"—the most liberal state in the nation—Bush specified three things: his having vetoed, as governor, a bill requiring public school teachers to lead children in the pledge of allegiance to the flag; his being, by his own boast, a card-carrying member of the American Civil Liberties Union; and his having supported a furlough program for prisoners under which a murderer escaped and committed a rape and a murder.

Though the charges were often made in misleading form, implying lack of patriotism and sympathy with crime, they are essentially true portrayals of both Dukakis and contemporary American liberalism. The pledge of allegiance is to the flag "and to the republic for which it stands." It was not written until 1892 and seems to have been intended at first for immigrants. Its overt, compulsory patriotism represents a point of disagreement between liberals and conservatives today. Liberals take patriotism for granted and dwell on diversity, whereas conservatives seem more aware of the need for unity and are willing to use compulsion to attain it. The need for instilling habits is common sense, but the necessity of overt patriotism in a country constituted by its republican principle is especially, though not peculiarly, American. It is just because liberals believe that America is founded on principle that in controversies with other nations they tend to "blame America first" (in Jeanne Kirkpatrick's phrase). Liberals should be grateful for the reminder that a free people is one as well as many, and that the unity is not automatic but needs to be constituted or pledged.

The ACLU, and most liberals, believes that a right is not secure unless it can be exercised to an extreme. The ACLU therefore teaches that respect for the rights of others requires respect for extremism. This doctrine, which, for example, transforms the right of free speech into a right to protest against others' free speech, is contrary to common sense and even hostile to diversity. For diversity is refreshed by a reminder of the principles a free people shares in common, and its moderation is a sign of health, not apathy. Criminality is unhealthy diversity, and furloughs given to murderers suggest a loss of the will to punish—and, men being what they are, a loss of will, simply.

Bush's three attacks on Dukakis exposed not only a liberal but also a liberalism that is politically exhausted and bored with itself. It is not unpatriotic, but it sees no need for patriotism. It is not extremist, but it is tempted or titillated by extremism—as shown by the unwillingness to denounce Jesse Jackson's campaign. And though it knows crime is wrong, it is sympathetic to criminals. Bush did not accuse liberals of being attracted to socialism, but he might have done so. The War against Poverty that began in the Johnson administration was inspired by a socialist's book, Michael Harrington's *The Other America* (1962). For some time now, liberalism has been uncertain of its definition and, in particular, unmindful of its boundary on the Left. But this was the first presidential campaign in which the L-word was repeatedly made an article of accusation: quite a change from the days of Kennedy and Johnson (let alone Roosevelt and Truman), signaling a realignment in the governing ideas of American politics if not a new majority party.

Dukakis could have campaigned under his true colors as a liberal. But he was constrained by the deficit, that is, by the opportunity to make an issue of the deficit; so he put forth modest programs for student loans, housing, and medicine of a kind described as "leveraged liberalism." Rather than requiring government outlays, they relied on compelling private business to shoulder the costs of providing entitlements. Two weeks before the end of the campaign, Dukakis finally admitted he was a liberal and said he was proud of it. But by then it was too late; he seemed merely to confirm what his opponent had been alleging. He made his appeal to patriotism by attacking the trade deficit, but, to his credit, he was a halfhearted protectionist. And in any case, he could not support American workers without seeming to blame American consumers. At the end of the campaign, he made some headway by claiming to be "on your side." This was an appeal, however, to the old Democratic majority which no longer exists for presidential elections.

Each party had the candidate—not that it wanted to run—but that it wanted to run against. The Democrats saw George Bush as burdened with the mistakes of the Reagan administration and involved in none of its successes: "Where was George?" asked Senator Edward Kennedy. Bush had a country-club background and could not speak articulately or forcefully. The Republicans, for their part, could not believe that the Democrats had nominated a northeastern liberal from the only state that had gone for George McGovern in 1972.

In the event the Republicans were proved right. In the primaries Dukakis survived by making no mistakes. Then he devised a winning strategy for the election. When it obviously was not winning for him, he was at a loss: a competent man, running on his competence, and appearing incompetent because he had thought competence was enough. His intelligence did not prevent him from appearing to be superior. In the second debate, it is reported, he intended to say: "Some people say I'm arrogant, but I know better than that." But he forgot, and the moment of self-deprecating humor he had planned eluded him. Bush, meanwhile, thrived in the bright light and hot air of the campaign, showing himself personable, warm, and grandfatherly. He easily survived, if he did not quite face down, the furor over his error in selecting Dan Quayle for vice-president. To put it gently, Quayle was not ready for the attention he received. But Bush was, and it did not matter.

The Mandate

Since Bush had based his campaign on values, not policies, there was a general movement after his election, led by Democrats in Congress, to deny that he had received any mandate from his victory. One could answer that he had based his campaign on the Reagan administration's policies, and that he had said he wanted to continue the Reagan revolution. This was sufficient notice of his plans. No more information was available from candidate Dukakis, who, as I said, reiterated the necessity of making tough choices without giving an example of one that would be tough for him (in the second debate, Dukakis gave examples of choices that would be difficult for Bush). In regard to the deficit, neither candidate had a convincing solution, though Bush was more definite in ruling out any new taxes ("read my lips"). But perhaps in treating so intractable an issue—necessarily subject to bargaining, change, and external factors— we should not require a detailed plan or even a plan of any kind.

What was lacking in the campaign was not so much the specifics of policies as argument. The candidates sought to array themselves on our side, that is, on the side of a majority. They said little to enlighten or instruct the American people or the part of it they were attempting to attract. I do not mean that a politician can or should treat voters as if they were pupils in school. He wants to win the election—but he also needs to govern once he has won. What is wrong with the liberal positions on patriotism, civil rights, and crime that Bush attacked so effectively? He did not say, nor did Dukakis defend them. Differences over foreign policy were deep and clearly marked in the case of specific incidents, but they too were unexplained by the candidates. In sum, the problem is not that Bush lacks a stick with which to beat the Congress; he has the Reagan mandate reasserted. But what is the meaning of the Reagan revolution? By failing to restate the arguments behind the policies, Bush allows the change to lose its momentum and its sense of direction for the American people. Worse, he risks losing direction in his own administration and in himself.

The notion of a *mandate* is old enough to have been refuted by Edmund Burke in his noble *Speech to the Electors of Bristol* in 1774. In Burke's view, the issuance of a specific mandate from the voters to their representative violates the space needed for the reason and judgment representatives owe to voters. Similarly, the American founders understood the function of representation as adding reason to popular will. When they sought a strong presidency, for instance, they wanted strength not from the backing of the people but against the people's momentary inclinations. Alexander Hamilton spoke of "extensive and arduous enterprises" (*Federalist* 72) that would attract noble spirits to that office; nothing was said about disclosing such enterprises to the people while campaigning for the presidency. Indeed, nothing was said about campaigning.

For good or ill, the days of high-minded representation are over. In America we live under what Jeffrey Tulis calls, in a brilliant new book, the "rhetorical presidency."[2] Although the constitutional structure remains in effect, it has been overlaid (not replaced) by the expectation, established since Woodrow Wilson, that presidents will carry their programs to the people. Such programs, one might add, are not likely to be "extensive and arduous" for the people, however much they exercise presidents. They will address an obvious problem of economics or peace within the range of the goals comprised by the "pursuit of happiness."[3] Nothing taxing will be proposed: no military glory, no empire. Modern Americans and their like will not mount a daring expedition against Sicily, as did the ancient democrats in Athens. It will take a crisis to make any sacrifice seem reasonable.

Then, since representatives today who ignore or act against popular will cannot reject the notion of mandate in the name of reason, as did Burke, perhaps the mandate should be made as reasonable as possible. To do this, a presidential candidate must develop a principle supported by argument simple enough for the public to understand and broad enough to gather a majority. He must make use of television's sound bites and visuals, but must realize that they dilute rather than concentrate the message because they rob it of its reasoning. The candidate must try to fight his way through the "voice overs" of dull-witted media interpreters, as President Reagan did with his weekly radio broadcasts.

If a candidate does not establish or renew a mandate for himself, he allows himself to be judged by someone else's mandate. He can appeal to a neutral performance standard, as Bush did when he contrasted the high rates of inflation, interest, and unemployment under the Carter administration with Reagan's economic achievement. But if you think that the budget deficit is crucial, you can be talked out of your sense of prosperity to the conclusion that the performance is not what it seems. Moreover, democratic leaders need to be believed when things go wrong—especially then. At such times your supporters need an argument to tell them why you should "stay the course" (Reagan's slogan for the 1982 congressional election, held during a recession). When the graphs turn down and the "misery index" goes up, a mere performance standard—asking the people whether they are better off—will suggest that your supporters should desert you. These are the perils of pragmatism: the pragmatic choice is open to interpretation (for even pragmatism is a philosophy), and it is faithless.

Sooner or later, of course, your supporters will depart. All the enterprises of democratic leaders today are subject to replacement. They appeal to a modern people's love of novelty and eventually they die by the same appeal from another leader. After the election of Bush, the Reagan era continues; but it will end. In the interim between mere pragmatic adjustment and philosophic detachment lies the enterprise of a democratic mandate, in which honor and reason are partners.

Part II

Constitutional Conservatism
in the Reagan Era

6

Pride versus Interest in American Conservatism

If I begin by calling the Reagan revolution "the revolt of the stupid," it will be clear at least that the following is not intended as a value-free survey of American conservatism today. Less clear, perhaps, will be my general approval of the revolt, although that will emerge soon enough. It remains to announce that I want to offer some friendly advice to American conservatism regarding pride and interest and to recommend to its attention the American Constitution, which so beautifully combines them. American conservatives, perhaps because of the manipulations of American liberals, have lost some of their attachment to the Constitution, and much of their understanding of it.

The Anti-Intellectualism of Intellectuals

Recently I overheard someone say that Harvard University was wrong to have invited Ronald Reagan to its three hundred fiftieth anniversary in the fall of 1986 because of Reagan's "anti-intellectualism." What could this comment have meant? Reagan had reduced student loan programs and university research programs, and wanted to cut them further. He invited many actors and very few professors to his White House dinners. Like the Democratic president he frequently praised, the one who began the practice of using ghostwriters for his speeches—Franklin D. Roosevelt, he himself should have been, and probably was, a C student in college. In sum, Reagan does not sufficiently respect the intellect.

To this charge many Reagan followers of a populist bent would respond by accusing liberal intellectuals of "elitism." But this action on Reagan's behalf deepened his guilt, because *elitism* is an epithet invented by liberal intellectuals; it is too fancy for redneck populists. Reagan thereby added responsibility for plagiarism to his anti-intellectualism, though in a manner that makes us wonder whether he and his followers were so stupid after all. Notwithstanding the tentativeness of Reagan's programs, their partial enactment, and their imperfect success, America had seen a complete revolution in sixteen years from the landslide defeat in 1964 of the Goldwaterites, universally despised by intellectuals, to the landslide victory in 1980 of their successors, the Reaganites, still generally if not universally despised by intellectuals. In the making of the revolution, Goldwater was the champion, and very little more; Nixon was a manipulator and an inconstant contributor; and Reagan, who captured the Republican party before he took over the presidency, was leader as well as spokesman.

To return to the epithet *elitism*, we can infer that the revolt of the stupid was not unprepared by the intellectuals. To be known as an intellectual is to accept praise for one's intellect—to take pride in it and, as we have seen, to demand respect for it. Yet in our day intellectuals too seem to have lost respect for the intellect and seem to be guilty themselves of anti-intellectualism. They no longer believe in social progress led by scientific discoveries and by artistic creations, and above all, they no longer believe that the human intellect has the capacity to find answers to life's deepest or most urgent questions. Then for intellectuals to give currency to accusations of elitism in the hope that they will land only on "reactionaries"—who, incidentally, are today both greater believers in and greater contributors to progress than intellectuals—reveals complacent disregard for their own vulnerability, and their own interest. Intellectuals themselves may no longer respect the intellect, but they have not yet abandoned their conviction that democracy can and should respect it, that democracy need not necessarily suffer from anti-intellectualism. Liberal intellectuals, particularly, take pride in their promotion of democracy, and in the programs they have conceived and sponsored for the "least advantaged" in a spirit of headlong compassion. They were perhaps vaguely aware that the democratism in which they took pride did not promote their own interest, which is that of the better or most advantaged. To that extent, their pride was increased, for pride takes pride in rising above interest. They became earnest, loving, and generous taxpayers.

The trouble, however, is that they learned to justify and helped to create a society of entitlements and a nation of dependents. Due respect to intellectuals compels one to assume that they know what they are doing, by contrast to politicians who stumble over expedients or imitate one another by coming forward with fashionable ideas whose time has come. It was intellectuals who redefined individual rights that one had to exercise for oneself as entitlements whose exercise is guaranteed to a certain degree by the government. The beneficiaries of entitlements are excused from the exercise of their rights on their own because their disadvantaged backgrounds, it is said, prevent them from competing on an equal basis. In other words: once a slave, always a slave (this is not said). Since the beneficiaries are incapable of individual responsibility, they are not treated as individuals but instead are identified according to their differing interests as perceived from outside by intellectuals and thereafter bureaucrats with the wisdom to discern such interests; or, ironically, interests sufficiently capable to organize themselves as interests claim the protection due to the incapable and the disorganized. In this way entitlements are extended from the disadvantaged simply to those who *feel* disadvantaged by preferences shown to the disadvantaged, and a competition ensues in appeals to compassion or just plain whining.

When the government declares war on poverty, everyone wants to be poor. Individuals driven into their interest dependencies try to find shelter in their weakness, both as individuals too weak to receive the equal treatment the government is handing out to everyone but themselves and as groups too weak to reform the system. In this system it is weakness that gets public attention. Individuals and groups who can take pride in, and can boast of, their contributions to the common good do not receive political recognition as such; their strengths are forgotten. Though it matters to have clout, one gets it or justifies it by claiming need. In sum, entitlements conceived or conceptualized by intellectuals are designed to serve the *interest* of the American people, but by making them a nation of dependents, they take no account of their pride.

The intellectuals who take pride in disregarding their own interests of course do not allow the disadvantaged this same aristocratic privilege; they do not even allow them the democratic right of asserting their interests on their own. We take note of a political truth our intellectuals have forgotten (forgotten, because it is featured in the liberal political philosophy of John Locke): that the satisfaction of one's interests is compatible with the loss of one's freedom. Liberalism, which began with the rejection of paternalism on behalf of religion and virtue, now has returned to paternalism to ensure safety and comfort.

In the face of this performance by intellectuals, and (to repeat) with a view to their own lack of esteem for the intellect, anti-intellectualism might seem a reasonable response. One could simply have given one's loyalty to President Reagan, who seems to have done much for both the pride and the interest of the American people. But even if we do not make the common mistake of underestimating Reagan—a mistake almost unavoidable by intellectuals—it must be admitted that his intelligence has to be inferred from events and results: it does not shine in his words. What shines in his words is common sense, but the ideas come from elsewhere, from conservative intellectuals. So far I have spoken of intellectuals as if they were necessarily liberal, but conservative intellectuals do exist.

Conservatism and Reason

Conservative intellectuals are, at the least, uneasy about their status as intellectuals. They share in the anti-intellectualism that liberal intellectuals, to their amazement, find in the common people of America. They had doubts about social progress led by scientists and intellectuals soon after the idea was first announced, and when the idea became real in the French Revolution, their doubts hardened into opposition. Conservative intellectuals did not have to wait for Nietzsche and Nietzsche's left-wing translators to teach them to doubt the power of the human intellect. From the first—let us say, from Hume on—they denied the notion that the human intellect could grasp society as a whole in order to reform it in accordance with the rational principles governing the whole. Such a reform would be, or would soon lead to, a revolution in which the furies of passion, not reason, would triumph. Reason in its place, when not attempting to grasp the whole—of society, of the world, of everything— was acceptable to conservatives. Reason could be prudent in the management of human affairs, in the manner of Edmund Burke, or could calculate one's interest as with Adam Smith, but reason that attempted deliberately to construct a whole, as through the social contract, was the greatest boast of human folly.

Conservatives believed that reason was necessary and useful in things up close to us, in front of our noses, but farther away things in the big picture have to be understood as in the domain of nature, when *nature* is understood as beyond human control, that is, as including both nature as classically understood (the intelligible) and chance. Nature so conceived can either be grasped with a single swoop of unreason—the romantic imagination—or be left to take care of itself under the control, if one wishes to think so, of an Invisible Hand. In this overall consideration one can say that conservatism, with its hostility to reasoning about the whole, begins as a doubt about the extent and even the possibility of self-government: we humans can govern ourselves in small matters only.

The Libertarians

How does American conservatism today fit this view of the fundamental trend of conservatism? We remark first that, although romanticism had an effect in America, not many American conservatives today come from the romantic type of Burke and his successors. (Burke, I can tell you, does not sell well in Reagan's America.) A hardy band of academic conservatives does exist in the environs of William F. Buckley's *National Review*, but they have not come to the prominence in the Reagan revolution to which their long service and suffering in the liberal era entitle them. Obviously conservative intellectuals of the libertarian variety who, descended from (if not equal to) Adam Smith, such as Ayn Rand, Friedrich Hayek, Robert Nozick, and political economists of the "public choice" school, have fared much better. The market has favored preachers of the market. The libertarians have attacked government subsidies, government transfers of income, and government regulation as inefficient and also as incompatible with liberty. These are two different considerations, as different indeed as interest and pride, but they tend to be presented as one. If too much government has been consented to, as clearly was the case under the Democrats and so continued under Reagan, the libertarians answer that this consent was against reason; but if much government could be found efficient, they would say it is against consent.

The libertarians cannot conceive the sociability of man; when asked to explain why people seem to like to live together, they come up with hypothetical insurance policies against the chance of having to put out a conflagration by oneself, perhaps also against the disagreeableness of solitude. When most reasonable persons hear things like these, they throw up their hands in dismay. But such gestures will not impress libertarians. They do not believe in compromise and they have made their way in the world without making concessions to what "reasonable," that is, confused persons think. They are gaining more and more adherents and, if they become a majority, it will be without having attempted it. They surely believe in *limited* government, but it is doubtful that they believe in government. They will ply you with arguments, but to impress you rather than to persuade you, so that you can join them on your own. (Also, they do not want to *be* persuaded.) They believe in the sovereignty of the self but not in the self-government of the self; so they are liberal on the social issues or on the general question of permissiveness, while conservative on economic issues.

Libertarians claim to be consistent as opposed to both liberals and conservatives, whom libertarians will accuse of unprincipled partisanship in their advocacy of liberty—liberty for the soul and not the body, or for the body and not the soul. Thus libertarians are not firmly in the Reagan camp, or in any camp but their own; they are not partisans in the Republican party, but use it. Reagan understood this: he spoke on behalf of the social issues but did nothing; and the libertarians in turn understood him.

The Fundamentalists

The conservative camp opposite to the libertarians is the Moral Majority, consisting of Protestant fundamentalists and led by the Reverend Jerry Falwell among others. (Falwell has dropped the somewhat self-righteous name of Moral Majority.) The leaders are preachers rather than teachers, and therefore do not qualify as intellectuals; but they somehow think nonetheless and their thoughts have great influence among the many who attend their churches and listen to them on television. The fundamentalists are the best and truest believers in the American Dream still left in America, apart from recent immigrants who have the advantage of observing from experience and do not need to believe. The fundamentalists have more faith in the worth and attainability of material progress than do the liberal intellectuals whom they scorn as men, or "persons," of little faith in anything. But the fundamentalists consider that the goal of material progress must be reached through immaterial means, with the help of God and by salvation in Jesus. Divine providence gives the guarantee of the attainability of material progress which secular intellectuals can no longer find in material causes, as, for example, in the study of history or in the science of economics. One should not forget that Nietzsche proclaimed the death of God and the death of liberal progress together, and as connected. So the hostility of liberal intellectuals to the fundamentalists suggests that liberals would rather keep God dead than explore how to revive liberal progress.

Fundamentalists are concerned for the virtues of the soul as well as for its salvation; they oppose the permissiveness of the entitlements society. They argue, as against liberal and libertarian individualism, that individuals are not individuals unless they are strong individuals, and that they can become strong only with the help of other human beings and of training in habits: individualism requires a good upbringing in the family. Humans are made not more independent, but instead more dependent, when they are given rights against the family. The family, in turn, needs the support of the church to enable it to hold fast against the rampant temptations of vice in this liberal society which lead individuals into dependency. Since fundamentalists regard the family as the friend rather than the enemy of the individual, they see a sorry contrast between the Welfare State that is doing its offhand, unconsidered best to destroy the family and the church that seeks actively and deliberately to foster it.

Family values are justified less for themselves than for the sake of individuals, and they remind us that pride and interest are not merely opposed. Before any individual can have an interest he must have the pride to be an individual. Such pride is increased when shared with other individuals in a nation of individuals; and fundamentalists above all others exhibit an unabashed, unsophisticated American patriotism (the only kind there is). They are passionate anti-Communists because communism is both godless and collectivist. They are not favorably impressed by Communist indoctrination in family values because Communists use the family to serve an atheist state. Although doctrinally opposed to Judaism, the fundamentalists favor and admire Israel more than liberals do. They like its informal democratic patriotism, which resembles the fundamentalists' populism. Their populism is for a people of honest individuals with good upbringing who do not need fancy constitutional contraptions in order to be honest, much less to restrain them from acting on what an honest people honestly sees. This is to say not that fundamentalists oppose the restraints of the American Constitution, but that they feel betrayed by them, above all by the Supreme Court; and their remedy is to infuse these restraints not with revived constitutional doctrine but with populist virtue. They see the American people as better than their government, perhaps accidentally for now, perhaps intrinsically. In this sentiment one can find both common sense and a touch of romanticism.

Goldwater gave little attention to family values, but Reagan has distinctively combined them with libertarian individualism in a manner that seems to emphasize morality as much as free choice. As I said, he has done little to purge the country of pornography and easy abortion, but perhaps it is enough, and certainly it is more than nothing, to speak of the immorality of these things. Morality is necessary to self-respect, which is the same as pride; and it is difficult to be proud of that behavior in a country by which one and a half million people every year sacrifice motherhood or fatherhood to their sense of their own interest, that is, convenience. No one is proud of having had an abortion, though some may never give it a second thought.

Responsible Conservatives

Another group is prudent or responsible conservatives consisting of Washington politicians such as Senator Robert Dole and a number of economists who give this position an intellectual tinge, but no more than that. Economists are not intellectuals unless they attack the bourgeoisie, but in that event they stop being economists. These conservatives are *responsible* because they take responsibility for things others have caused, not because they are responsible for causing things. Instead of mongering ideas themselves, they take as their vocation the task of cleaning up the mess others' ideas have left. They reject supply-side economics and worry about the deficit. They distrust ideological conservatism, which they think too much resembles the liberal ideas they have devoted their lives to opposing. They have, therefore, a reactive attitude more suited to a minority than a majority party, as the more eager conservatives have pointed out to them. Nonetheless it is too much to believe that the responsible conservatives will always be wrong, and that their sober, Burkean prudence will never be needed. The Republican party has to decide whether to try to retain the Reagan presidential majority with a prudent, responsible conservative or to seek to extend it to a congressional majority with an idea man (if not an intellectual).

Neo-Conservatives

Last but not least are the neo-conservatives, refugees from socialism and liberalism who voted for change with their mouths and pens. The neo-conservatives often come from more prestigious universities than the hardy conservatives, many of them having received their academic appointments before it was realized how conservative they were or would become. They themselves have turned conservative only gradually, as if in response to slowly mounting evidence; and the name *neo-conservative* was not chosen by them but fastened on them by their enemies and former friends. Only fairly recently has it been accepted as accurate by Irving Kristol, their acknowledged leader. None of the neo-conservatives supported Goldwater in 1964; almost all supported Reagan in 1980, though often in private. To the extent they are Republicans it is because they believe in political parties and not because they like other Republicans. Between 1964 and 1980 their own studies of the various, expanded government programs of that period, published particularly in the journal they founded, the *Public Interest*, began to pick apart the liberal Great Society. And in foreign policy the disastrous turn of the Democratic party to the Left in 1972 was recorded and condemned especially in *Commentary*, edited by Norman Podhoretz. Most neo-conservatives are Jews, and they naturally feel the danger to Israel from the inaction of a craven, guilty America. Neo-conservatism as a process of self-conversion is not yet complete, and the inroads that have recently been made at the *New Republic* are of universal interest, divided into concern and satisfaction.

The neo-conservatives have the education and confidence of intellectuals, but probably in reaction to liberal intellectuals, their work lacks the sweep one expects from intellectuals. They have given themselves over to social science with a supplement of common sense (a mix of oil and water if there ever was one), and they stay away from philosophy. The *Public Interest* proclaims that the public interest is "not some kind of pre-existing, platonic idea" as if big ideas rather than wrong ones were the source of our troubles. This allergy—for it is not thought out as a conservative critique of the power of reason—perhaps accounts for the peculiar backward motion of the neo-conservative movement, always glaring indignantly at those from whom it is retreating and never turning around to salute and embrace those into whom it is retreating. William F. Buckley, when asked whether he resented the neo-conservatives as Johnny-come-lately's, answered tolerantly: "We had the ideas; they supplied the facts."

Although neo-conservatives have rediscovered and documented the value of market incentives by contrast to blundering government regulation, they differ from libertarians in emphasizing also the importance of the noneconomic, in particular the necessity of moral character, in a free people. They have offered a political, that is noneconomic, defense of capitalism, which has led them to a broader appreciation of it than capitalists (and libertarians) can achieve. To defend the bourgeoisie one must transcend the interest of the bourgeois; one must look at the whole to which their freedom contributes, and so one must not simply equate their freedom with freedom simply, as do the libertarians. Neo-conservatives, especially the less academic ones such as Kristol and George Gilder, have attempted to restore the breadth of consideration to be found in Adam Smith; but since they remain chary of the boastful intellectualism of liberals, they (except for Kristol) hesitate to seek out a still more comprehensive consideration that might be called constitutional. Freedom in the economic view is a matter of interest, but in the political view it is a matter of pride. The trouble is that interest and pride appear to be in conflict, and the problem is to combine them. Freedom is secure, or as secure as it can be, only when they are combined. To explain this recommendation to conservatives, I shall briefly contrast the conservatism of Adam Smith with the constitutionalism of the American Constitution.

Adam Smith and Constitutionalism

Smith makes it clear, as economists and libertarians today do not, that interest is opposed to pride. For him, the "system of natural liberty" operates when each individual is permitted to pursue his own interest, that is, the "uniform, constant and uninterrupted effort of every man to better his own condition" as opposed to both his ambition for greater things and his desire for present enjoyment, which are the two aspects of pride. "Sober undertakings" from which one can expect a "solid and profitable" return are preferable to "spirited undertakings" that promise something "grand and marvelous" (*Wealth of Nations*, 2:2–3). Today economists and libertarians are liable to the influences of positivist science and value relativism from which Smith was nobly and blessedly free; so they usually define one's interest as whatever one believes one's interest to be, even if it is the desire for "mere trinkets of frivolous utility" (Smith, *The Theory of Moral Sentiments*, 4:1.8). Since Smith understands that one's interest is opposed to something else in one's soul, he sees that it must be transformed into a virtue: to pursue one's interest is to be industrious and frugal; to revel in one's pride is to be prodigal. From the standpoint of one's interest, the classical virtue of liberality, by which one showed one's freedom from excessive love of money, appears to be the vice of prodigality, to which Smith adds the vice or alleged virtue of hospitality. Whereas nobles and priests in the dark age of feudalism were hospitable, the rational man is frugal.

Thus we see that the consideration of interest as virtue leads to its political consequences, in regard to which Smith remains faithful to his view of the superiority of interest to pride. Politics is the arena of pride: individuals seek honors and offices that will elevate them above the need to pursue their interest, and nations follow mercantilist policies of specious advantage and false glory that blind them to their true economic interest. To combat the dependency of free peoples on aristocratic delusion, Smith proposed an understanding of politics that would deprive it of its glamour, or would sublimate this glamour in the aesthetic appreciation of the political scientist who admires the beautiful intricacy of the constitutional machine. If only our political arrangements could be made to resemble as nearly as possible the activity of the Invisible Hand in economics—complicated yet unintended—then the pride of domination would be divided up and disposed in separate but mutually dependent motions. The beauty of such a constitution would lie in the convenience of its "system"; it would be a whole that never appears or acts as a whole, hence one that never indulges or encourages the pride men take in rising above their private interests in order to act for the common good.

Unfortunately, or fortunately, Adam Smith never attempted, much less completed, a political science of this kind. According to a current interpretation to be found on both the Left and the Right, however, the U.S. Constitution is based on a similar political science that sets interests to check one another in order to avoid reliance on our higher, but more prideful nature. If this were a correct interpretation, Americans would be stuck with a system that offers no way out of their present difficulties; for a system of interests is far from inconsistent with—it is the very definition of—a nation of dependents. As we have seen, it can easily be in one's interest to accept satisfaction at the cost of one's freedom, when the exercise of freedom is costly or irksome or dangerous. Why not take a government check instead of work? Why not let someone else take the trouble to vote or run for office? Why not pay a "volunteer" to fight for your country?

Or, to the contrary, is freedom necessary to one's interest, since we have also seen that self-interest requires a separate, independent self? If so, then one's interest entails a willingness to *sacrifice* one's interest when freedom requires self-defense either as an individual or for the sake of one's country. In this view interest is defined not against pride but in company with it. But this is a pride that allows for the pride of others and does not seek merely to dominate them. It is a pride in self-government expressed in "that honorable determination, which animates every votary of freedom, to rest all our political experiments on the capacity of mankind for self-government" (James Madison in *Federalist* 39). Such pride is not indignant when confronted with the pride of others, for *their* pride is in *your* interest as well. It is a matter of both pride and interest to allow them the same freedom one claims for oneself. This freedom includes the right of consent even to those who may be petty, irrational, and prejudiced, because their pride must be respected even in their errors. And it includes a right of self-advancement granted even to one's rivals and especially to one's superiors. Ambition is usually assumed to be in one's interest, and often said to be against one's interest. Both opinions are correct: ambition is self-advancement, but with extraordinary trouble and pains. Free government needs to allow for the ambiguity of pride and interest in the ambitious, as well as in ordinary citizens.

Living under a constitution means taking pride in seeing our interest in freedom. Not every people has the virtue to do so, and those who do should take pride in it. To accept a constitution, its law, and its established forms is choosing to have limited government, one that tempers our pride with our interests, yet ennobles our interests by combining them with pride. Neither the conflict nor the cooperation of pride and interest must be lost sight of. A constitution, if well-drawn, will make allowances for human weakness and also for human intolerance for human weakness.

To see the virtues of constitutionalism, conservatives must retract their refusal to use human reason to grasp the whole of human affairs. Perhaps that refusal is futile in any case, if in fact we are driven to find and explain the Invisible Hand that guides them. Reason will come to terms with unreason by its reverence if not by command. Then to consider how or whether the *American* Constitution embodies the virtues of constitutionalism becomes a timely question for American conservatives—one that touches both interest and pride.

7

Pride and Justice in Affirmative Action

Affirmative action is settling down in our constitutional polity like a determined guest seeking to establish squatter's rights. Though the issue is far from settled, controversy has subsided. The Supreme Court has pronounced indecisively on several occasions and in several voices, lately with some discouragement. The Democratic party, trying to exist on a faded and confused memory of itself, has lost its early enthusiasm for affirmative action, but remains "committed" to it in the routine sense of that word—stuck with it. The Reagan administration, elected in a spirit hostile to affirmative action, found it necessary, or merely convenient, to tolerate it, even to truckle to it. And the Bush administration seems to accept affirmative action in principle if not with enthusiasm.

Affirmative action is perhaps the most interesting policy issue of our day because it best reveals how we understand our Constitution. How we understand our Constitution shows how we understand ourselves as a free people, what our condition is, and where we are tending. As an issue of public policy and as a question of constitutional law, affirmative action is not held to be a critical matter requiring immediate attention and a definite commitment. Though surely a delicate matter, it has not been, and may never be, an election issue. But for what it reveals of our polity as a whole, affirmative action is a "regime question" reflecting a new theoretical understanding.

Even the phrase *affirmative action* is interesting. It seems redundant, for who would want a negative or passive action? But *affirmative action* implies that the business of government is to make things happen and not just to lie back and let them happen. Indeed, it implies a deliberate change of policy by government, in the way it secures rights, from "negative action" to affirmative action. How does this change affect the Constitution?

A Question of Pride

The most revealing incident in this regime question remains the one by which the first Interior secretary in the Reagan Administration, James Watt, lost his job in 1983. Watt set off a furor by remarking that he had appointed to a coal-leasing board "a black, a woman, two Jews, and a cripple." It was a remark of shameless cynicism, and deliberately subversive, but it was also true. He should have appointed the same people and not said why. He should have known, indeed he surely knew, that to state the true purpose of his appointments was to render them useless. An affirmative action appointment does not serve its purpose unless one denies that it has been made for that purpose. The denial is necessary in order not to hurt the pride of the beneficiary, because an affirmative action appointment necessarily implies something lacking in the appointee. This lack, to be sure, is not the fault of the appointee—rather it is the fault of white, male America. But there is nonetheless a lack, and it must be denied.

Affirmative action is obviously a way of helping people who are considered insufficiently capable of helping themselves. But just as obviously, this fact cannot be admitted. Or, if it is admitted in general—as when Justice Thurgood Marshall said in the *Bakke* case that "meaningful equality remains a distant dream for the Negro"—it must be denied in all particular cases. The reason for wanting to help people is that we hold them to be equal in some sense, hence deserving of equal treatment. But if we help them, we imply that they are unequal in some sense, hence undeserving of equal treatment. Government and management must therefore give help through affirmative action while denying that they give it, indeed *by* denying that they give it, in order not to hurt the pride of the beneficiaries. Their pride, and America's recognition of their pride, is not beside the point: it is the point.

More than has been realized on either side of the debate, affirmative action is a question of pride. So far, most of the argument has been about its justice. Proponents point to past injustices done to blacks, women, Hispanics, and others on a lengthening list of victims who deserve compensation—partly for revenge, and partly because their suffering has left them unprepared to take advantage of the new opportunities now admittedly available in American society. Opponents reply that one cannot remedy past injustice with new injustice; that with such group justice, one may benefit an individual who has not suffered at the expense of an individual who has not been guilty; and that affirmative action is thus in truth punitive justice rather than the distributive justice it claims to be.

A sign of concern with the justice of affirmative action is the description of blacks and others as *victims*. Even, for example, in *Firefighters v. Stotts* (1984), a Supreme Court decision unfavorable to affirmative action, the description appears. In that case the Supreme Court decided that a federal court cannot require the city of Memphis to ignore workers' seniority for the sake of affirmative action quotas when making layoffs. Justice Byron White's majority opinion contained a statement that relief could be provided under the Civil Rights Act "only to those who have been actual victims of illegal discrimination." Affirmative action, of course, provides relief to *presumed* victims of illegal discrimination without their having to show actual discrimination. If this statement—which is doubtful and disputed—should be applied to affirmative action in general, it could call for a welcome return to the principle and language of the Civil Rights Act of 1964. As is well known, the act's legislative history contains a remark by one of its sponsors, Senator Hubert Humphrey, partially quoted by Justice White, denying that its intent was to set up a system of racial quotas or to achieve a racial balance.

Yet whether remedies should be confined to actual or broadened to presumed discrimination, one should note that the beneficiaries of affirmative action are referred to as victims. More and more, our legal system is coming to regard American citizens as victims rather than free agents and to substitute the imposition of punitive justice for the democratic choice of policy. The expansion and the transformation of tort law make the tendency apparent to all, as Americans increasingly sue and are sued not for wrongful acts—implying responsible actors—but for victimization in which the victims, who are not expected to do or understand anything on their own, are treated as passive and uncomprehending recipients of injustice. *Victims* do not behave as *citizens*. Citizens are busy with what they can do for themselves and others; victims are concerned with what has been done to them and with what they can get from others.

By a recent "consent decree" Prudential Insurance Company was required to send an offer of free remedial training to 8,000 minority job applicants who had been rejected because they could not pass a test. This event should have sent a shiver of fear into the hearts of teachers everywhere. Teachers, like other consumers, are used to demanding warranties from businesses and corporations: when things do not work, pay me back! But when this idea is carried into teaching, the result is not so agreeable. Students or former students might insist on a warranty providing them relief for the consequences of any remaining stupidity or ignorance after they or their parents or the public have paid their tuition, and teachers might have to provide free remedial training or more. In this situation, as with affirmative action in general, the law makes victims of the alleged victimizers.

Still, regardless of the winner of the debate over the *justice* of affirmative action—even if affirmative action is just (distributively) and is required by (punitive) justice—justice cannot be the only consideration. It remains a question whether it is good for blacks and other beneficiaries of affirmative action to regard themselves and to be regarded as victims. For as we see from that Watt incident, it seems a strange and unsatisfactory act of justice that cannot take pride in announcing whom it has benefited and why.

Advantages of Affirmative Action

To see how affirmative action affects the Constitution, let us consider it from the standpoint of pride. In what follows I confine myself to blacks, and leave aside women and Hispanics. Blacks are the only group that was brought to America against its will, then enslaved while here, and after being emancipated, held down in segregation as second-class citizens. Their case is quite different from that of women, who, I must say, suffered no such oppression. As proof of this hardy assertion I offer that great surrender of American males to the women's movement in the last two decades: no confrontation such as at Little Rock or Selma; no Governor Wallace to be a hero of the male chauvinist pigs. The women's revolution has been accomplished by "raising consciousness"—first the consciousness of women, then of men. But an oppression that can be overthrown by complaints is hardly oppression. That the Equal Rights Amendment did not pass was more because women did not agree about it than because men opposed it; and if now the women's movement is changing its character in a "second stage," from unisex to job and motherhood, this too is because women are having second thoughts about their own first thoughts. As for Hispanics, they have come to America voluntarily and are making great strides except that they are hindered by programs of bilingualism. Their difficulties, and those of other minorities as well as the female majority, do not belong in the same category as the wrongs done to blacks.

The advantages of affirmative action might appear to be the following. First, it is revenge for the denial of the birthright of blacks as Americans. That birthright of full citizenship with civil and political rights was first expressly then tacitly taken away, and whites now should have to pay for this injustice. Revenge is not very pretty, but it is very human; and most criminals are punished for lesser crimes than enslaving other human beings. Revenge, usually under the name of "compensation" or "reparation," is certainly part of the appeal of affirmative action to blacks.

Second, one must face blacks' insistence on affirmative action. This program, which was not invented by them but invented for them by whites, is now *their* program, their right, their entitlement. To abandon it now would be a "takeaway," a reaction against the progress achieved by the Civil Rights Movement, perhaps even a sign that this progress was never really secure, that whites were never really serious about civil rights. As one who has spoken on affirmative action at universities, I can testify that this feeling is strong among the most educated blacks, including black students. The black community, as defined by those who speak for it—the effectual definition of a community, is in favor of affirmative action. Any politician who speaks against affirmative action is understood as not interested in appealing, or at least as not appealing, to blacks.

Third, affirmative action enables blacks to learn and improve by doing. They can bypass the slow system of apprenticeship in which many get bogged down while gaining allegedly necessary qualifications. They can learn on the job and take pride in acting on their own and doing by themselves instead of always submitting to tests that have been laid down by others. These tests, together with the whole system of "qualifications," it is often said, were not imposed on whites when they were on top or making their way to the top. The whites on top had the old-boy network, and the immigrant whites on the rise had informal control of certain jobs, such as the Irish in the police force. Affirmative action for blacks merely makes public and formal policy of preferential practices that were not found so objectionable, or are not objected to today, when done by whites. Besides, so-called unqualified appointments are often good ones, and "qualified" characters often turn out incompetent.

Fourth, blacks can become responsible Americans by getting their share of the best jobs and highest positions in America. They will be proud to be Americans when they are respected, for *respect* is the essential thing, not money or standard of living. When blacks are respected, America can then respect itself and no longer suffer guilt for the American dilemma. The gap between America's ideals and the American reality is essentially revealed in its treatment of blacks.

Disadvantages of Affirmative Action

Nonetheless, there are disadvantages of affirmative action, which, I believe, outweigh the advantages. To begin, we should return to the necessity that affirmative action programs conceal the help they render to their beneficiaries. Such programs cannot claim success, we have seen, because to do so would insult those whom they have just benefited. One does not see a smiling executive introduce "our new affirmative action appointment" to his fellow employees. Affirmative action beneficiaries are described in contradictory fashion: They deserve the help of affirmative action because they are equal; but they need it because they are not equal. The only way out is to accuse the rest of American society of racism in order to explain why potential equality does not become actual.

Surely it is true that racial prejudice remains in America, but it is almost as sure that it will not be cured by accusation. To whom does one make an accusation of racism? To people who believe racism to be a bad thing, not to racists. Thus the very accusation that America is racist presupposes that most Americans are not racist. In consequence, those who accuse do not really believe their accusations of racism, and the accusations tend to become routine. An example is the accusation of "institutional racism," in which actual racists are not sought, let alone named. Well, this is no way to get on with one's fellow citizens. Such accusations deny the real progress that has been made, and they overlook the real good will most Americans have for blacks, the admiration for their courage and endurance, and the genuine longing for community with this wronged people.

Affirmative action does not find racism but imputes it to Americans as the sole cause of remaining inequalities. It claims to be a temporary program, but it sets no limit on itself other than the eradication of prejudice, that is, the achievement of perfection in human community. At Harvard University (my "place of employment"), the official policy is to continue affirmative action "until we have demonstrated to our own collective satisfaction that hiring decisions are absolutely color-blind and neutral." *Absolutely* is a word not often heard at Harvard, where many people commonly say they do not believe in "absolutes." But meanwhile—in the interim before absolute suppression of prejudice has been attained—the benefits of affirmative action depend on imperfection, on the continuance of racism as asserted in accusations of racism. We might suspect that those accusations will continue as long as the benefits of affirmative action are desired. But with a view to the bureaucracy that has been created to enforce affirmative action, both in government and with private employers, we can be *sure* that accusations will continue out of both self-interest and professional duty. Affirmative action lives and thrives in an atmosphere of suspicion and accusation. It wants to make us less conscious of race by the route of making us more conscious. On the face of it, to reach that goal by this route is not likely.

Second, affirmative action tends to make blacks irresponsible by encouraging them to blame others for their difficulties. It is of course not always incorrect to blame others for your troubles, but it is almost always counterproductive to do so. You cannot easily reform those whom you blame, but you can do something about yourself. Blacks can and should take responsibility for what they can do, even against the hostility of the white majority (to the extent that this majority is truly hostile). What blacks can do is limited, but this is the case with all human actions, and responsible action includes accepting what one cannot do so as to do what one can. Blacks, therefore, should not wait around for whites to take affirmative action to change their attitudes when blacks can change their own attitudes by affirming their own actions. The problems of blacks are not going to be solved by whites; indeed, it is better that they not be. This truth has been recently addressed by several thoughtful blacks—Jeff Howard, Ray Hammond, Glenn C. Loury, and Shelby Steele. And, of course, Booker T. Washington long ago made it the centerpiece of his doctrine.

Affirmative action also leads to a patronizing, condescending attitude in whites toward blacks. Whites do not hold blacks to the same standards as other whites because they do not expect them to perform so well. For if one expected as much from blacks as from whites, there would be no need for affirmative action. So affirmative action tends to confirm the idea of black inferiority in the minds of whites even while its purpose is to erase it. Blacks tend to get preferences of the kind that do them no good because they serve as excuses. Blacks, for example, are hired as affirmative action officers rather than in jobs that lead somewhere. Charles Murray has rightly called this frame of mind "the new racism," and it is found in people who could never bring themselves to utter a racial slur. Blacks are said to be equal, but as a practical matter are held to be inferior. In an answer to Murray's argument, Harvard's President Derek Bok asked whether equal opportunity, if returned to now, would produce any more progress for blacks than the little it accomplished before 1965 (i.e., before affirmative action). I think it would, because of the decline of racism, the success of the Civil Rights Movement, and the passage of the Civil Rights Act of 1964. But at some point—and why not now?—it is necessary to put confidence in blacks themselves.

As a result of blaming others and of being patronized by whites, blacks come to think of themselves as victims, hence as essentially passive. The solution seems to be, then, to make claims on white America on the basis of their sufferings, needs, and wants—in sum, on the basis of their inadequacies. But, instead of regarding themselves as victims, blacks should think of what they can *contribute* to America, and make claims (for all of us make claims) on the basis of what they have contributed and can now contribute.

To claim 11 percent of every activity on the principle of affirmative action is to say that blacks make no contribution of their own and that America would have lost nothing distinctive if it had sent all its freed slaves back to Africa. But blacks have one sure contribution to make, a valuable addition to their other valuable contributions to our culture. They have been the victims of democratic injustice and have seen freedom from underneath, and in consequence they know what most other Americans can hardly imagine, that democratic majorities can do terrible wrong. This is valuable information for a free people.

Affirmative action makes blacks accentuate the negative and appear helpless in order to build a case for aid, but in fact blacks have made many contributions to American culture. They have played a dominant role in our popular culture for some time, and their intellectual leaders, such as Booker T. Washington, Frederick Douglass, and William E. DuBois, are worthy of more appreciation and study than they receive. Blacks should think of the contributions they have made, and then think them *over*: What does the black community want to contribute to America? This is thinking positively, and it can be done only by blacks for themselves. As an example of thinking it over, an outside observer might ask whether it is such a good thing for educated blacks to rush into the professions from which they have been excluded, such as medicine and law, and also into business, but forget the traditional professions in the black community. It used to be that preacher and teacher were the only professions open to blacks, yet these two were important to the dignity and morale of the black community. Now they are not so well respected as before, with consequences possibly detrimental to blacks. For the sake of American education in general, I particularly worry about the minute number of blacks studying to become college teachers.

The black community has indeed become wedded to affirmative action, but is this a good thing? It is not necessarily permanent; polls have shown that, though most black leaders favor affirmative action, most of their followers oppose it. This finding does not mean that black leaders are not leaders of the black community, because leaders should lead, not follow; but it does suggest that, if affirmative action is unwise, black leaders are not bound to it by the demands of their constituents. In their present frame of mind, black leaders see affirmative action as a measure of their power; but it has to be said that most whites see the same thing as a sign of blacks' dependency. Reinforcing the appearance of dependency is the political isolation of blacks. In the 1984 presidential election two-thirds of the whites voted for President Reagan, but nine-tenths of the blacks voted for the Democratic candidate. Blacks have become conspicuous as the most loyal adherents of the Democratic party; they have become, as the congressional Black Caucus says, the soul of that party. Though there is nothing wrong in favoring one party rather than the other, there is disadvantage in doing so when a group can be so readily identified as privileged dependents or a "special interest." This is especially true when a different opinion is taken for disloyalty to the black community. Those few black leaders who oppose affirmative action have had to suffer for having betrayed the common interest in their standing with other blacks.

When that common interest is defined as affirmative action, the idealism of the Civil Rights Movement in its heyday is transformed into the defense of rights and privileges in jobs, positions, and offices. Its nobility is lost in calculation of mundane advantage. Since it is hard for blacks to work up enthusiasm for affirmative action in anyone else, they turn to making alliances with women and Hispanics. Let others in on affirmative action, and blacks will have a stronger political base, even a majority, to support them. But such alliances dilute the special case that blacks can reasonably make on their own behalf to the conscience of the nation. All too often, affirmative action produces jobs for white, middle-class women—a group that has never been enslaved or even underprivileged.

There is nothing particularly shocking in politicking to protect one's self-interest, and immigrant and other groups have in the past established informal, do-it-yourself affirmative action programs. But there is nothing edifying in such practices. Though some have attempted to justify them, no one has attempted before now to dignify them. On the contrary, every movement called "reform" has opposed and tried to uproot them. Those who have criticized the reformers, for example, political scientists who find hidden merit in big city "corruption" in the good old days, have not proposed a formal program of "corruption" to help us return to those golden times. Instead, they have counseled prudence and a greater willingness to let things be and let things happen. In this spirit, one can see an obvious difference between the prudence of using black policemen in black neighborhoods, for example, and the erection of a formal requirment that this concession to human nature be generalized and insisted on as if it were a moral principle. If it is asked why blacks should not benefit as much as whites from such a concession, the answer is that they do: look at big-city government today.

Despite what proponents of affirmative action say about the difficulties of defining merit, they rarely admit that merit is no longer the first consideration. Instead, they try to redefine merit: it no longer means the best, or the best available; it means acceptable, or beyond a certain minimum. Sometimes merit is divined as what society needs, and society's needs are more big shots who are blacks and women; ergo, promoting them is promoting merit. They serve as "role models," and the role they model is that of being patronized by white males.

The last-mentioned disadvantage of affirmative action sums up all the others. Affirmative action makes blacks conspicuously dependent on the rest of America by becoming dependent on government. Blacks are not alone in this dependency; all of us have become more dependent on so-called entitlements. But blacks have become more so, for affirmative action is the most outstanding example of an entitlement.

Affirmative Action as Entitlement

What are entitlements, and what is the matter with them? The term entitlement, as we have seen, has escaped from the language of the federal budget into American politics and even into political philosophy. There it designates a right whose exercise is guaranteed, to a certain degree, by the government. What does this mean?

The U.S. Constitution is based on rights that are prior to itself. These rights are secured by government and exercised by citizens in their private capacity; for example, the government secures the right of free speech by preventing interference with it, but it does not tell the citizens what to say or how to exercise their right. This distinction between the right and its exercise is the basis for the distinction between public and private or between state and society that characterizes constitutional democracy. By means of this distinction, government is limited because it acts for society, that is, for citizens in their private capacities; it facilitates the exercise of those capacities but does not prescribe how they are to be exercised. Government remains limited insofar as it maintains and respects the distinction between securing rights, which is the business of government, and exercising them, which is not.

The distinction between rights and their exercise is essential to limited government, but it can leave a situation in society in which limited government, for example, might make it illegal for any employer to discriminate on grounds of race in hiring, but it would not require employers to hire blacks since this requirement would infringe upon their freedom to contract. So to blacks, an equal right to a job might seem merely formal. The government does not secure them an actual job, only the right to compete for one from which without any overt act of discrimination, prejudice may effectually exclude them. Then, blacks might ask, why should not America live up to its ideas? And why should not government close the gap between its ideas and its reality? The Constitution is indeed based on rights, but rights are not rights unless one can exercise them effectually. The right and its exercise must be brought together so that the ideal becomes real and profession becomes fact. Thus, instead of "equal protection of the laws" as in the Fourteenth Amendment, one must provide "laws protecting equality." Affirmative action by government is ne-

cessary to close this gap because minorities and women have a background of disadvantage that keeps them from exercising their rights effectually.

The importance of *background* is the key to the argument. One's
background is commonly distinguished as part nature and part nurture.
Nature is the human capacities we have, plus the innate bent and talent
of each individual. *Nurture* is the custom and history of one's group and
nation, plus individual upbringing. The political philosophy behind limited government affirms that nature is more important than nurture: that
humans have a fixed nature enabling them to overcome a background of
poverty or deprivation. With the equipment of nature and given the
chance to succeed, an individual can overcome, perhaps even disregard,
the past history of his nation and long experience with oppression. Since
his identity is more in his equipment, which is a positive capacity, than in
his history, which may have been unfortunate, he has the means, as we say,
for a "fresh start."

In general, America has claimed to be, and has been to some extent, a
fresh start for mankind, the New World. Though the American polity
contains ethnic groups, it does not *define* itself in terms of ethnic origin.
This is the beginning point of Nathan Glazer's classic study of affirmative
action, *Affirmative Discrimination* (1975). In this view, the individual
must be given the chance to succeed, as I said, by removing barriers to
advancement characteristic of feudal or status societies which make more
of one's conventional than one's natural advantages. Because of these
natural advantages liberal political philosophy holds, a disadvantaged
individual does not need to be put on his feet by government, much less
given a push in the right direction. He can pull himself up by his own
bootstraps, of course, with the aid of family and friends. The dominance
of nature over nurture provides the basis for the liberal argument for
equal opportunity and limited government. *Limited government* implies
that government should not be used as much as it might be, and *equal
opportunity* implies that not all succeed, or not all equally. Politically, then
the promise is for a series of partial reforms that open up opportunities
but do not attempt to make everyone happy.

Affirmative action, however, comes from a political opinion and a
philosophy that are not satisfied with partial reforms. It wants to close the
gap between the ideal and reality, and to do so it understands a right not
as a formal opportunity that may or may not succeed, but as an effectual
guarantee from government, an entitlement. In the view of its supporters,
partial reforms are no use because every extension of rights is canceled by
the inability of those with a disadvantaged background to exercise their
new rights, which to the supporters means to exercise them equally. For

them, only absolute reform is real reform. Real reform requires government action not merely against discriminatory actions but against the attitudes behind those actions.

The Right of Consent

When government proposes to change or rather, *attack* attitudes, it encounters the right of consent, the basic right in the Constitution. Consent is the basic right because all other rights depend on it. Without the right of consent, other rights are merely the gift of the government, possibly to be withdrawn at the government's convenience. The right of consent is the right by which, when it is exercised to establish a constitution, other rights pass from *natural* rights (or human rights) to *civil* rights, rights enforceable by law that are more limited but more effectually protected than abstract natural rights. The right of consent is a matter of justice, because it is just to count each person as one. But it is also a matter of pride, for to count as one, each person must count *for* something, must be *worth* something.

The right of consent presupposes that each adult is worthy of being taken seriously as a rational creature capable of choice, hence worthy of being persuaded and not taken for granted. His dignity requires that his consent be sought through persuasion, and neither ignored nor presumed. Affirmative action both ignores and presumes. Usually enforced by the judiciary, the branch that is furthest from consent, it ignores white males because they are presumed to be racist and it presumes the consent of blacks and women because of their race and sex. Affirmative action is not yet fully applied to voting, but there is a trend in that direction. In the Voting Rights Act of 1982, Congress flirted with the idea of giving protected groups the representation it presumed they should vote for: black representatives for blacks, and so forth. This attempt at mandated racist voting was narrowly and only partially defeated. More recent court decisions and legislative activity have brought us still closer to the practice of presumed consent.

One cannot rightly presume how the right of consent will be exercised. One cannot suppose that blacks, because they are blacks, must want this and not want that. Of course, it is not always practicable to take a vote. It may be defensible to presume tacit consent in a situation from which one draws benefits, but consent that is presumed because of one's social and economic characteristics is an outrage. Whereas the first presumption declares what you have apparently consented to, leaving intact your right to withdraw consent, the second says what you *would* consent to, thus making actual consent unnecessary and bothersome. It is hardly surprising, and not reprehensible, that blacks should vote for blacks, but for them to do so automatically is no merit and deserves no praise. For the government to presume, as a matter of law, that blacks will do so is no mere prediction of how they will vote but an unthinking usurpation of their right of consent. According to this bright idea, the government should no longer confine itself to guaranteeing the right to vote, but should now look to see how that right is exercised, in case voting by one method or another should deprive a minority of its fair share of representation, *as calculated without reference to elections.*

It is not enough to describe our problem as a gap between reality and our ideals. Such a description overlooks the right of consent, which is the key to all our other rights. Our problem is in one way greater than a gap between reality and our ideals, and in another way more honorable. It is a gap within our ideals, a gap arising from the right of consent and reflecting the reality that free men are not free of prejudice.

Since this is so, and is likely to remain so, do we want to conclude that freedom should be withheld until all prejudice has been abolished? That is the totalitarian way, which says, in contradiction of itself, that men are worthy of freedom but not of gaining it on their own. But then, if we avoid this contradiction and allow that people should have "freedom now," and not have to wait until government has declared them worthy of it, we must respect their right of consent. We must respect that right even in those who are prejudiced (and of course in those we merely disagree with). To do so is not merely a practical necessity—as if we were merely recognizing the gap between reality and our ideas—but a moral imperative derived from our central ideal, the right of consent.

Living together in freedom requires more than justice, for after justice has been exacted, people are not always in a mood to live together. To put ourselves in the right mood for free society we must recognize the dignity of being persuaded. This morality of consent requires us to consent, for the sake of our morality, to a gap between reality and our ideals. It also provides a necessary check on our moralism, when we try to rush into reform too confident that those who are opposed are merely prejudiced. Moralism gives morality a bad name and makes free citizens angry and impatient with one another.

Properly understood, the right of consent neither prevents us from resorting to compulsion when necessary nor disables us from attempting reform when desirable. In this proper understanding, consent has its forms and procedures whose observance makes it necessary to persuade one's fellow citizens. Consent must be registered in legal elections to offices in bodies established by law so that it is clear who are the winners and losers. The point is to leave the majority capable of action after the minority has been heard. A person's right of consent is not violated when he has been outvoted, and his dignity has not been denied when he has been outargued. The forms and procedures of a free government give definition to the dignity of free citizens. It knows when it can act, and we know when we have been consulted.

All these forms and procedures, together with the spirit in which they are practiced, have been called constitutionalism. They ensure respect for the means by which the right of consent is exercised, and thereby they secure respect for the right of consent. They *constitute* a free society; without such forms a society might be tempted to believe that freedom is doing as one pleases, or doing what someone thinks is required by justice.

Affirmative action has no regard for the forms and procedures that serve as protection of the right of consent. It has no patience with them when they seem to get in the way of justice, and no compunction about multiplying them when they are thought to advance justice. Any old procedure may be altered, any new procedure may be added; all that matters is the result. What is worst about affirmative action is the Machiavellian *underhandedness* of pretense and manipulation with which it aims to secure a good result.

The gap between the ideal and reality was deliberately planned and fixed in our Constitution. It arises from the right of consent, since that right both obliges us to respect the rights of others and enables us to insist on our own. That right, therefore, serves to perfect our rights, but also permits prejudiced resistance to progress. Government can attempt perfection by overriding prejudice, but when it does so it can develop a self-serving tyrannical—or bureaucratic—definition of perfection. More important and more urgent for us, government makes its citizens depend on government for their rights, for the entitlements we are beginning to take for granted. A free society is necessarily imperfect; if it became perfect, citizens would no longer have to exert themselves to be free. What is affirmative action but an attempt by government in its least consensual branches, the bureaucracy and the judiciary, to redo what the Civil Rights Movement did voluntarily and on its own responsibility? Surely the contrast is remarkable between the free, popular movement that led to the Civil Rights Act of 1964 and the arbitrary, bureaucratic misinterpretation of the act that gave rise to affirmative action. Affirmative action may or may not be "unconstitutional" because it violates a clause of the Constitution, but in the broader sense it is unconstitutional because it undermines the basic principle of our Constitution.

Part III
Constitutional Origins

8

The Religious Issue and the Origin of Modern Constitutionalism

The religious issue was deeply and hotly contested at the origin of modern constitutionalism in the seventeenth century. The three great founders of constitutionalism to be considered here—Hobbes, Spinoza, and Locke—devoted much of their studies and large portions of their most famous political works to the Bible and its political implications. Two of the four parts of Hobbes' *Leviathan* (1651) concern the Christian theology required for or compatible with his notion of sovereignty. Spinoza's *Theologico-Political Treatise* (1670) is entirely an analysis of Scripture with a view to the consequences for free inquiry and free government. And the first of Locke's *Two Treatises of Government* (1690), together with his *A Letter Concerning Toleration* (1690), reveals the same interest in repelling the claims of divine right.

For the *religious issue*, or the *theologico-political* problem (to use Spinoza's term), is whether men are ruled by God or gods, hence by divine right, or by themselves on principles they discern without necessarily referring to the Word of God in Scripture. If rule derives from divinity, all government is theocracy, more or less, since even if priests are not rulers, rulers are required by the principles of divine right to serve, in some sense, as priests. If rule is made by men, government is constituted by human choice out of human nature, and "constitutional government" so understood, though it may seek or accept the support of religion, is not based on—is indeed constituted against—divine right.

To see the continuing importance of the religious issue, however, is not so easy as to recognize its original importance. In our day, the *social issue* appears to be dominant. The social issue dates, perhaps, from the end of the eighteenth century, and through the nineteenth century, as socialism gained force, it increasingly preoccupied the politics of constitutional governments. Generically, the social issue is the age-old conflict between the rich and the poor, but in constitutional government it has taken a specific form that is reflected in the word *social*. The social issue arose when it was observed or alleged that society, which is private (as we say today, "the private sphere"), was not autonomous because it was not providing for the poor; hence political intervention, either welfare legislation or revolution, was needed to restore the balance of society. This issue now appears paramount because it is the crux both of party conflict within constitutional regimes and of international conflict between constitutional and Communist regimes.

But why should one expect *society* to exist separately, if not altogether independently, from the *state*, and thus to have its own autonomy or balance? To appreciate the social issue today, one must understand why we assume society to exist. This assumption was first put forth in arguments that Hobbes, Spinoza, and Locke used to confront the religious issue; thus to understand the social issue, one must understand the religious issue. One could even suggest that the religious issue *was* the social issue in its first appearance, and that the social issue as it appears today is the consequence of the religious issue. If politics is defined by its issues, the religious issue at the origin of modern constitutionalism is still at the heart of modern constitutionalism.

The State-Society Distinction

Modern constitutional government is limited government, in which the limitation on government is expressed in the distinction between *state* and *society*. Invented by Hobbes and developed first by Spinoza and Locke and then by Adam Smith among others, this distinction has become, with the success of liberal constitutionalism, a fundamental belief rarely questioned in our time. We in the liberal democracies do not agree on what government should do or how far it should go, but we do agree that certain things, however we define them, are not the business of the state. The state, which is public, is in the service of society, which is private; and the state is limited to this service as a means is limited by its end. This is not the whole truth, because we do speak of *the public* as having authority over merely private, that is, individual, inclinations, and because constitutional formalities, such as due process of law, cannot be understood merely as means to an end. The subordination of state to society, however, is the main truth of constitutional government, which is shared by liberals, conservatives, and even radicals, despite the various pet projects of intervention in others' liberties cherished by all three parties. That these projects are known as "intervention" indicates the general expectation that government be limited; and their intent, as with the social issue, is to restore the balance of society and enable it to function on its own with only minimum regulation and without being ruled by government.

The basis of the distinction between state and society was stated clearly by John Locke in his *A Letter Concerning Toleration*: it is the further distinction between body and soul. The magistrate, Locke says, has jurisdiction only over "civil interests" such as "life, liberty, health, and indolency of body," together with property, and his power "neither can nor ought in any manner to be extended to the salvation of souls." Society is the realm of the soul, or today what passes for the soul, the self. Thus the distinction between body and soul responsible for the modern constitutional distinction between state and society is stated in the context of the religious issue. But what of private economic activity concerned not with the soul, it would appear, but with material well-being? Constitutional government encourages it, we find, not only because it makes people rich but also because it keeps their souls occupied with harmless, or at least bloodless, acquisition and prompts them to put aside contentious recipes for saving their souls. Today, the economy is said even by economists to be determined by tastes, preferences, or other attitudes of soul in consumers and by enterprise and opportunity seeking in producers: it is affected and regulated, but not prescribed or ruled, by government.

Difficulty arises for the constitutional distinction between state and society when the soul, in its unruly desire to rule itself, tries to rule other souls: that is, when a part of society seeks to use the power of the state to rule the whole of society. For it seems unreasonable not to apply the rule one follows for oneself to others, especially in a matter of importance that is not to be decided by mere idiosyncratic taste. For example, in the abortion debate in America today, the pro-choice party is as eager to rule fellow citizens as is the apparently more prescriptive pro-life party; one wants a society in which abortion is respectable, and the other wants one in which it is abhorred. These are two very different societies because they would be ruled differently. From such examples it may easily be inferred that the desire to rule others has its root in the desire to rule oneself; thus in societies attempting to maintain a distinction between state and society, in time one hears less of *soul* and more of *self*, then less of self-control and more of *self-expression*.

Our constitutionalist distinction between state and society seems to promote, if not require, a distinction between body and soul in which the soul gradually abdicates its ruling function. This is the apathetic *individualism* Tocqueville feared, which we see in the wishy-washy liberal and the uncaring conservative or, on the contrary, the rebellious and aggressive self-expression of angry radicals, which equally endangers the constitutional distinction between state and society. How can the state serve society if society craves the state? If government is to remain limited, individuals must be able to rule themselves, at least to some extent, and to do this, religion—which reminds us of the importance of our souls—might seem indispensable.

We have therefore uncovered, in the principle and in the probable history of modern constitutionalism, both a hostility to religion and a positive function for religion. Hostility to religion produces the constitutional distinction between state and society, in order to prevent the state from attempting to save our souls in accordance with the demands of religion. That distinction leaves concern for souls to private individuals in society. But if individuals are not to be responsible for others' souls, why should they be responsible for their own? To enjoin citizens from tyrannizing over their fellows, constitutional government runs the risk of leaving them unconcerned, both for their fellows and for themselves. This risk will appear in the social issue as well as in the religious issue since one can ask, Why be responsible for poverty in property if not for poverty of soul? The answer that religion gives to the question Why be responsible? will always be more convincing to more people than any fancy, theoretical calculation of self-interest. But then, if religion is required to maintain responsibility and autonomy in society so that society does not become dependent on the state, how do we keep religion within constitutional bounds? For religion, as religion, is primarily concerned with saving souls, not with constitutional freedom. With this difficulty in mind, let us see what can be learned from Hobbes, Spinoza, and Locke.

Hobbes: The Question of Sovereignty

Modern constitutionalism, having its origin in Hobbes, was from the first opposed to a rival constitutionalism that began with Plato, was most highly developed by Aristotle, and had its proponents in the seventeenth century (Philip Hunton, George Lawson, Marchamont Nedham, and John Milton among others). This constitutionalism shared the fear of fanatic religious partisanship that animates modern constitutionalism, but instead of finding the solution in limited government, it aimed at a mixed government. Instead of limiting what government might do in response to the demands of *any* party, it attempted to mix what was reasonable and just in the claims of *all* parties. To this end, Aristotelian constitutionalism laid emphasis on the soul and its individual responsibility, because it was only by virtue of some such universal element in all human beings that partisans might be persuaded to do justice to the claims of rival partisans to establish a common or more common good in a mixed constitution. To educate and cultivate just souls was, therefore, so far from prohibited to government as to constitute its main business, and the realm of the *political* was understood to comprehend both state and society as now conceived (*state* meant constitution or regime in the wider sense, and *society* referred to a particular group within the political).

According to Hobbes, this Aristotelian constitutionalism did not work. Rather than moderating, it endorsed and even intensified religious partisanship. The common good, which is intended as the goal to which the parties of a mixed constitution would contribute, becomes in fact an external standard with which to criticize and attack every existing regime. Various parties offer diverse interpretations of the common good, so that the "common good" has no effectual force against their partisanship; tyranny, for example, said to be contrary to the common good, is merely "monarchy misliked." Similarly, the soul, which according to Aristotelian constitutionalism makes men responsible for their actions and capable of justice, according to Hobbes is often captured by vainglorious imagination that makes men strut, boast, and fight one another over senseless issues. Our fears as well as our hopes turn us from the care and perfection of our souls to a more down-to-earth concern for what will happen to us. Under pressure from this concern, yet too lazy to think the problem through, we quickly settle on an invisible cause of our well-being and personify it so that we can assume it is as interested in us as we are in it—calling it "God." Thus, care for the soul's perfection is transformed into anxiety for its salvation, and individual responsibility is handed over to God, or rather to those who claim to speak for God—prophets and priests.

Against this mixed constitution and its disastrously unsuccessful (as Hobbes deemed it) program to moderate religious partisanship, Hobbes raised the question of *sovereignty*. He raised that question with an extremism never before seen, for he demanded that, to secure government against partisans, not any particular party or combination of parties should win, but someone, *anyone*, should win. The condition necessary to establish sovereignty is that all parties recognize that winning in politics is all-important or that human power (Hobbes was the first political scientist to make a theme of *power*) is the sole consideration. The pride of all parties based on some (religious) principle that leaves them content to lose or prompts them to fight to the death—indeed, all parties in all politics hitherto, Hobbes shows, is vanity, and their partisans should surrender their otherworldly or utopian goals and put peace foremost. Because men are impelled by religion and vain philosophy to fight over a vision of perfection they never actually see, the establishment of *civil* sovereignty requires the establishment of *human* sovereignty. To seek peace, men must set aside anything supernatural or invisible that might make demands on them and look to their own necessities. The sovereignty of man means the sovereignty of human necessities as opposed to human perfection.

Hobbes demonstrates this truth with the famous *state of nature*, a notion he invented that was adopted by Spinoza and Locke and has been fundamental to modern constitutionalism and liberalism (broadly defined) ever since. The state of nature is a prepolitical condition in which men live without conventional restraints or advantages, using only the advantages of their human nature. Though such a state will not ordinarily be before our eyes, we can easily and reasonably imagine it, by contrast to the prophetic dreams of divine revelation. From the fact that we lock our doors and even closets within doors when a government exists, we can infer that, without a government, no uncoercive human association could subsist, and we would live miserably in a state of war. And in such a war we can readily imagine that the best or strongest individual would be as vulnerable as the weakest, since cunning would be equal to wisdom and muscle. The state of nature would be a condition of war and equality altogether contrary to that set forth in the Bible in which the first humans, before they sinned, lived in peace and were perhaps equal to one another but, above all, creatures of God, subject to him, and, after they sinned, in need of divine grace. That Hobbes's state of nature is a state of war indicates that men were forced to sin out of necessity, that therefore they did not really sin when scratching or fighting for their lives.

The remedy for *sin*, moreover, is not divine grace but a human sovereign with adequate power, that is, human power so plainly visible to men in its execution as to be uncontestable by them. How can such a sovereign be found? Hobbes—this is his utopian revolutionism—does not believe that any actual sovereign has ever had the requisite authority. All sovereigns have rested their authority, in the Aristotelian manner, on the claim of a particular political party that has attempted to suppress the claims of rivals. As we have seen, however, the very virtue claimed for such regimes serves first as a standard with which to judge them, then as a lever with which to overturn them. Uncontestable authority can be established only by an appeal to the state of nature, in which men are equal and no claim to rule, whether monarchical, aristocratic, or democratic, can reasonably be made. In this state of equality and war, each person has by nature an equal right of self-preservation and, to maintain this right, a further right to be the judge of the means of his preservation. Thus quite precisely, according to Hobbes, nothing is sacred in the state of nature, and each has a right to everything; neither God nor fellow human has property that one must respect. Any claim to sovereignty must be constructed from the ground up, for no conventional claim can be valid in the state of nature, and an examination of that state leads certainly and obviously to the conclusion that no claim of any man to rule another based on a natural superiority can be valid either.

The sovereign authorized by the exercise of men's natural right of self-preservation is wholly artificial and absolute: wholly artificial in order to be absolute, because only natural superiority might be contested by partisans. Since no actual sovereign has ever been absolute, however, Hobbes's doctrine of sovereignty cannot rest on experience but must be expressed in a natural law that calls for the first simply unlimited and undivided sovereign known to history. Although this doctrine has a realistic beginning in the state of nature, it issues in a surprising legalism. Hobbes's natural law consists in what is reasonable for men in the state of nature to do—to seek peace by subjecting themselves to a sovereign; and this reasoning is powerfully supported by fear of violent death should it not be followed. Yet despite this reliance on an unexalted reason and the passion of fear, Hobbes's doctrine of sovereignty teaches, even exhorts, men to act not as they have, or as they would, but rather as they should. His realism does not simply endorse the world as it is, but seeks to transform it by a novel legalism that requires men to shed their illusions and be their real, as opposed to their actual, selves. This legalism tries to compel us to ignore the actual facts of politics, which always limit the sovereignty even of the most tyrannical governments; for those powers in Hobbes's society that are denied the rights to challenge the sovereign will nonetheless have to be respected by the sovereign in practice. It is an odd realism that exhorts men to behave as they never have before and an equally odd legalism that defines the law as anything the sovereign wills; but both the one and the other are the essence of Hobbes's sovereign.

Thus Hobbes's doctrine could hardly be more ambivalent in its attitude toward constitutionalism. On the one hand, nothing appears more opposed to constitutionalism than a teaching that every sovereign must be obeyed regardless (almost) of what he does and that there must be no formal constitution of institutions to ensure limited government. On the other hand, Hobbes's doctrine of natural rights establishes a distinction between state and society by removing every duty of the sovereign to educate or compel men to live more virtuously than they would without him, except as virtue is defined as obeying him. As long as men obey the law, they will have considerable liberty in the silences of the law, for Hobbes tells his sovereigns that it is in their interest to require as little as possible from their subjects. Moreover, the natural right to self-preservation has *constitutional* effects in Hobbes's system; he is, for example, the first to allow a right against self-incrimination. And when, far from want-

ing to abolish Parliament, Hobbes encourages the sovereign to seek coun-
sel from it, he permits a latent constitutionalism to moderate the absolute
sovereign in practice.

Hobbes's disposition of religion reflects his ambivalence toward constitutionalism. Religion, according to him, is based on fear of invisible
spirits as opposed to fear of the visible sovereign. It causes trouble both
by challenging the sovereign, thus disturbing the peace, and by flattering
the sovereign, thus tempting him into tyranny. Yet Hobbes does not
believe it possible, necessary, or desirable to abolish religion. Even though
his doctrine replaces the Bible with the state of nature as the foundation
of politics, he expounds in the second half of *Leviathan* a Christianity that
serves the purposes of his sovereign while answering human need. There
is a "natural seed of religion" in the human propensity to seek an invisible
cause of one's well-being. This seed is tirelessly cultivated by the three
classes of big talkers to be found in civilized societies—lawyers, priests,
and scholars. While attacking them, Hobbes admits religion into society
despite its basis on the principle contrary to that of true sovereignty.
Although he tries to prove that Christianity neither needs nor challenges
the state, there is no guarantee that his proof will be successful, and in the
event, of course, it was not.

As to the soul, Hobbes defines it away. Soul cannot be found in the
world of Hobbes's science, which recognizes only bodies in motion. Human beings are moved by necessity—both by reason, which compels them
to see how things must be, and by fear and other passions, which bring
necessity into the next moment of one's life. True choice and true elevation are equally impossible, and so, therefore, is human responsibility.
Hobbes's doctrine of authorized sovereignty seems to be a system of
human sovereignty by which men for the first time take control of their
lives, but in fact it is not. The sovereign is irresponsible because he does
not have to answer to anyone, including God; and the people, though
formally responsible for every act of the sovereign they have authorized,
are actually irresponsible because they must do nothing themselves but
accept everything he does.

Spinoza: Natural Right Entire

In Spinoza's works, criticism of revealed religion is even more prominent
than in Hobbes's. His *Theologico-Political Treatise* is a criticism of superstition, first by appeal to the Bible and then by appeal from the Bible to
reason, the philosopher's reason. Superstition is invented and used by
rulers and priests to suppress political freedom in the people and free

inquiry among philosophers. In the preface to this book, Spinoza establishes a connection or alliance among religious freedom, democracy, and philosophy in opposition to suppression, hierarchy, and superstition. More precisely, since his philosophy establishes an alliance between religious freedom and political freedom, his politics can be called constitutionalist. By prudent forbearance, more than by respect for right, Spinoza's state does not attempt to impose itself on society. Although the distinction between state and society is not derived from the natural right of individuals, is not defined legally, and is not protected by constitutional forms and liberties, nonetheless it exists or can be made to exist in effect. Spinoza is known for equating right with might. Let us see how this equation arises from his treatment of the religious issue and how, contrary to our expectation, it results in a practicing constitutionalism.

Spinoza's criticism of the Bible begins with the quite orthodox statement that prophecy or revelation is sure knowledge. But then, by degrees of gradual but relentless insinuation, revelation is revealed to be mere imagination dreamed up to delude a vulgar people. Revelation is temporarily equated with natural knowledge and then, by comparison with it, rejected; next, revelation is relegated to moral truth and then, by comparison with that, again rejected. Spinoza carries this argument to an open denial of the miracles that attest to revelation. He says that, since God's power is infinite, we cannot know what is naturally possible, hence cannot know what is supernatural, hence cannot know what is miraculous. Hobbes had said this much, but the bolder Spinoza adds that since God is wise, he would not attempt miracles that would not be convincing as such. Therefore, miracles are impossible as well as unknowable, and it is presumptuous and *impious* to believe in them. Spinoza's premise in this mode of argumentation (which is an elaborate and impudent begging of the question) is that God's will is identical to his intellect, hence perfectly open to human inspection. If it is claimed that God's will is revealed in the Bible, then the Bible can be read as if it were a human book. So read by Spinoza, the founder of historical study of the Bible, it proves to be a very inferior book.

Now, since God's will is infinite, so too is his creation, nature. Nature has no limits defining what is possible; nothing that happens is any more natural than anything else. This means that nothing that happens is any more providential than anything else. The Jews are not God's chosen people; God cares equally for all, that is, for all nature, that is, for no one in particular. It is up to men to govern themselves, and thus Spinoza shares in the premise of modern constitutionalism that government is constituted by humans to answer human needs. Differing from Hobbes, however, Spinoza "keeps natural right entire." Since nothing is unnatural, everything has as much right as it has power; and men have no privileged exemption from this truth.

In consequence, Spinoza's politics lacks the legalism of Hobbes's. He does not agree with Hobbes that the artificial institution of sovereignty establishes the rule of law, supported by the promise to keep one's word as given in the social contract. For him, the sovereign is as natural as the "state of nature" preceding it; the rule of law is rule of the strongest, who made the law; and promises hold only so long as one is compelled to keep them. But if (or because) Spinoza's system lacks the advantages of constitutional legalism and formalism, it has a clearer, more consistent, more revealing realism. In place of Hobbes's authorized sovereign, who may be any form of government, Spinoza says straightforwardly that democracy is the "most natural and most consonant with the liberty that nature grants to everyone." This is so not because democracy is more just, but because the people will demand their freedom, and not because democracy accords with the equality of rights, but because men will insist on their equality despite the facts. The facts are, according to Spinoza, that men are divided into the rational few and the irrational many. But it is rational for the few, who are weak, to defer to the many, who are strong. Spinoza does not try to maintain that democracy can be seen by the many to be in their interest; so he does not forget that democracy needs to be sustained by republican virtue, that is, martial virtue, and also by charity. Charity, or love of one's neighbor, cannot be supported by reason, since reason teaches men to take and keep what they can; so charity depends on faith. The main work of charity being to counteract religious fanaticism, it is one delusion set against another, worse delusion. After beginning from the standpoint that religion is *the* enemy of human reason and freedom, Spinoza concludes that religion suitably redefined so that it amounts to charity and nothing more is a necessary foundation of a free community.

Spinoza's democracy can be considered liberal and constitutionalist because it keeps a place (though not public status) for the wise as distinguished from the ignorant. Together with the "foundations" that qualify simple rule by the ignorant many, the wise will enjoy free inquiry and free speech. Although these are not constitutional "rights," free inquiry cannot be prevented anyway, and free speech is useful because it is inconvenient to priests. The aim of the state is merely bodily perfection (including the low, instrumental virtues mentioned above) as opposed to moral or theoretical perfection. The few who desire theoretical perfection in the life of a philosopher cannot ignore their need for bodily perfection but will not be hindered by demands for moral perfection, nor will the vulgar many who desire merely bodily perfection. In Spinoza the distinction between state and society is constituted by the absence of such demands (except for minimal martial and charitable virtues needed for bodily perfection). Most human souls want vulgar pleasures; some few want contemplation of the whole of nature. The freedom that both want unites them politically, but only in an external sense. The irrational many are irresponsible, and the rational few are responsible to the whole but not to humanity as humanity. The distinction between state and society does not allow—or require—philosophers to become kings.

Locke: Rule of Law

Locke's constitutionalism is close to ours and feels comfortable to us. Either it feels comfortable because it is close, or it is close because it feels comfortable, or both. Locke does not puzzle us with the odd legalism of Hobbes's notion of absolute sovereignty, and he does not frighten us with the unsettling realism of Spinoza's dictum that might makes right. Locke argues his constitutional politics more directly on political grounds. He put the principles of his politics into his *Two Treatises of Government* and left psychology and epistemology for his *Essay Concerning Human Understanding* (1690) and biblical criticism for his *Reasonableness of Christianity* (1695) and paraphrases of St. Paul (1705–7). Thus he does not force us, nor did he force his contemporaries, to confront the religious issue and to oppose religion with constitutionalism. Rather, he provides two arguments for a liberal constitution, religious and nonreligious, and presents them together, mingled and, it often seems, confused. On inspection, and after disentangling the two arguments, the same unsettling problems Hobbes and Spinoza bring to the fore may be seen lurking in the shadows of Locke's talkative prose. The confusion, then, is perhaps not his but ours and is intended for our comfort. We should be wary that Locke is known both for his caution and for his confusion.

The first of Locke's *Two Treatises of Government* is on paternal power, the second on political power. The argument from the inadequacy of paternal power to the adequacy of political power does not seem to raise the religious issue—but in fact it does. Locke's *First Treatise* is devoted to an attack on Sir Robert Filmer's *Patriarcha* (1680), in which Filmer tried to argue that political authority comes from God, hence is passed on, beginning with Adam, from father to father. In this view paternal power is the manifestation of God's rule among men, and true political power resembles paternal power as closely as possible. To refute this conclusion, Locke points out repeatedly that the Bible says "Honor thy father and thy mother," not merely father; so it grants not a single paternal power but a divided parental power. Moreover, Locke asks us to consider the nature of this grant: does it require us to obey our parents no matter what they command, or is the grant to our parents limited by God's other commands? Does the Fifth Commandment stand alone, or is it to be taken with the other commandments? In the latter case, surely the orthodox interpretation, God's grant of power to humans is given with strings attached, and human government is required to put God's commands above human needs. One should obey one's parents, and by extension the political authorities, only when they obey God. Thus Locke's discussion of the absurd doctrine of an obscure polemicist raises the same question of human sovereignty that we saw stated more directly by Hobbes and Spinoza.

Whether Locke answers this question in the same way as Hobbes and Spinoza or follows the Bible has been much disputed, and the doubt that Locke permits, or encourages, on this point is the prime instance of the confusion that has been attributed to him. At the beginning of the *Second Treatise*, Locke brings up the same unbiblical "state of nature" featured by Hobbes and Spinoza and describes it as a "state of perfect freedom . . . within the bounds of the law of nature." A state of perfect freedom is the contrary of a state of obligation toward one's creator, but what are the bounds set by the "law of nature"? Locke does not make it difficult to find them out; they are to preserve oneself and the rest of mankind. He does make it difficult, however, to see whether the source of the law of nature is God or human nature regardless of God; so he makes it difficult to see whether following the law of nature is obeying or disobeying God. In any case, one can say, on the one hand, that he does not base his politics on the Bible or on divine right in any sense that overrules merely human needs and, on the other hand, that he expresses his politics not in terms of mere self-interest, but rather in terms of rights conjoined with duties. The duty to preserve others yields to the right to preserve oneself when the two come into competition, but Locke does his best to prevent them from doing so. The duty to preserve mankind in the state of nature is transformed into the duty to obey a constitutional government in civil society.

Constitutional government establishes the rule of law in the modern sense, best described by Locke. It is not mere sovereignty, as with Hobbes, or mere power, as with Spinoza; nor is it a mere voluntary association resembling an insurance company to serve as conduit from rights to policies, as with libertarian theorists in our day. The rule of law in its modern sense means not the rule of certain ancient laws or of a higher law of divine origin; nor does it mean the rule of natural law, for Locke says that in civil society the natural law is simply the preservation of society or of the majority. It means rule by *declared laws* that have been made by the legislative power, which must therefore be both supreme and public. This rule of law is the rule of lawmaking by a *due process* visible to all. On second thought, as it were, Locke admits that declared laws have to be complemented by prudence and discretion in the executive and federative (foreign affairs) powers; so the supremacy of the legislature is modified to secure a separation of powers. Thereby, government acquires a formal structure, respect for which is by itself a reassurance (if not a guarantee) that liberty is not endangered. The distinction between state and society, which in Hobbes and Spinoza is merely in the *interest* of both state and society, acquires a formal boundary of procedure to help decide when the state is rightfully intervening, or wrongfully intruding, in society. Whereas with Hobbes the sovereign "represents" the people whatever he does, in Locke's constitution due process in government, as well as elections to Parliament, give *representation* a more determinate meaning. Though the structure is formal, it bears a convenient resemblance to the Constitution of England (with a few alterations), so that Locke does not have to appear to be as revolutionary as do Hobbes and Spinoza. And with England as his model, Locke (in contrast to Hobbes) can forge an alliance with lawyers and allow the common law to specify the rights of citizens when Parliament does not decide. The problem of securing responsible sovereignty still remains, but it is muted and somewhat concealed. Just as today in constitutional democracies, when people elect but constantly denounce politicians, the question of who is responsible gets lost between the people and the government.

With a formal boundary to demarcate state from society, Locke can rely on the voluntary motion of society to secure its own autonomy more than could Hobbes and Spinoza, whose governments had to create their own supports, particularly official religions. The voluntary motion occurs in economics, education, and religion—three great concerns formerly political but treated extrapolitically as private matters in Locke's writings. In regard to religion, he argues against a civil or established religion and for a toleration of religion or sects now to be considered voluntary. Government cannot promise not to interfere with religion because it must ensure that religion does not interfere with government, since it tends, perhaps inevitably, to do so. Why does religion tend to be intolerant and to seek, against the very idea of modern constitutionalism, to use government as its instrument? The answer is that religion teaches, inevitably, that men's souls belong to God. Locke says, however, that "the care ... of every man's soul belongs unto himself." And what if he neglects the care of his soul? Locke answers, What if he neglects his health or his estate? The magistrate cannot force him to be rich or healthy against his consent, so cannot force him to save his soul. This is as much as to say that it is of the essence of the soul to be free to refuse responsibility for itself. It is not of the essence of the soul to cultivate or perfect itself, much less to obey God. The result is a negative freedom or self-satisfaction expressed not so much in gaining what one wants as in the power to refuse. The problem for education (see Locke's *Some Thoughts Concerning Education*, 1693) would be to make something positive of this power and to convince men (or children) who believe they are already independent that they must *learn* to be independent. This is not easy, because to admit one needs to learn is to acknowledge one's dependence.

Modern constitutionalism as we see it in Hobbes, Spinoza, and Locke does not have a solution for the religious issue. A solution would be a society in which the highest human aspiration, the divinity in man, would thrive while human freedom was preserved: the rational society, perhaps, of Hegel, if that could be made to work. Our three constitutionalist philosophers had their hopes for a permanent improvement in human freedom, but they were too sober to believe that it could be achieved without cost. But did they correctly reckon the cost in human irresponsibility—even to their own project—when men are no longer required or expected to take care of their souls? The measures these philosophers adopted to contain religion by diminishing the soul seem also to endanger freedom.

9

Separation of Powers in the American Constitution

Separation of powers is the chief of the "auxiliary precautions" necessary against oppression by government, according to James Madison in *Federalist* 51. It is especially a precaution against government, but also, as will be seen, a necessary means to effective government. As a precaution, it is auxiliary to "dependence on the people" or to representation, the primary precaution. In *The Federalist*, in which separation of powers is best expounded, the American Constitution is shown to be republican government that is wholly popular, because all parts of it are derived from the people, and yet wholly representative, because in no part do the people govern directly. Separation of powers is the form or structure of republican government in which the people are revealed as not governing directly. While Madison in *Federalist* 10 refers to representation and extensive size as a republican remedy for republican diseases, separation of powers might best be described as a nonrepublican auxiliary to republicanism, its "interior structure," as Madison says in *Federalist* 51.

Separation of powers, according to Alexander Hamilton in *Federalist* 9, is a modern invention, indeed an invention of modern political science. Although as a doctrine separation of powers is indebted to the medieval parliaments and modern, limited monarchies whose practices give substance to abstract categories, it did not emerge as it were naturally from the conflict of social groups for political power. In this regard and as a whole, separation of powers must be distinguished from the mixed regime dear to ancient political philosophers such as Plato, Aristotle, Polybius, and Cicero. Set forth as a guide to statesmen, the mixed regime results from an assessment of the rival claims to rule of social groups or classes in which each claim is found to be partial, hence in need, and yet worthy of being mixed with its rivals to achieve a better or truer whole. This assessment presupposes both an existing whole and the existing political parties that claim to rule it. But the doctrine (for such it is) of the separation of powers begins with a theoretical analysis dividing political power into categories not found in uninstructed political practice. For it was clear from the first that legislative, executive, and judicial powers do not correspond exactly, and often not even roughly, to the actual powers of parliaments, kings, and judges. This analysis, then, is critical in its initial stance and not merely after consideration. *The Federalist* presents its version of the separation of powers not as emerging from the practice of republics, let alone of the English monarchy, but as one cure for the weakness and disorders of previous republics, including the American states which had been independent since 1776 and above all the federal government under the Articles of Confederation. Although it borrows from practice, separation of powers was originally, and remains essentially, a theory—but not, as we shall see, a utopian theory.

The most famous theorists of the separation of powers, besides the authors of *The Federalist*, are Locke and Montesquieu. But the theory had its origin in certain writers who published before Locke during the English Civil War, and, surprisingly, its essential precondition in the political science of Thomas Hobbes. Hobbes was the furthest of any political thinker from believing that power ought to be separated, but he prepared the theory of separation of powers by arguing that power pure and simple, without reference to the ends for which it will be used, is and should be the central concern of politics. Hobbes's political science reduces the social claims to rule heard in politics, which are the basis of a mixed regime, to individual desires for power. Reasoning from these desires, men create a sovereign or government that is wholly artificial and wholly representative, presupposing no prior society or social group. This sovereign is defined by his power to make laws for his subjects unlimited by any claims of their subjects to rule.

As Hobbes was writing during the English Civil War, and to some extent with a view to his absolutist solution, the separation of powers first appeared in the 1640s as a distinction between legislative and executive powers in writings by Philip Hunton, John Sadler, John Milton, and (later: 1656) Marchamont Nedham on the parliamentary side. Thus, the original and perhaps essential separation of powers was twofold, between legislative and executive, not threefold as we know it today. It was made for a double purpose: to separate the executive power (which was usually held to include the judiciary) from the legislative and, not incidentally, to subordinate the executive to the legislative. In both respects the end was to maintain the rule of law, so that the one or those who made the law could not apply it, and the one or those who applied it could not change it to suit themselves. But since the executive in Britain was the king (and would be likely anywhere to be one or few), and since "executive" means carrying out the will of someone else, the king was by implication reduced to a subordinate, and the doctrine of separation of powers, despite the seeming impartiality of its end, had from its origin a republican bias. More radical writers, such as the Levelers Isaac Penington and Sir Henry Vane, used it to criticize the invasions of a republican executive (Cromwell) or republican legislature (the Long Parliament), but this usage hardly made it less a republican doctrine. Moderate royalists at this time, such as Charles Dallison and George Lawson, also used it in defense of the king, but to do so they had to combine it with some version of the mixed regime in order to elevate the king from the rank of mere executive.

The problem of the separation of powers in its original statements was its republican animus against the executive: this animus made it subversive in a monarchy and, as Americans were to discover from bitter experience with weak executives in the federal government and in the states from 1776 to 1787, useless and dangerous in a republic. The doctrine itself was self-defeating, for how could the executive power be kept separate from the legislative if the legislative was encroaching and the executive was subordinate? To turn to a "mixed monarchy" or a "balanced constitution" was an inconsistent, makeshift arrangement because it admits the claims to rule of several parties and thus is forced to mix powers to satisfy the parties as well as separate powers to promote the rule of law. Harmony gets in the way of security, and it is not clear which comes first.

Locke and Montesquieu, the two greatest promoters of separation of powers (Madison called Montesquieu the oracle on the subject), saw this problem clearly and attempted solutions. They were obliged to add a third power, to compromise the purity of the separated powers, and to "fortify" the executive (Madison's expression) well beyond the literal meaning of the word. But when they complicated the original twofold distinction, they did it for the sake of that distinction, and while complicating it, they clarified its end.

Locke achieved a synthesis of Hobbes's political science and the constitutionalist opinion of the 1640s and 1650s. In his *Two Treatises of Government* Locke makes the same beginning as Hobbes from a prepolitical state of nature, and thus, like Hobbes, obviates all claims to rule that might proceed from existing groups and that might justify a mixed regime. But in contrast to Hobbes, Locke believed that men could be governed by "declared Laws," hence that they need not be required to consent to government regardless of its lawlessness. The reasonable desire of each to know what is his, and to keep it secure, can and should be satisfied with such laws. Locke thought it safe to define the legislative power as sovereign rather than insist, as Hobbes did, that every act of the sovereign be considered a law. Rule of law in Locke's understanding is the rule of the lawmaking power, governed only by the natural law that society must be preserved and not by any higher law containing specific commands or prohibitions. When formulated in this way, as rule by legislation, rule of law calls for a separation between legislative power and executive power to ensure that the legislature is not exempt from the laws it will often be making.

Yet, mindful of the weakness of a subordinated executive, Locke added a third power, the federative, dealing with foreign affairs, which he called the natural power because it corresponds to the power every man had in the state of nature. This power was conceptually distinct from the executive, yet since it required the whole force of society for its exercise, as did the executive, the two powers were placed in the same hands. They are distinct, Locke says, because laws can direct the exercise of the executive, whereas the federative must be left in great part to prudence. As Locke discerns a practical alliance between two powers against a "sovereign" third, he justifies a prudence that can support the rule of law but cannot be directed by law. This appreciation of discretion, as distinct from law, culminates in *prerogative*, which is acting for the public good without direction from a law or even against the law. Prerogative applies to domestic as well as foreign affairs; so the need for discretion, which supports executive power, becomes an equal, countervailing, and complementary consideration to the rule of law, which demands the sovereignty of the legislative.

We see that Locke's seemingly abstract constitutional doctrine makes a very practical appeal to the two sides of the Civil War—legislative supremacy for the Whigs and prerogative for the Tories. But although each side can recognize its slogan in Locke's argument, it will not find that Locke endorses either claim to rule. Neither the law-abidingness of Parliament nor the virtue of the king is presupposed. Instead, Locke traces the three separate powers to be found in civil society to one general power, called "political power," which in turn he derives from the power that each man has in the state of nature to execute the law of nature, his natural right and duty conjoined. Underneath the supremacy of legislative power in civil society is the fundamental executive power in the state of nature.

This fundamental power, which reminds us of Hobbes, becomes divided in civil society between lawful power and discretionary power (these are not Locke's terms) in a balance that reminds us of the constitutionalist writers. But Locke, while avoiding the extremism and absolutism of Hobbes, clarifies the inconsistency of the constitutionalist inventors of separation of powers. With the notion of the state of nature, borrowed from Hobbes, he provides a ground for the separated powers exercised by government in civil society, and thus also a limitation on government through its wholly representative character. And since government has no right or power of its own, his political science can apportion its powers more from an analysis of the nature of political power than from a need to satisfy the demands of existing powers. Locke shows that separation of powers and representation are necessary to each other, and that both are necessary for limited government.

The influence of Locke can be seen in a small group of early eighteenth-century radicals, including John Trenchard, Anthony Hammond, John Toland, Walter Moyle, and William Hay, called "Commonwealthmen." They opposed corruption of the House of Commons by the king's ministers through "placemen," members of Parliament given offices and pensions to influence their votes and to secure their loyalty to the ministers. The arguments against such corruption (and also against standing armies that might overawe Parliament) were made on behalf of the independence of the legislative power, but not so as to subordinate the executive. Indeed a Tory, Henry St. John, Viscount Bolingbroke, could use the same arguments to promote the policy of a "Patriot King" who would govern independently of Parliament without resort to "corruption" and without regard to parties.

These writers have mechanized Locke's more subtle and complicated ordering in a government in which legislative and executive powers are balanced so as to be kept independent of each other. Speaking generally, one might say that the seventeenth-century clash of monarchical and republican regimes, moderated by appeals to a mixed regime, had become a dispute between powers of government to be resolved by finding a balance. The older claims to rule were now advanced, as they are today, in terms of Lockean political science, and parties, rather than claiming to rule the whole regime, formed around the two visible powers within a limited government in order to redress its balance—as Montesquieu remarked.

Montesquieu's contribution to the theory of separation of powers was above all in his formulation of the invisible, or less visible, power, the judicial. In reaction to Hobbes and Machiavelli, and in some degree to Locke, Montesquieu denied that fear could have a prominent and positive role in free government. He accepted the Lockean understanding of the rule of law as requiring government limited to the securing of rights, and he insisted more than Locke on the mildness and moderation of such a government. "A constitution," he said in the *Spirit of the Laws* (1748), "can be such that no one will be constrained to do things the law does not oblige him to do, and not to do things the law permits him" (11.4). Its end should be political liberty, defined as "that tranquility of spirit that comes from the opinion each has of his safety" (11.6). The government must be such that one citizen will not fear another citizen. To achieve this, the separation of the "three sorts of powers" is necessary, and particularly the independence of the "power of judging." The latter punishes crimes or judges differences among individuals, and it must be separated from the other two powers so that the judge neither legislates nor has the force of an oppressor.

Montesquieu makes it clear that the power of judging has its origin in the executive power (they were together in Locke), and thereby draws our attention especially to that separation. He remarks that European governments are moderate because the prince, who has the first two powers, leaves to his subjects the exercise of the third. When subjects themselves exercise the power of judging—in juries—that power, "so terrible among men . . . becomes so to speak invisible and null." Citizens fear the magistracy, but not the magistrates: in accordance with political liberty, they do not fear other citizens. At the same time, since punishment has been subtracted from the executive power, that power no longer appears to have the "force of an oppressor."

Montesquieu transfers the terrifying aspect of government from the executive to judging, and from judges to juries, so that it nearly disappears from view. This is perhaps why he speaks of the *power of judging*, not the *judicial power* as did Lawson and Bolingbroke, who anticipated him in describing the three powers as we do today. The third power is different in nature from the other two; lacking a will of its own, it is the power that hides power. In this respect it seems to epitomize the mildness of free government, and Montesquieu seems to suggest that the separation of the third power from the other two, and particularly from the executive, is the essential separation.

Yet Montesquieu cannot leave the power of judging without political strength against the other two powers and against the people. So he allows the hereditary nobility (in the House of Lords) to stand up for it, defending itself while defending the power of judging. It is to have a negative "faculty of preventing," as opposed to a "faculty of enacting," at least in taxation. For the sake of securing the independence of judging, Montesquieu compromises its separation from the legislature and also admits, contrary to the principle of wholly representative government, a distinct hereditary interest in government—though not because "nobles" are noble. Such compromising moderation was not inconsistency, but it was not agreeable to Americans, who borrowed much else from Montesquieu. Separation of powers was originally a republican doctrine that Locke and Montesquieu rationalized, neutralized, and cleansed of its partisan animus. But to do so they reinterpreted the English Constitution rather than abstracted from it, and in their political science they left items of unreason, unacceptable to rational republicans, such as prerogative and the House of Lords. Certain improvements remained for grateful Americans to effect so that the separation of powers could be adapted, not to the peculiar circumstances of America but to the universal requirements of an experiment "on the capacity of mankind for self-government" (*Federalist* 39).

At the time of the Revolution, Americans were agreed on the necessity of separation of powers, but unclear as to what separation meant. Their colonial inheritance was a hostility to executive power in the royal governors which they often expressed in the language of the radical Commonwealthmen, using *separation of powers* to demand the end of executive corruption in the appointment of "placemen" from the assemblies to serve on governor's councils. Then, in the Articles of Confederation and in their state constitutions made immediately after the Revolution began, Americans reverted to the weak executive of seventeenth-century republicanism. After sad experience during the war with domineering or hesitant legislatures (felt and denounced by Thomas Jefferson among others), they were ready to be instructed in a design that for the first time would justify a strong executive to a republican people. But those favoring a strong executive could not make it seem fully republican, for example, Theophilus Parsons in the "Essex Result" (1778), who advocated representation for property as well as men, and also John Adams in his *A Defence of the Constitutions of Government of the United States of America* (1787), who combined separation of powers with balance of the natural orders of society—one, few, and many. Yet the Antifederalists, who recognized the difficulty and were more dedicated republicans, could find no convincing republican justification for a strong executive and a complex structure of offices (for example, *The Federal Farmer*, Letter 14).

Through common deliberation the framers of the Constitution came to a better solution and a clearer understanding. Comparing the government they had made with Britain's mixed government, James Wilson said that in principle the new government was "purely democratical. But that principle is applied in different forms; in order to obtain the advantages, they exclude the inconveniences, of the simple modes of government." Madison argued in *Federalist* 10 and 51 that a certain material basis of diverse sects and interests was required for a successful republic. But this material basis is called forth and kept in being by the "different forms" of the Constitution, so that the Constitution does not depend on a certain prior social order. Its material basis is diversity rather than hereditary conventions. Nonetheless, as was said above, part of its formal structure—the separation of powers—is not distinctively republican.

Two arguments for separation of powers appear in *The Federalist*, but one of them, which is closer to republican distrust of outstanding men, is much more obvious. This argument is that separation of powers is needed as a precaution against the ambition of those holding power. It refers to the "encroaching" (a word used frequently) nature of power as such, and does not examine sorts of powers. It is satisfied when power is checked by power, and its concern is negative, the prevention of tyranny. In Madison's famous statement (*Federalist* 47): "The accumulation of all powers legislative, executive, and judiciary in the same hands, whether of one, few, or many, and whether hereditary, self-appointed, or elective, may justly be pronounced the very definition of tyranny." He assumes (with Montesquieu), not that all men are hungry for absolute power (as Hobbes), but that absolute power actually held will be abused. In this matter he departs from the classical tradition that holds open the possibility of a wise man who would not abuse absolute power.

The other argument for separation of powers, less obvious in *The Federalist* but implied by Hamilton's mention of the "regular" distribution of power (*Federalist* 48), is that separation makes the powers work better. In this mode power is not generalized but kept distinct in sorts or classes and understood as power to perform some definite function (well). Montesquieu is the source of the first argument, Aristotle (in his discussion of the parts of a constitution at the end of *Politics*, book 4) the source of the second. While maintaining both, and without departing from republicanism, *The Federalist* gradually shifts its main reliance from the first to the second.

In *Federalist* 47 and 48 Madison refutes the simplistic republican doctrine of separating powers that says that each power should be located in its own branch and kept in isolation from the other powers in their branches. Such a doctrine overlooks precisely the encroaching nature of power that republicans ought to fear. Because power encroaches, and powers do not merely work at their own functions in isolation, the three branches must be given means of self-defense to ward off encroachment. Such means necessarily involve the branches with one another, but only for the sake of the independence of each. Independence is secured not by innocent reliance on "parchment barriers," but only by mutual checks, such as the president's veto and the Senate's consent to executive appointments and treaties, requiring legitimate contact in order to prevent illegitimate collusion. The simplistic doctrine in fact leaves the legislature dominant and unchecked, "drawing all power into its impetuous vortex." Thus, the simplistic doctrine is the one confused.

If power encroaches, Madison's argument continues, it must be because men love it, or have ambition. But the spirit needed for defense is the same as the motive behind encroachment. Separation of powers by the self-defense of each, then, makes use of the ambitious in order to watch over the ambitious. The principle is "Ambition must be made to counteract ambition" (*Federalist* 51). Although republicans distrust ambition, Madison has brought them, by means of their distrust, to see that ambition is useful, perhaps indispensable, to republics at least by counteracting itself. One might also reflect that ambition is in a sense republican, being hostile to fixed, hereditary interests in the community. Although ambitious individuals constitute a class, as a class they help maintain diversity. Ambitious persons distinguish themselves by leading groups of men to do new and different things. Again, we see that the forms of separated powers create their own social support.

The negative argument in *Federalist* 47–51 shows the advantage that separation of powers presents to the people: a precaution against oppression by their rulers. It speaks to their distrust by setting forth a "policy of supplying by opposite and rival interests, the defect of better motives." But this statement, as it were to the people, already suggests opportunities for the ambitious. Ambition counteracting ambition means ambition *vying* with ambition, not thwarting it. Unlike simplistic republicans and the Antifederalists, Madison does not frown upon ambition. The argument in *Federalist* 51, as David Epstein has pointed out, "cannot be considered a summary of the whole book (*The Political Theory of "The Federalist*," 1984, p. 146). The rest of *The Federalist*, describing the three branches of government and the different qualities required for success in each, speaks to the ambitious as well as to the common people, and not merely to their ambition. In its positive argument for separation of powers, *The Federalist* evokes "better motives" than ambition by dwelling on the qualifications required to succeed in each constitutional situation. This is neither empty exhortation to virtue nor rash reliance on virtue: as the negative argument connects private interest to defense of one's constitutional place, the positive one connects private interest to virtue in carrying out one's constitutional duty.

The Federalist does not make a theme of its discrimination of the separate powers. To do so might seem to endorse the claims to rule of those who claim virtue in those powers, in the manner of the Aristotelian mixed regime. Instead, *The Federalist* presents those virtues through an analysis of the two modes of power, energy and stability. The forms of power—legislative, executive, and judicial—must be constructed with these two modes and with an eye to their difference and their balance. Energy and stability are categories of political science (indeed of natural science), not political opinion. In directing the virtues of politicians through scientific categories *The Federalist* makes them means to a republican and constitutional end; virtue is encouraged but subordinated to liberty. Liberty is understood as the end of a distribution of power in the Constitution which gives not only security from fear of other citizens but also, through elections, a share in rule for all and an opportunity for ambition in some. Although scientific, the system is not mechanical, and does not merely connect selfish interests seeking calculated utility on the model of a free market.

Thus, the "fit characters" Madison mentioned in *Federalist* 10 as likely to emerge in greater number from a large republic are called to the tasks of the three branches, not so much for what they are as for what they will do. The merits required in each branch are, in turn, described as the expected consequences of merely formal characteristics: the relatively lengthy term and small size of the House of Representatives (relative, that is, to republican tradition and Antifederalist objections); the number and term of senators and of the executive; and the lifetime tenure of judges. As with all constitutions, the ordering of quantities produces probable qualities (Aristotle, *Politics*, book 4, chs. 11–13), but *The Federalist* is careful not to identify the result in terms of a regime. Its argument moves from what is republican to what is good for republican government, leaving it to be inferred that "the more permanent branches"—the Senate, the executive, and the judiciary (*Federalist* 52)—are not the ones republicans would claim as their own even though they enable republics to be more permanent.

Even, or especially, in regard to the popular branch, *The Federalist* makes a point of the merits for which the people will elect their representatives. If one trusts the people, it says to the Antifederalists, one should trust their choices. Legislating is generalizing, but rather by combining various local conditions than by abstracting from them. Legislators need knowledge of their locality, the ability to communicate this knowledge to other legislators, and a capacity to combine interests to make a general law, not to mention the majority needed to pass a law. The Senate, with its longer term, is a force for stability, likely to "possess great firmness" against the evils of mutable government existing from the tendency of legislatures to legislate too frequently. The executive will have energy because he is one rather than plural, and firmness because of the length of his term and his eligibility for indefinite reelection. *Energy* is now a characteristically American term of praise; in *The Federalist* it is a scientifically neutral word free of monarchical resonance (Epstein, 1984, p. 171) and justified as a means to stability. If republican government is naturally both slow and flighty, executive energy quickens it and executive firmness solidifies it.

These descriptions of what legislative and executive powers do reveal reasoned justification for what might have seemed to be, from the negative standpoint, departures from separation of powers. Seen positively, the bicameral legislature appears not as a check irrelevant to legislation but as an aid to wise legislation, and the executive veto is seen not to violate separation of powers but to contribute to the legislative process experience and firmness that otherwise would be lacking. Even for the negative purpose of checking, the positive distinction of functions now appears necessary; for an undefined legislative power or executive power leaves encroachment undefined and thus excuses or invites it. "Parchment barriers" are not enough, but they are necessary to real barriers so that the three branches can defend themselves from defensible positions. As a whole, separation of powers creates "responsible" government in a sense now familiar but new with Madison and Hamilton (*Federalist* 63, 70) of responsible *for* rather than responsive *to*. Government with separation of powers is derived from the people but also separated from the people, responsible for the people *because* it is at a distance from them. There, government can serve the people without being servile, and the people can hold it to account without preventing it from governing.

This new notion is at its height in the judiciary, hardly mentioned in the account of separation of powers in *Federalist* 47–51; in *Federalist* 49 one learns that breaches of the Constitution should not be submitted to conventions of the people for judgment. The judiciary is the "least dangerous" branch, least able to injure or annoy the other two branches, hence not a player in the system of ambition counteracting ambition. It checks the other two branches, but not in the way that they check. It has "neither Force nor Will, but merely judgment" (*Federalist* 78). Judging, as distinct from legislating and executing, is the measuring of laws and actions against a preexisting standard, the Constitution or a law, and includes interpreting that standard. If the judiciary is to be separate, it must be independent; and if it is to be independent, its judging must reach to judicial review of the rest of the government.

Thus the judiciary passes from one power among three, and that the least dangerous, to the one above the others, the only one with its eye steadily on the whole, monitor of the separation of powers and guardian of the Constitution. So far from automatic is the working of separation that two of them must yield, when required, to the supremacy of the judiciary. To do so is not unrepublican, because it puts "the intention of the people" shown in their solemn act of establishing a constitution above the intention of their agents (that is, the other branches which have force and will) and, perhaps, even above their own "momentary inclination." But judicial review will not *seem* unrepublican, despite such high authority and lifetime tenure for judges, because it offers the possibility of relief from the injustices of government to individuals. As with Montesquieu but not in his way, government seems more tolerable with an independent judiciary, for the judiciary guarantees to each citizen not only trial by jury, but, far more valuable to Americans, the right to sue. In the American version of separation of powers, reason and republican pretensions are both satisfied, and antirepublican ambition is given its due.

To recite the history of separation of powers in the American Constitution would require a review of all American political history and an analysis of no small part of it. It would begin with the conflict that soon developed between the two principal authors of *The Federalist*, Madison (taking the side of Jefferson) and Hamilton, over presidential power; and it would continue through the recent Supreme Court case on the legislative veto, *Immigration and Naturalization Service v. Chadha et al.* (1983). Such would be a history of conflict within the system of separation of powers among partisans of the two or the three branches, defending their constitutional positions or seeking unconstitutional advantage. Apart from this history, however, critics have increasingly offered challenge to the separation of powers itself. The first, and most powerful, was Woodrow Wilson in his *Congressional Government* (1889) and *Constitutional Government in the United States* (1908). He reduced the separation of powers to its checking function, attacked it as mechanistic, Newtonian, and obsolete, and proclaimed the need for leadership to override the checks, overcome the separation, and put the system in motion toward progress. He was followed by other political scientists, E. E. Schattschneider in *Party Government* (1942) and James MacGregor Burns in *Deadlock of Democracy* (1963) who argued that party responsibility, more or less on the British model, would cure the immobility that they alleged was the aim and consequence of separation of powers. Richard E. Neustadt, in *Presidential Power* (1961), has provided a widely used definition of separation of powers—"separated institutions sharing powers" (p. 330)—which denies that the powers are separated according to function. The dislike and distrust of constitutional formalities are more systematic and more pronounced in the behavioral movement in political science led by Robert A. Dahl. In his *Preface to Democratic Theory* (1956), he maintains that the formal, institutional separation of powers presented in *The Federalist* adds nothing except confusion to the material, behavioral analysis of factions in *Federalist* 10.

In sum, whereas separation of powers in the American Constitution was above all an achievement of political science as understood and improved by the framers, today's political science is unconvinced of that principle and, if not persuaded of any other, is yet ready to abandon it in favor of some more seemingly progressive proposal. Without attempting to judge which political science is better, one can remark that the framers of the Constitution perhaps underestimated the risk they took when they grounded their construction on political science. But it is not easy to take account of the immutable truths of politics without relying on the fashion and fancies of political science.

10
Choice and Consent in the American Experiment

We Americans, with our worries in the present and unmindful of our past and future, may have lost all sense that, at its beginning, our government was intended to be an experiment for mankind. Today, our politics is divided between liberalism and conservatism in such a way that any grand common project engaging us all seems out of the question.

Liberalism (as used today) I take to be the happy view that life is mainly a matter of *choice*. As a liberal, you may live as you please, keeping your options open; or taking the longer view, you may choose a "life plan" as recommended by liberal philosophers such as John Stuart Mill and John Rawls. Conservatism, by contrast, is the belief that life is mainly a matter of *consent*, in which you must recognize your duties and live as duty requires. Your duties are not chosen; they come from the station of life in which you have been placed. Conservatives do not rule out all change, but they change only when it is necessary, and not out of choice.

These are extreme positions, perhaps, but they supply the fundamental biases of liberalism and conservatism from which liberals and conservatives are difficult to budge, to which they always like to return. (Libertarian conservatives are mainly partisans of choice.) Yet when we look at the "American experiment" as originally conceived, we see a combination of choice and consent rather than a division of parties between liberals and conservatives (those names were not yet in use). Parties there were, of course, and liberals and conservatives there have always been, in some sense. But Americans may learn something about themselves if they try, for a moment, to look beyond this division.

Responsible Choice

In our day many theories of choice explain how choice is exercised and how it might be rational, but if we want to understand what choice is, we must look to Aristotle's *Ethics*. There we find choice defined as voluntary rather than merely spontaneous, a reasoning specific to humans, even to adults, uncompelled by forces outside them. There are several things choice is not: it is not desire, which may be opposed to choice; nor is it anger, which is sudden; nor is it a wish, since we may wish for the impossible but may choose only what we can do; nor is it opinion, which is true or false whereas choice deals with good and bad. When we choose, we deliberate, and we deliberate over means, not ends, and over changeable matters within our control, not over eternal truths we cannot effect.

Our ends, according to Aristotle, are not chosen by us; they are given to us. For example, health has to be an end for a human being; even a martyr or a suicide has to be concerned with health in order to perish when he likes. We may wish for the attainment of such ends, but as said above, we may wish for the impossible. It is better to say that we accept or consent to possible ends, those ends that constitute our humanity, such as health and happiness. In consenting to the end of health we accept the limitations of our bodies in their susceptibility to disease—something we might prefer to have otherwise. We choose the means to become healthy. Thus every choice is made in a context in which something is not chosen but consented to. Our power to choose is real but it is limited by the ends we must consent to when we choose one course of action rather than another.

To choose responsibly, therefore, we take account of things that necessarily accompany our choices. In doing so we assume responsibility not only for actions we have chosen but also for their consequences, which we have not chosen. Indeed, in a sense, we *have* chosen these consequences. Aristotle said: A human being appears to be the origin of his actions. Thomas Aquinas, explaining this, said that if you choose to walk in the hot sun you choose to perspire. Though in one sense you did not choose to perspire, since it is not given to us *not* to perspire in the hot sun, in another sense you chose to perspire as a known consequence of walking in the hot sun. Choosing and consenting are distinct but also connected, so that choosing assumes or takes over consenting and we seem to will even our limitations. By consenting to our limitations we do not overcome them, but we adopt them. They are ours, not imposed from outside but constituting our identity. Instead of regarding nature as an alien tyrant, we make it our nature—our friend and our ward.

The combination of distinction and connection between choice and consent explains why we use the word *responsible* in so paradoxical a way. If someone chooses to do something foolish, we call him responsible for that action; but we also consider him *irresponsible* for choosing to do something foolish. Similarly, a responsible person is someone who takes charge precisely in a difficult situation he did not cause—for which he was not responsible. The responsible person "knows what he is doing" in the double sense in which we use that phrase: he knows what to do and he is aware of his limitations. His contraries are not only the person who does not know what to do but also the person who wants everything his way and will not accept what he does not like. Somehow, indeed, the fool who acts wrongly is less irresponsible than the willful and the selfish person who refuses to act except on his own terms. At least the fool knows that he cannot do everything and that he cannot avoid doing something.

It almost seems that the essence of human responsibility is accepting responsibility for things one is not responsible for. Surely our choices will not issue in actions if we insist on having everything our way, and our choices will bring us to grief if we seriously mistake their consequences. Responsible choice requires that we know our limitations and the constraints in the situation, and then, accepting them, that we choose well.

The American Experiment

How do these reflections on choice and consent apply to the American regime? We can see on the first page of *The Federalist* that, according to its author, America is carrying on an experiment for mankind to decide the question whether men can govern themselves by "reflection and choice" or must be governed through "accident and force." This theme has been played many times by American statesmen, most notably and nobly by Lincoln in the Gettysburg Address, in which he interprets the Civil War as a "test" to see whether a nation conceived in liberty and dedicated to the proposition that all men are created equal can long endure.

What is the American experiment? As an experiment, it is first of all something chosen. America did not come about gradually in the course of time; it was *founded* at a certain time by certain men known as founders who deliberated together in a constitutional convention. Although all looked to George Washington to be the first president, he was not the sole founder choosing the regime by himself. The Constitution was proposed by a few, then debated, and ratified by many.

Second, as an experiment the American regime was something new. Although much was inherited—institutions of the British Constitution and of state constitutions, and ideas from political philosophers in Europe—America was not a regime devoted to tradition. Its best inheritance—the space of a continent—was an opportunity. The first Americans, the Puritans, chose to come to the New World, and they were followed by waves of immigrants. Although these immigrants came over to escape persecution and poverty in their homelands, they were not mere refugees or exiles wandering where chance might take them. The Puritans came to live a life of their own, and later immigrants were attracted by the promise of America. The essential Americans have been not those born in America so much as those who chose it, or those, once in America, who left for the frontier. Today, Americans choose their residence; few of us live where we were born, and none of us does so without ever thinking of moving.

Third, the American Constitution is an experiment on behalf of all mankind. It would fail if it proved to be valid not for all peoples but for Americans alone because of their particular circumstances or national superiority. Whereas the English pride themselves on the rights of Englishmen, Americans take pride in the rights of man, or as we say today, in human rights. Americans say to the world: you can have what we have, and we are superior only because we have shown this possibility to you. Americans are not content with liberty merely for themselves, but they would be untrue to their principles, especially the right of consent, if they were to attempt to force their way of life on others as do most other revolutionaries. So they tout it or "sell" it to the world.

The American experiment is an experiment of an hypothesis. When America was founded, one could not be sure that self-government would work. At that time the question was not "decided," as we tend to believe today. And it was an innovation to found a nation by constructing a government that had not yet been tried, indeed to make its founding the trial of a theory as yet untested in experience or tradition. American political practice has not merely been shaped by theory, but it was deliberately intended to serve as the test of theory.

Last, America is an experiment of self-government, of human beings governing themselves. However much Americans at the founding may have sought the guidance of God, or prayed for his blessing on their undertaking, their principle was not divine right, their laws did not come from above, their government was not a theocracy, and their people were not chosen by God for a divine mission.

Self-government in America was popular government—but of a new kind. All previous popular government had failed (as we learn from *Federalist* 9, 10, 14), when the majority of the people behaved tyrannically as a faction hostile to the rights of others or to the interest of the community. Two new remedies for this general failure were found in modern political science, the principle of representation and the idea of an extensive republic. A "wholly popular government" is derived in all its parts from the people, on the one hand, but on the other, being wholly representative, it never allows the people to rule directly. Thus it gains the legitimacy of democratic consent while not sacrificing the advantages of aristocracy arising from the election of representatives who choose better than the people would choose on their own. Or is such a happy combination of choice and consent, of liberalism and conservatism, too beautiful to be true? If the people choose others to govern for them, thus to choose on their behalf, can the result be called self-government? The people seem to be passive, the government active, and popular choice seems to have dissolved into consent. The American regime seems to contain within its principle the danger of passivity and apathy in its citizens of which Tocqueville spoke in his *Democracy in America*.

The American Volunteer

To understand the danger of passivity, we must return to the modern political science on which the American regime was based. This political science held a fundamental notion in common with modern natural science, a notion with two aspects. First, science was expected to extend human power over nature. Nature does not have to be accepted as it is; it is neither our friend nor our master. Nature can be subdued and made to serve our needs. But at the same time, science is expected to narrow human responsibility. Men are not responsible for the universe as it is because we did not make it. We are responsible only for what we make. The fundamental distinction that can be applied to everything is between what is natural, which comes about by chance and is imposed on us, and what is artificial, which we make to be useful to us. The artificial is the intelligible essence of things, so that when we know something, we know how to make it.

What happens to choice and consent in the system of modern science? It would seem at first that we do not have to consent to the way things are, or appear to be. We can remake things, for example, improving the species of fruits and grains through hybrids. But there's a rub to this new-found power to make: once we learn how to make something, we must choose according to our ability to make. Television, for example, gives us new power to see things at a distance, but once we begin to watch television, we lose our capacity to concentrate on things around us. Indeed, as we reflect on it, we realize that we did not ever choose to have television. It was invented for us, and we accepted it. Our choice was determined by our power to make, by technology; and technology seems to have become our master instead of remaining our servant. Accordingly, it is often said, and truly, that television makes us into passive citizens, choosing less and consenting more.

According to modern political science, men can make their governments from the ground up. Aristotle had said that man is by nature a political animal, from which it follows that we cannot choose *whether* to have government, but we can choose *which kind*. Thomas Hobbes, however, denied that we have to accept our alleged political nature. We can imagine ourselves in a nonpolitical or prepolitical state of nature; so we can decide whether to have government at all, not merely which kind. But this extended choice proves to be a delusion. The state of nature without government is so harsh that necessity compels us to construct a government. Once we know how to make a government, we have no choice but to make it in that way. Therefore, our making is a kind of consenting, and making a government is consenting to its being made. We start out by refusing to accept what we have not made, and we end up being forced to accept whatever we can make.

Thus, Hobbes understood a citizen to be someone who votes himself into subjection. An active conception of government suddenly turns into the very idea of passivity. If we try to choose everything from the ground up, we fall into accepting everything that has been made. The modern idea of responsibility is that we are responsible only for what we make, but thereupon we become responsible for all that has been made. The responsible voter who helps to make a government becomes responsible for what it does, regardless of what it does; every citizen becomes responsible for the necessity of government, as if he had made that necessity.

Or one may refuse responsibility and become a rebel, since after all, *I* have not made the government, or anything else. A world I never made is one to which I owe nothing. But then I must make my own world by means of a revolution. The revolutionary character of modern political science comes from its attitude toward responsibility. For Aristotle, one must accept some things in order to choose others. For this political science, however, one must accept nothing in order to choose: so choice requires a revolution. But after you make a revolution, then what? You make a new government, accept responsibility for it, and settle into passivity. One can dream of being a permanent revolutionary, but this is nothing but the irresponsibility of someone who wants always to be in charge and never suffer the consequences.

Yet perhaps some middle course can be found between the passive citizen and the permanent revolutionary. This is the way of the volunteer. The volunteer is the person who takes charge in a situation he did not choose. His way combines consent and choice because, as regards consent, he does not try to remake everything and, as regards choice, he does not accept passively what others have done or what chance has wrought.

He looks to see in what way his actions can make an improvement and chooses to do what he can.

One problem remains: it is wise to volunteer? This is a reasonable question because those who volunteer run risks that can be avoided by remaining passive. Is it not one's self-interest never to volunteer but to hang back and be a "free-rider" on someone else's volunteer action? The answer depends on what kind of self you want to be or have: passive or responsible. A responsible self must be understood in both senses: responsible for what you can do and for what you have not done. The reason for becoming a volunteer is not to save your life, much less to make money, but to be a volunteer. It is no doubt too much to expect everyone to be a volunteer in every situation; so to volunteer is not a universal duty. But we can be sure that free government will not survive, that the American experiment will not endure, without responsible volunteers.

Part IV
Constitutional Forms

11

Social Science and the Constitution

But it is not to be denied that the portraits [the advocates of despotism] have sketched of republican government were too just copies of the originals from which they were taken. If it had been found impracticable to have devised models of a more perfect structure, the enlightened friends to liberty would have been obliged to abandon the cause of that species of government as indefensible. The science of politics, however, like most other sciences, has received great improvement.

(Federalist 9)

Our fifth proposition is that insofar as there is any general protection in human society against the deprivation by one group of the freedom desired by another, it is probably not to be found in constitutional forms. It is to be discovered, if at all, in extra-constitutional factors.

(Robert Dahl, A Preface to Democratic Theory, p. 134)

Here is a distinct contrast. On the one hand is the political science of the American Constitution, given credit by the author of *The Federalist* for a saving contribution to republican government, without which the friends of liberty would have had to abandon its cause; on the other is a nearly complete dismissal of the importance of our Constitution, together with the political science that, according to *The Federalist*, made it possible. The weight of the contrast is on the importance of constitutional models or forms. Though Dahl declares his support for the American "system" because of its peculiar "extra-constitutional factors," he does indeed abandon republican government as a *cause*, that is, as an example for the rest of mankind.[1] Since, for him, the Constitution is not the cause of American political behavior, in the sense of determining it, it is not a cause, in the sense of an end which he or we should be devoted to promoting or should recommend to the world. Dahl calls the extraconstitutional factors "social prerequisites"[2] from which we receive a hint about why his political science, in contrast to that of *The Federalist*, is generally regarded as a branch of "social science."

Political Science versus Social Science

What, then, is the full extent of the contrast between *The Federalist*'s political science and American social science today? What are the various differences in method and results and how do they combine to make the one science the creator and savior of the Constitution and the other its detractor and indifferent observer? To carry out this inquiry, we are aided by the critique Dahl himself made of "Madison's political science" in *A Preface to Democratic Theory* (1956). Although American social science is not at all preoccupied with its history, it has one nonetheless.[3] It has roots in the German philosophy it despises a priori and in the Scottish political economy that its liberal majority considers inhumane.[4] It has an embarrassing ancestor in Arthur F. Bentley, whose antics in *The Process of Government* (1908) seem now to mock, like the imitations of an ape in a tree, the modern battalions of sophisticated scientific explorers. It has a prophet and propagandist in Harold Lasswell, who set forth in the 1930s all the promises of social science for an earthly paradise of safety, income, and deference, and displayed an imagination not yet equaled by his successors. But Dahl's book was published in the heyday of American social science, shortly after World War II when it decided it wanted to rule the universe—of departments of political science in American universities.

Dahl's book has been criticized by defenders of Madison (among whom I count myself), but his good humor under attack has kept him true to his intent, which was progressive rather than exegetical. One should be grateful for a founding document of American social science that seeks to displace *The Federalist* rather than ignore it or merely disparage it. Other social scientists, having left to Dahl the task accomplished or attempted in this document, have thereby left to him the mantle of founder. Social science is now as diverse as any other successful movement of thought in a liberal democracy—I mean successful in its political, not its scientific, objectives. Since I cannot cover it all, I shall concentrate on Dahl's *Preface* because of its foundational character and on the *public choice* school. The latter, we shall see, makes a nice contrast with the *reflection and choice* claimed for the Constitution by *The Federalist*. But before considering how social science relates itself to the Constitution, we need to remind ourselves of the role and character of political science in *The Federalist*.

Political Science in *The Federalist*

Political science, we have already seen, is not merely in the background of the Constitution, providing implicit assumptions; *The Federalist* expressly acknowledges it and gives it credit for making the Constitution possible. This should help recall to us that liberalism in its origin was primarily a doctrine of political science. Although liberalism was based on rights and interests, it was not primarily a doctrine—as we often suppose today—asserting that men should have their rights guaranteed and their interests satisfied. Liberalism was originally about self-government in which men attempt to exercise their rights and pursue their interests by themselves, in freedom. The manner in which they exercise rights and pursue interests—the *forms* of self-government—were, we shall see, as important as the securing of rights and interests because rights and interests had to be secured *freely*. So although liberalism began its reasoning from prepolitical rights and interests in a state of nature, from that beginning it looked forward to the constitution of government under which rights and interests would be exercised and pursued politically, in constitutional channels. Liberalism was originally a doctrine of constitutionalism discovered and set forth by political science.

The Constitution can be said to be based on "liberalism" (in a generic sense that bears little relation to today's "liberals" as discussed in chapter 10) because it puts liberty over virtue as did the original seventeenth-century liberals Hobbes (not himself a constitutionalist), Spinoza, and Locke. This does not mean that the Constitution has nothing to do with virtue. On the contrary, the Constitution uses virtue, relies on it, and attempts to call it forth both from the people at large and from the more virtuous among the people.[5] Moreover, *Federalist* 51 asserts that "justice is the end of government." But this means that justice will always be *demanded* by the people, and government must respond to the demand.[6] Similarly, *Federalist* 55 supposes that there is sufficient virtue among men for self-government. But it is not the business of government, or of the federal government (which will become more powerful than state governments) to cultivate virtue and to improve souls.[7] Thus the Constitution is based on a kind of behavioralism. It relies on what can be expected in human behavior rather than exhorting to deeds that can only be wished for. But what can be expected is not the worst or even the lowest common denominator: it is a modicum of virtue in the people and outstanding virtue in a few, both of these cooperating with, and under the direction of, an insistence on liberty that can be found in the nature of every human being and cultivated in a free people.

What can be expected in human behavior is not the same as what has been seen. *The Federalist* makes it quite clear that the Constitution is not based on past experience. Past experience is almost entirely discouraging to a new republic, for republics, both ancient and modern, have lived alternatively in the extremes of tyranny and anarchy. They have been weak abroad as well as unstable at home. Previous "celebrated authors" in modern political science, too much impressed by this inglorious experience or unable to overcome it, have been unfriendly to republics and have based their constitutions on monarchies, in recognition that the modern state was everywhere the work of a monarchy.[8] The Constitution, therefore, is avowedly an "experiment."[9] It is a departure, the application of a new theory or hypothesis, and its success is not assured. It is an experiment to see, as we learn on the first page of *The Federalist*, "whether societies of men are really capable or not of establishing good government from reflection and choice, or whether they are forever destined to depend for their political constitutions on accident and force."

Reflection and choice: what do these mean here? We may begin with *choice* because, we shall see, the reflection necessary to free government concerns mainly the bounds to choice. Choice is not merely will. Although choice begins from a will, it is a reasoned will with inconsistencies and momentary inclinations refined out. Government by choice is settled and stable; when it changes, it does so deliberately by design and for a definable purpose. Such a government is even capable, through its executive, of undertaking "extensive and arduous enterprises" (*Federalist* 72, p. 437). Reflecting "the deliberate sense of the community" (*Federalist* 71, p. 432; 63, p. 384), it is as much opposed to governments by popular will alone as to monarchies, both of which belong to the company of constitutions depending on "accident and force." Certainly the "passions" of the public "ought to be controlled and regulated by the government" (*Federalist* 49, p. 317). The element of will in choice gives it a grounding in the universal human insistence on having things one's own way, but if that will were unaccompanied by reason, it would bring anarchy (=accident) and tyranny (=force). The work of reason is to give direction and solidity to the insistence of will, both to elevate it above whim and to settle it into determination. In this view the American Constitution does after all attempt to improve men's souls, but the method peculiar to it is to elicit reason from the people rather than to impose it on them.

The Constitution, therefore, is not a mixed constitution giving different classes separate powers in accordance with the sense of honor or faculty of reasoning they might be expected to oppose to popular will. The Constitution is "wholly popular," which means that all its branches are derived from the people (*Federalist* 14, p. 100; 39, p. 241). But since all branches are derived from the people, none of them is the people (as with the democratic assemblies of ancient republics); and the wholly popular Constitution is thereby "wholly elective" (*Federalist* 65, p. 396; 63, p. 387). The American Constitution establishes the first republic that derives all powers from the people, but also the first that withdraws all powers from the people. The people's choice is to be governed by those whom they choose in "elections." Government by choice, as explained in *The Federalist*, appears as a species of the genus government by consent, but it is equally opposed to pure democracy on the one hand and government by a single act of consent on the other.

Single consent is a species of government by consent invented and elaborated by Thomas Hobbes. Hobbes had criticized the ancient democracies for being actual oligarchies ruled by whoever could sway the passions of the people, the demagogues. He thought it necessary to seek the consent of the people; but to prevent them from having any active share in the government, he conceived that they must consent once, and once only, to the absolute power of a sovereign. A choice that cannot change, however, is not a settled or determined choice. It is not a choice at all, but a submission. While repeating Hobbes's criticism of demagogues (*Federalist* 1, p. 35; 6, p. 54; 10, p. 79; 55, p. 342) and accepting his conclusion that government must be withdrawn from the people, *The Federalist* maintains a middle ground between demagogues and Thomas Hobbes in government by choice through elections and the structure of government. This middle is constituted by the choice of a people in its constitution, for a *constitution* is lacking in both pure democracy and Hobbesian sovereignty.

Americans, with their "republican genius" (*Federalist* 37, p. 227; 66, p. 403), were of course not drawn to Hobbes's solution. They preferred the constitutional tradition revived by Locke and Montesquieu. But in making their Constitution wholly popular, they improved on Locke and Montesquieu with a demonstration by experiment that the people are capable of self-government without the aid of a hereditary monarchy or Senate. Such "aid" is both accident and force when juxtaposed to the choice of the people, for only a wholly popular constitution is wholly elective. Nonrepublican and mixed constitutions depend on the accident of heredity, and when they are not lucky, on force (*Federalist* 39, pp. 240–1; 51, p. 324).

Thus the American Constitution, by republicanizing the constitutional tradition of Locke and Montesquieu, perfects the liberal constitution of consent into a republican constitution of choice. (Here I use "liberal" and "republican" in their original generic senses.) But most Americans were instinctively republicans; through practice and prejudice they were captives of a republican tradition hostile to monarchy and to mixed constitutions. They had no difficulty in supporting a wholly popular constitution, for the state constitutions they had spontaneously (undeliberately) adopted after 1776 were wholly popular.[10] They were not, however, wholly elective, even though they made ample use of "elections," because they did not establish, through extensive size and separation of powers, the necessary and proper distinction between the people's will and their intention or choice or "election."[11] Since most Americans were instinctive republicans, the primary rhetorical and political task of the framers of the Constitution was to constitutionalize the republican tradition. They did this by republicanizing the constitutional tradition. But to republicanize the constitutional tradition, the primary feat of the framers' political science, *The Federalist* had to soften republican hostility to institutions outside the republican tradition.

The essential political distinction in *The Federalist*, therefore, is that between democracy and republic, a distinction *within* republicanism. Although today such a distinction may seem "conservative," it is endorsed and explained principally by the "liberal" Madison in *Federalist* 10, 14, and 39, as well as implied by the "conservative" Hamilton in *Federalist* 9.[12] The usual opposition between republic and monarchy or aristocracy, characteristic of both constitutional political science and republican polemics, hardly appears in *The Federalist* because republican Americans do not need it and would in fact be harmed by it.[13] For the essential difficulty of the Constitution, only partly revealed in *The Federalist*, is that certain nonrepublican institutions and practices in bad odor with republicans must be appropriated from the constitutional tradition, and made republican, in order to make good the distinction between democracy and republic. For *The Federalist*, the republican tradition is the problem, and the constitutional tradition the solution.

The republican tradition, with its dependence on a small territory, a homogeneous people, and cultivated virtues, exaggerates the extent of human choice. Those seemingly choice-worthy qualities are too easily transformed in practice into weakness, majority faction, and aggression or intolerance.[14] The task of *reflection* in political science, then, is to take account of things in nature and by chance that cannot be chosen and to match them with things that can be chosen. Since, for example, a republic cannot choose to avoid foreign relations, it must be large enough to succeed in them. Since it cannot choose a human nature that will keep the homogeneous majority from domineering the minority, it must have a diverse people. And since it cannot expect that virtue will always come out moderate instead of self-righteous, it must encourage interest and ambition. A republic, then, must be taught to choose what, abstractly, it would not have chosen—precisely to found government by choice. A large, diverse, commercial republic is a more deliberate and rational choice than a small republic chosen from the republican tradition (and out of Antifederalist sentiment) because with such a republic a people does not try to choose everything. Prompted and taught by reflection, it chooses to limit choice.

To choose to limit choice in this way might be called *constitutionalizing or formalizing behavior.*[15] It would be fine if one could solve all the problems for which men consent to government simply by establishing a republic, that is, a republican form of government. A people could then use its form of choice to choose how to deal with the world. But certain necessities of the kinds mentioned above—foreign enemies, the human desire to domineer, the human interest in security—intervene. Then a choice arises as to how to deal with these necessities: to keep them out of the constitution, so that the choice to be republican remains pure and noble, if frequently frustrated; or to bring them into the constitution so far as possible in order to anticipate necessities before they arrive. *The Federalist* praises the American Constitution for anticipating necessities.

According to *The Federalist*, the republican form is so far from solving all problems that it itself is the main problem in a republic. For the republican form of the republican tradition suggests that every majority produced by that form is legitimate and wholesome, which is far from the case. Thereby the republican form conceals the factiousness of a domineering majority and the usurpations of the legislature it dominates.[16] The form makes people believe that the main danger to republican government comes from an aristocratic minority desiring to rule, when in fact the very establishment of the form has made this danger both unlikely and easy to defeat. Republicanism, in its assertiveness as well as in its complacency, is too attached to the republican form. It was necessary, then, for the framers of the Constitution to bring to republicans, smugly satisfied with the republican form, an awareness of the actual behavior of republican majorities. Up to 1787 in ancient and modern history, republican majorities, while adhering formally to the republican form, had destroyed republics with their actual behavior.

Thus we find in the political science of *The Federalist*, as in social science today, a certain dismay with the naiveté of republican citizens and a central concern with the difference between forms of government and actual behavior. But in considering how to give effect to this concern, *The Federalist* wanted to maintain respect for republicanism, partly out of deference to its obvious force in America, but also because it had in view another, opposite concern. Having been too much attacked to the republican form, the people might become too little attached to it. Perhaps even through remedies adopted to counter the first danger, the people might fall into the second. In that case, the Constitution might seem to become an instrument, a mere means to an end outside itself. If all human behavior, including that of republican majorities, is self-interested, then any political form, even the republican, will be maintained only so long as it seems to promote the self-interested ends of individuals or groups. Yet if republican government is to be obeyed, it must be seen to be over the people whom it controls,[17] not as a mere factor in their calculations; it must be something they prize as worthy for its own sake, an authority for them, which they even venerate (*Federalist* 49, p. 314). How can the people venerate a constitution they regard as a mere instrument? How will they defend that constitution? This was the difficulty on which Hobbes's political science foundered: a sovereign consented to for the sake of self-preservation will be abandoned, when danger comes, for the same end of self-preservation. A republican people could also abandon the republican form for the sake of security with a conquering despot or an all-powerful government if it had no attachment to the form as such, if it had no republican genius or spirit. Therefore, despite the delusions inspired by the republican form in its traditional sense, Publius takes care to maintain that the new Constitution is "strictly republican" (*Federalist* 39, p. 240; also 10, p. 80).

The problem faced by the political science of *The Federalist* was this: on the one hand, one must never question "that fundamental principle of republican government which admits the right of the people to alter or abolish the established Constitution whenever they find it inconsistent with their happiness" (*Federalist* 78, p. 469). Yet, on the other hand, when this right is admitted, it seems to imply that the people can do what they like with the Constitution and that republican government and the rule of law continue only at their option for their convenience. This problem may reflect an ambivalence in choice itself between the human desire to choose for oneself, protected by the right of choice, and the rationality in choice that distinguishes it from mere will. Too rational a choice may seem to foreclose choice; too choosy a choice may seem to demean it.

As soon as one states the problem in this way, however, the solution adopted in *The Federalist* begins to reveal itself. Government by choice, we have seen, must take account of the actual behavior of men in which they frequently subordinate their choice, and the republican form that protects it, to their interest in security. As *Federalist* 51 reminds us in the famous passage defending the Constitution's appeal to the interest of an officeholder—or its *constitutionalizing* of self-interest—men are not angels (p. 322). But the same human nature that keeps men from being angels prevents them from being messengers or slaves of higher authority and inspires them to insist on their freedom. Those who demand that forms of government be judged by actual behavior must admit that men actually insist on their freedom as well as their interest, and that they will often go to great trouble, against their interest, merely to have things their own way—or even to feel they have had their own way.[18] The Constitution, according to *The Federalist*, adopts both motives of interest and motives of freedom. It appeals to the interested behavior of men as it seeks to satisfy the universal necessity of security and the need some feel of attaining an ambition (*Federalist* 51, p. 322), but also it takes account of the universal human need for the "liberty which is essential to political life" (*Federalist* 10, p. 78) as well as "that honorable determination which animates every votary of freedom to rest all our political experiments on the capacity of mankind for self-government" (*Federalist* 39, p. 240).[19]

Regarding one's interest, the Constitution is a means to an end outside itself. It provides avenues for the pursuit of one's interest in its political offices, in the rights it guarantees, including the right to vote, in a national commerce, and in a free economy. Regarding one's freedom, however, the Constitution becomes an end in itself in which the people provide for their interests through self-government. Self-government in this regard is not merely a means to their happiness but an essential part of it, since to live as a slave however rich or famous would be inhuman and dishonorable. The republican forms of the Constitution which allow free pursuit of one's interest make the Constitution an end in itself as well as a means to private ends because it satisfies the "capacity of mankind for self-government." In *The Federalist*, the Constitution becomes an end *as well as* a means. To forget that the Constitution is a means to the people's happiness would exaggerate the power of human choice to the point of supposing that men could form a permanent arrangement regardless of necessities that might arise. It would also diminish choice (in accordance with the ambivalence of choice noted above) by implying that the right of the people to choose a government, once exercised, no longer exists. Thus *The Federalist* emphasizes several times the sovereignty of "absolute necessity," hence of substance over form in politics; it declares the "transcendant law of nature and of nature's God . . . that the safety and happiness of society are the objects at which all political institutions aim and to which all such institutions must be sacrificed."[20] This necessity was the substance of *The Federalist*'s case against the Articles of Confederation, and in a general sense, as we have seen, against all previous republics.

Yet again, the choice for a new constitution must not be made lightly for transient partisan advantage, as if a constitution were a disposable convenience, made for obsolescence. A new constitution must be made "by some solemn and authoritative act" (*Federalist* 78, p. 470) to show respect for mankind's capacity for self-government. To make it work requires an "honorable determination" (as we say today, a commitment) rather than a hasty, passionate decision or a cool, standoffish calculation of what it may do for me. A constitution needs loyalty as opposed to ignorant enthusiasm or a temporary investment, and insofar as it satisfies our capacity for self-government, it deserves loyalty even when the benefits are unclear or far-off. To allow the people's happiness to become an overspecific standard by which to criticize the output of the Constitution on a daily basis—like a misery index for the health of the economy—would be to ignore that the very working of the Constitution, apart from its policies, is part of the people's happiness. Government by choice prizes choosing as much as the things chosen.

The ambivalence of the Constitution as a means and as an end in itself can be seen in the various statements on the ends of the Constitution in *The Federalist*. It is not enough, in the first place, that the Constitution merely be republican; it must aim at, and achieve, ends that are beyond republicanism, and that therefore put republicanism to a test, in keeping with the experimental, as well as the instrumental, character of the American Constitution. For a people wholly absorbed in republicanism cannot convincingly recommend republican government to the rest of mankind who may not be so absorbed. These ends beyond republicanism in *The Federalist* (carefully described and analyzed by David F. Epstein)[21] are justice and the public good. Justice is respect for private rights and is the end of "civil society" as well as government; the duty of government is the "protection," not the perfection, of men's diverse faculties, especially but not only in regard to property (*Federalist* 10, p. 78; 51, p. 325). The public good is the end only of government; hence it is narrower than justice. The concern of government for the public good, however, amounts to "pursuing" or "promoting" (*Federalist* 45, p. 289; 57, p. 350). The public good consists first of all in safety (*Federalist* 3, 23), for which government needs both "energy" and "stability" (*Federalist* 37, p. 226)—two modes of political power that are neutral as to regime, not necessarily republican. Promoting prosperity and commerce is the other element in the public good to receive mention (*Federalist* 12, 30).

Yet if these are ends beyond republicanism, so that republican government cannot attain them merely by being republican, they are not altogether separated from republicanism. The ends in themselves seem designed to maximize the choice of ways of life left to the people. Justice is mainly the prevention of crime, a negative duty for government; and the public good, though positive, is limited to those activities such as national defense and general welfare which allow or make it easy for people to lead their own lives.[22] Liberal individualism and republicanism, two erstwhile enemies, are shown how to make friends with each other as government by the people's choice is revealed, in the Constitution, to be the government that leaves the most choice to the people. Republican government that formalizes the behavior that people insist on, their living in security and their having a choice, will also be the limited government that liberals have wished for and sometimes found but never been able to cheer for.

The "true test of a good government," according to *Federalist* 68 (p. 414), is "its aptitude and tendency to produce a good administration." This would be recognized today as a behavioral test of government—of what it can produce or show. Yet Hamilton introduces it by disagreeing with the "political heresy" which says that only fools contest for forms of government.[23] The republican form— of the American Constitution—has an aptitude and tendency to produce a good administration of the ends of government. The Constitution achieves these ends indirectly by the tendency of its form rather than directly through indoctrination in the ends or imposition of a way of life.

What, then, is the general character of the republican form of the Constitution as *The Federalist* explains it? It is to establish government by choice by introducing forms that take account of behavior arising from necessity or from human nature, not from choice—representative government with separation of powers in a large, diverse country. This paradox is required by the human insistence on free choice and the natural limits to such choice. By constitutionalizing the limits to choice the Constitution secures choice better than all previous republics, according to *The Federalist*. Thus, in embracing the imperial size and representative structure previously thought fatal to republics, the Constitution provides a "republican remedy" for the diseases of republican government (*Federalist* 10, p. 84), though it might be more accurate to speak of a *republicanized* remedy when referring to the "more permanent" parts of the government, the Senate, executive, and judiciary, which seem to operate by their own choice apart from the people's.

It is in the nature of form, however, to leave open the content or behavior it formalizes. A constitutional form, whether it is an institution such as the presidency or a right such as the right to vote, leaves open whether the president will provide an effective administration and the voter will prefer "fit characters" to demagogues. Thus, once one incorporates into the Constitution the necessity for a strong executive and the necessity to avoid pure democracy, a choice of how to deal with those necessities is established. Behavior thus formalized is no longer simply determined by necessity, so long as the Constitution is successful in developing an *aptitude and tendency* to good administration; a poorly made constitution will of course aggravate troubles by spreading the delusion of choice. For example, in explaining the separation of powers, a republican device in origin, *The Federalist* shows at first (*Federalist* 47–51) that separate powers must be independent, and to be independent, each power must have means of defense, especially the more permanent powers.

Thus, contrary to republican tradition, separation of powers compels Americans to abandon the supremacy of the legislature. The traditional republican form of a dominant legislature is made to face necessity, and to do so by accepting a necessity—the self-interest that officeholders will predictably connect to the constitutional rights of their offices (*Federalist* 51). But then, as *The Federalist* goes on to explain and defend each of the three branches, it becomes clear that much more can be expected of officeholders than a merely stubborn defensiveness toward one another: virtue in congressmen (*Federalist* 55), character and moderation in senators (*Federalist* 62, 63), energy in the president (*Federalist* 70), knowledge and judgment in the judiciary (*Federalist* 78). How far one can expect these qualities varies with the office and finally remains uncertain;[24] altogether, one can speak only of an "aptitude and tendency" to produce them, argued by *The Federalist* not from the character of a certain class expected to hold the Constitution's offices but from the formal characteristics (term, appointment powers) of the offices.[25]

As befits an experimental Constitution, there is no guarantee of success. No constitution of a government by choice could guarantee success without depriving the people of choice or demeaning their choice to mere whim. All it can do is to set up a tendency to responsible government (*Federalist* 63, p. 383), in a new sense of *responsible* now somehow familiar to us as "choosing to be responsible for," rather than merely "responsive to," the people.[26] The Constitution exists in its aptitude and tendency, as conceived by political science, to elevate the will of the people to their intention; the achievement is up to us.

The Social Science Model

Our social science will not tolerate the indeterminacy of a situation in which the Constitution may or may not achieve its end. Social science wants a guarantee that it will do so. When social science cannot find certainty in the individual case (as often happens), it insists on a calculation of statistical probability to discount that uncertainty. It would never be satisfied with the shrug of the shoulders in the ordinary man's "probably" or with the careful forbearance in *The Federalist*'s "aptitude and tendency." Social science objects, therefore, to the use of terms or ideas over which people disagree; social science will replace these vague, contestable ideas with agreed-upon definitions, so that social science can progress without always having to go back to reconsider old disputes.

Social science will be cumulative, which means that the advance of knowledge will necessarily go together with agreement on its findings. Social science proceeds by causing consent to itself; as science, it is not only irrefutable but also undeniable. And what is it that can be neither refuted nor denied?—the facts of behavior, as opposed to the promises, the oughts, the open authorizations of formal statements, especially those in a constitution. Hence the first rule of social science is *behavioralize the formal*. Always look for the actual behavior resulting from a formal authorization or definition, and when you catch people at what they do—for you must watch what they do rather than listen to what they say—you will have a truth that will gain agreement.

Behavioralizing the Formal

In the first chapter of *A Preface to Democratic Theory* Dahl behavioralizes the forms and formalities of the Constitution and the formalized explanations of *The Federalist*. Beginning with his chapter title "Madisonian Democracy"—for who can say that the founders or Publius had a consistent intention?—Dahl cuts both of them down to size. The forms of the Constitution can be summarized as the separation of powers (including federalism, which gives separated powers to the states and the federal government), but since one can prevent tyranny without this device (as in Great Britain)[27] and since one cannot surely prevent tyranny with it, one must seek the social conditions of behavior that make separation of powers work or fail to work. Whereas the constitutional device is indeterminate because it depends on the chances that founders will discover it and get it accepted, and then that it will be used sensibly and constructively rather than stubbornly and obstructively, the social conditions are determinate because they do not depend on human intentions. If they did, then one would have to wait to see how men dealt with their conditions, and political science would have to abandon prediction as the test of its success and return to retrospective praise and blame.

Whether these conditions "work," Dahl points out, cannot be judged by using terms such as "tyranny" or "faction," because those terms are subject to partisan definition and therefore "remain mere untestable assertions."[28] The first rule of social science requires a reduction of boastful rhetoric, of ambiguous terms, and of offices defined by their supposed functions—in sum, of the formal—to its actual results, its unarguable meaning, and its testable operation.[29]

This reduction, however, is not enough; it is only half the story. In order to guarantee the working of a political system, social science cannot allow things to happen as they will, for to do so too would be a surrender to chance. Social science must show that it can replace faulty, bombastic explanations with realistic, operational ones; it must project into the future, and to do so it must develop models with the capacity to predict. Historical explanations are cluttered with historical circumstances, thus always to some extent accidental. True explanation is universal, and the best test of universal knowledge is not being surprised by an unexpected event; for a social scientist, to admit surprise is to confess a culpable ignorance. Models with the capacity to predict, then, are universal conditions cleansed of their historical manifestations, which are accidental and arbitrary: these models are *formal*. Hence the second rule of social science is a reversal of the first: *formalize the behavioral*. Always state the behavior one has found in a form that guarantees its universality.[30] To generalize is not enough, because generalizations have exceptions and the chance exception may change everything in a particular case. Only a formalization that does not merely add particular instances can discount, and therefore overcome, the particularity of those instances.

Formalizing the Behavioral

When the social scientist formulates his pattern or model, he is freed of dependence on accidental fact while free, too, of ambiguous values. He can project into the future without waiting for events to occur, yet also without "prescribing" what he merely likes or wishes. He can be contemptuous of both historian and philosopher (as traditionally understood), while at the same time claiming to be both empirical and formal. When a social scientist claims to be both of these things, he is talking out of both sides of the same mouth. From one side he deflates phony formalities pretending to transcend reality, from the other he condemns "journalists" who are satisfied with particulars and do not know the methods of formalizing. The paradox of aggressive humility combined with calculated hybris is the essence of a social scientist. It is true that he might be embarrassed to say which comes first, the fact or the model. For how can we check our model with the facts if we cannot find facts unless we first have a model? And how can we generate a realistic model unless we first have facts? This difficulty (which cannot be resolved by uttering the phrase *ideal type*) reveals an ambiguity in *behavioral* and *formal*. If the one can be so readily converted to the other, perhaps they are not so clearly distinct from each other as behavioral science supposes when it insists that we progress from political responsibility that may or may not appear to scientific explanation that is determinate and guaranteed.

After Dahl has behavioralized the formal, by resolving constitutional forms into the behavior they wrongly claim to cause, he proceeds to formalize the behavioral. He introduces the model of *polyarchy* with which, through subtle elaboration in several books, he has come to be identified. Polyarchy, not the Constitution, supplies the categories in which American politics is to be understood, or more precisely, its "conditions." Instead of learning, with the help of *The Federalist*, what we *ought* to do in order to make the Constitution work, we are told what we *shall* do, given the conditions of the American polyarchy. If the American polyarchy does not function according to one's preference, one can— under certain conditions—change the conditions that make it what it is and must be. But, in the view of Dahl, one cannot make a constitution.

To make a constitution, one must make a comprehensive choice, a choice to limit choice, in our case a settled intention solemnized in a written document to which constitutional officers take an oath. Such a choice is a choice above other choices establishing a fundamental law above ordinary laws; and it is therefore to some degree unconditioned insofar as it is intended to shape and anticipate conditions, and to do so in a characteristic mode. In the view of social science, the people cannot make a constitution because by their conditioning they have only one suitable constitution, the one they already have. In the view of *The Federalist*, however, the people, to their enduring cost and shame, may choose not to make a choice, through willfulness or bad advice or both: one cannot be certain about it.

In the analysis proposed here, *The Federalist* bears a considerable resemblance to modern social science, and it is no wonder that many social scientists, despite their criticism, feel at home when they read it. *The Federalist* behavioralizes the formal by compelling the republican genius to face the facts of republican experience, and it formalizes the behavioral by bringing those facts and the necessities they represent into the form of the Constitution. Publius, though, corrected the republican principle out of fidelity to it; he was concerned to sustain the dignity of man's capacity for self-government by establishing the first successful republic. With its basis in the human desire and capacity for self-government, *The Federalist* formalizes the formal in us: our insistence on running our own lives even against our interests; our refusal to be bound by conditions that make us merely dependent, responsive creatures; and our belief in the possibility of honor and sacrifice. These things are *formal* because they are powerful in us regardless of our "preferences"; they constitute a desire for *self-*

government independent of what we may think government is good for. Although this formality of the will is often seen in stubborn and angry actions, precisely those actions confirm our capacity to rise above our interests; and although they can lead us in self-righteous idiocy to demean and even cast away our freedom, this formality is the basis of freedom in our nature.

Preempted Choice

Since Publius respects the desire for freedom, *The Federalist* offers a new republican political science to assist the choice of a free people. Consistent with republicanism, it can do no more than *assist* that choice; it cannot replace that choice or make it unnecessary by discovering the conditions determining how and when it would be made. *The Federalist* also finds a place, in its political science, for the founders and their fame ("the ruling passion of the noblest minds") as men without whom American politics would not be as it is today.[31] A free people, it appears, cannot choose a constitution for itself spontaneously or automatically; it needs to be assisted by political science and by statesmen, and by each in a manner so as not to exclude the assistance of the other. Dahl, however, finds no place in his model for a constitution; a well-drawn constitution and able statesmen to establish it are not among the conditions of polyarchy, even in the book he wrote to set forth the conditions of *becoming* a polyarchy.[32] In another book Dahl discusses the making of the American Constitution, and concludes that the founders created a framework that could be either a democratic or an aristocratic republic. He implies, however, that this indeterminacy was a fault to be corrected.[33]

In general, social science has had little or nothing to say about the American Constitution, constitutions, or constitutionalism. It does not accept that any difference exists between the founding of a constitution and ordinary politics, or that ordinary politics could be affected by the making or not making of a constitution. In keeping with Dahl's belief that the American political system is "endless bargaining," the Constitutional Convention of 1787 has been interpreted as an instance of bargaining and its outcome explained by the theory of voting coalitions, to wit, "an explanatory framework for the operation, impact and characteristic process of conflict in a serial decision-making situation."[34] If anything has been left to statesmanship by this theory, William Riker will take it away, in his talkathon Greek, with "heresthetics," the art of political strategy.[35] Such a framework, supplemented by such an art, both dissolves and replaces the Constitution, by behavioralizing and formalizing. Social science not merely assists a free people in constitution making, but it takes over their choice, first telling them that constitutions do not matter, then showing them the conditions that will in fact determine their behavior, that is, their lives. And to judge from the social scientists, the American people do not need their founders.

This conclusion has to be drawn from what the social scientists have said; they are not individuals of great ambition for themselves personally. Although their theories would replace the Constitution, they themselves do not want to overturn it. Indeed, on the great issue in deciding upon the Constitution according to *The Federalist*, whether to have democracy or a republic (with representation and extensive size), the social scientists were accused of being defenders of the status quo and were made to suffer furious assaults on their integrity by advocates of "participatory democracy" (who, in turn, retained many of the fundamental features of the American Constitution). Dahl assumes, too, that a polyarchy will have a strong executive, an independent judiciary, and something like a Bill of Rights.[36] For all their disregard of constitutional forms, social scientists seem to work, as it were, next to the Constitution, but oblivious of the shadow it casts on their work. If American politics is "endless bargaining,"[37] for example, is this not partly because the formality of separation of powers requires it? And are not the terms of bargaining partly determined by the formal, constitutional powers of the several institutions? In general, is not the "extra-constitutional" partly determined by the constitutional?

Institutions Wasting Away

Recently, social science has rediscovered the importance of *institutions*, impressed (it is said) by the obvious difference in behavior (and success) of the Democratic party before and after the McGovern-Fraser reforms of 1970 though none of the underlying conditions had changed. But to understand the institutions one would have to return to the Constitution that instituted them and raise the question of intent: has the institution evolved according to its original intention? In the case of parties, not mentioned in the Constitution, one would have to see whether they were nonetheless intended, and for what; and whether the founders of parties had intentions to carry out or improve the Constitution or merely tactics to manipulate or circumvent it. In general, one would have to ask, is government by Constitution possible, or does the comprehensive intention it constitutes waste away through the accidents of history? Dahl attributes the survival of the American Constitution to its being "frequently adapted to fit the changing social balance of power,"[38] but he does not give it credit even for adaptability. He does not think that the fundamental problem it should have addressed was that of *majority* faction; much more he fears *minority* faction from some source of oligarchy and therefore welcomes above all else the democratization of the Constitution.[39] In company with social scientists in general, he takes the conventional republican or democratic citizen's view, opposed in *The Federalist*, that the enemies of popular government are much more dangerous than its vices, if indeed it has any vices other than a disposition to tolerate its enemies. What is needed from social science is reflection parallel and rival to that in *The Federalist* to show why the people's reason should endorse, rather than seek to dominate or moderate, its will. What we get instead is an analysis attempting to determine what conditions the people's will, which simply assumes that the people ought to have what they want.

Non-Will and Unreason

Social science does not accept the distinction essential to *The Federalist* between the people's will and their reason or intention. It takes note, as we have seen typically, that we have no *assurance* from the working of the Constitution that popular will must become a reasoned intention. An aptitude to refine the people's will or a tendency in that direction is not enough, since what the Constitution does it must do unfailingly and indisputably. Therefore, instead of wasting time on study of promised tendencies in the Constitution frequently not delivered in fact—not to mention reflection on what the people's reason as opposed to its will might be—social science turns to a search for the *determinants* of popular will.

The Federalist describes the formal orders of the Constitution as having a tendency to further justice and the public good; hence it praises them in the act of describing. Politicians who read *The Federalist* and citizens who hear what it says will learn, in the subdued, nonhortatory way explained above, what is expected of them and what can be hoped from them. In particular, they will learn that republics are in need of seemingly nonrepublican institutions and that popular will must be checked and improved in its own interest to become something more reasonable than it frequently, temporarily is. The political science of *The Federalist* is, therefore, practical and edifying. It provides a guide—though one without passion or elaboration—for action toward something better, toward the good. But although political science of this kind may offer guidance to politicians and citizens, it is not universal, necessary, and exact—precisely because it partly depends on politicians and citizens to make it actual.

In order to achieve the determinacy of a science that is universal, necessary, and exact, social science looks beneath the popular will rather than beyond it, for what determines or correlates with popular will cannot be will. Social science reduces the people's will to non-will whereas *The Federalist* elevates it to an intention. It does seem that any attempt to understand the people's will leads above it or below it. Social science goes below, to find out why people will as they do—because of their income, sex, race, and the like. Most social scientists approve of constitutional checks on popular will, since such checks are based on a calculation of self-interest, a more determinate and predictable motive than virtue. But if asked they could not say why they approve of them. In practice their theories belie their sense of responsibility and their political acumen and result in a powerful but peculiar democratism. They see that the forms of the Constitution do not surely elevate popular will, as intended; they believe their analyses show that the only things surely elevated by those forms are certain groups, for example, property holders.

The consequence of social science, then, is to debunk those allegedly public-spirited minorities, actually self-serving, who try to justify their prominence, actually dominance, by claiming to refine the people's will or to contribute to the public good. These are *elites*. When social science rejects the explanatory value of the constitutional in favor of the extraconstitutional, it necessarily denies the political contribution of those who claim to use the constitutional forms as intended. In particular, it refutes the claim in *The Federalist* that the nonrepublican parts of the Constitution serve the republican whole: hence the democratism of social science, revealed in a Beardian view of the Constitution—not requiring the researches of Beard—as a shelter and headquarters for the privileged few.

Yet this is a peculiar democratism, because it does not, cannot, support the claim to rule of the people as a whole. For social science discloses a democracy without a people, that is, a democracy in which the people are not a whole. The people could be the whole only if their will made sense as an intention, only if they have a common good, but since there is no guarantee of this, one must seek the determinants of their will, as we have seen. In seeking the determinants of their will, however, social science dissolves that will into wills; different groups in the people have wills differently determined. Not only is there no common good, but even "majority rule is mostly a myth" because majorities are nothing but self-seeking minorities in combination.[40] They are, to use the technical term, *coalitions*. (Publius too spoke of majorities composed of minorities, but he was always ready to judge them by the standards of justice and the public good.) The minority or minorities that prevail do so arbitrarily, and if one considers the lack of a common good, necessarily so. Yet, if one considers the same lack, no other minority or minorities would win out any less arbitrarily. The elites that social science discovers dominating the people are both necessarily arbitrary and arbitrarily necessary. They cannot be justified yet cannot be imagined away: an elite-cursed democracy! Some social scientists try to wriggle out of this bind by settling for the status quo (though not defending it), others by hoping that, when all the elites except the social scientists have been melted away, a genuine people will be found in the pot.

Dahl seems to think he has got around this difficulty when he brings up, as opposed to constitutional forms, elections and political competition.[41] These operate against a background of "underlying consensus" that is "prior to politics" (hence extraconstitutional) to save the American system from falling under the rule laid down by the Italian Gaetano Mosca that claims that every society has a ruling class. Not minority rule in America, Dahl says, but minorities' rule. Just a moment, Professor Dahl! What guarantee do we have that minorities will not compete to establish rival schemes of oppression, or collaborate on one? How do we know that they will accept the result of an election?

An election is a constitutional form[42] bestowing popular approval on a government that it simultaneously withdraws from direct popular rule, as we have seen. An election as opposed to selection by lot is an essentially aristocratic device (because it presupposes that some people are better than others—a point to be learned from Aristotle).[43] The founders of a representative, constitutional republic appropriated it to help combat the vices of republics. Although elections do not always produce fit characters, or even soft, compassionate characters, let us hear some applause from social scientists for a nonrepublican constitutional form that works often and for the courage and perspicacity of those who saw how to use it on behalf of republics. As for the "underlying consensus," it is indeed political, though originally—yet surely not now—distinct from the details of the American Constitution. It is not merely a "social prerequisite" but a political one too. And what guarantee is there that the consensus will not justify slavery, to use Dahl's own example?[44] If one can dissolve "majority rule" into myth, one can do the same for consensus.

Consequences of Surveys

It is time to consider surveys. The survey is an extraconstitutional form, invented and propagated by social science, which has had a considerable, as yet unmeasured, effect on American politics and society. If we wished to decide whether social science assists American democracy, as Publius asserts his political science has aided American republicanism, we would have to judge whether this most outstanding innovation of social science has made the working of American democracy easier or harder. Its tendency is probably to promote the democratism discussed above. Surveys of popular opinions and attitudes resemble elections, but apparently have a contrary effect. Instead of asking, as in elections, who should be entrusted with government and for what ends, they encourage people to believe that their current opinions and attitudes should be immediately adopted by their government. Otherwise why ask? Or is it that survey data will be highly useful to power-seeking politicians who want to take advantage of what people feel?

Certainly surveys are at odds with the idea of representative government as it appears in *The Federalist*. There representative government is presented as an attempt by popular authorization to create scope to govern; but surveys have the effect (if not the intent) of closing this space. Surveys create pressure on governments to produce immediate results, sooner even than the next election; and they foster a mode of thinking (the economic indicators or misery index) that makes elections turn on immediate results or promises thereof. Politicians are encouraged to seek popularity and to do so they are given scientific means to make carefully modulated appeals to various and conflicting sections of the electorate. Citizens learn nothing useful; to discover that a certain percentage of other citizens of one type or another agrees or disagrees with them does not help them to judge the political questions they face. It is as if voting were the same as watching or betting on a race.

Social science in this aspect and as a whole is practical for politicians who want to manipulate and appear complaisant, but it is not edifying. Nor, apparently, do these devices of popularity actually make government more popular. They seem rather to breed dissatisfaction as the people are taught to demand popularity, and to produce cause for dissatisfaction as government is distracted into seeking popularity. In studying behavior as opposed to intention, social science specializes in the discovery of unintended consequences. With its surveys social science appears to have had some unintended consequences of its own for the working of the Constitution.

The End of Public Choice

Rather than ask the opinion of a scientifically sampled respondent—a formalized but still real human being— social science has discovered that it is possible to infer (with a certain mathematical sophistication) the choice of a rational individual without ever approaching a real human being. It is even possible, as James Buchanan and Gordon Tullock have shown, to conceive the rules a rational individual would choose for making choices, and thus to model a rational constitution.[45] This is the achievement of *formal theory*, so called to denote its distance from the arithmetic of actual measurement, including today a thriving school of *public choice* theorists. These social scientists study politics with the conceptual tools of welfare economics and especially of game theory, a mathematics originally applied to economics by John von Neumann and Oskar Morganstern.[46] Although the origin and character of this theorizing is economic, its adepts and pioneers differ as to just how closely politics resembles economics.

To speak of the pioneers: William Riker (*The Theory of Political Coalitions*, 1962) says that politics is essentially conflict, whereas economics is essentially compromise; to use the term of game theory that has passed into popular lingo, politics is "zero-sum" (one player's winnings are another's losses).[47] But Anthony Downs (*An Economic Theory of Democracy*, 1957) and Buchanan and Tullock (*The Calculus of Consent*, 1962) believe that the compromise achievable in economics can also be got in politics; so politics is non–zero sum and all can gain from it.[48] Those holding political compromise possible have been joined by theorists of international relations who conclude that politics among nations is essentially more irenic than it sometimes appears to be. Are we then left with a decision, made prior to scientific inquiry, over whether politics is peace or war? To avoid this embarrassment, it appears we must go with Riker. His assumption that politics is war is more determinate because it covers all cases; one can derive peace from war (since to seek peace is rational behavior) but not war from peace. The experience of peaceable economic exchange on which the others rely may be derivative and hence deceptive, because it depends on political peace. If so, it might be better to understand economic exchange as a device of politics, undertaken for political motives such as keeping government limited, rather than politics as an extension of economics. Riker, while revealing the most political perspicacity of these theorists, does not go so far, but in the main point he aligns himself with Hobbes (*De Cive*, 1642).[49]

The Federalist attempts in its understanding of government by choice to do justice to both the people's will and their reason—the main task of the Constitution. Constitutional government must be by consent, so as to recognize the human insistence on choice; but it must also refine and elevate consent, in order to face the necessity of providing good administration. The difficulty of making consent rational while keeping it choosy accounts for the indeterminacy of the constitutional system: government by choice depends on the chance that peoples and governments will choose well.

There is no getting around the dependence of choice on chance.[50] But getting around this dependence is precisely what the public choice theorists attempt to do. They want to provide "theoretical determinacy," the "logical foundations of constitutional democracy" (Buchanan and Tullock),[51] "a generalized yet realistic behavior rule for a rational government" (Downs),[52] "precision of statement" (Riker,[53] typically less optimistic). The consequence is disastrous for the understanding (and perhaps also for the practice) of public choice. The twin but opposite evils *The Federalist* wanted to avoid are both embraced by the theorists of public choice: their models are both so rational as to foreclose choice and so choosy as to demean it.

Instead of bringing together will and reason (which is a problematic undertaking, hence unscientific in their view), these social scientists keep them apart for the purpose of modeling undisturbed by this difficulty— that is, the main difficulty—and then hope at the end for a magical reconciliation. They begin with people's choices, including everything from the deliberate to the whimsical (for how could one define the difference scientifically?); these are also called "interests" or "preferences," and they add up to "utility." In common with the current usage of economists this *utility* has almost nothing to do with what is useful. It is merely what you think to be useful, when "useful" means "good" or rather, apparently good; the most useless luxury is part of your utility if you show by your behavior that you want it.

Thus utility loses the realism in the power to puncture and deflate spurious ideals that made it attractive, or useful, to the first utilitarians.[54] Similarly, *interest* is no longer the realistic alternative to passion, and *preference*, to insistence. All utilitarian realism must be sacrificed to the greater, postutilitarian necessity of relativism, because no social scientist now believes he can surely say what is realistic. Hence it becomes realistic to refuse to say what is realistic. What if the founders had adopted this attitude toward the Articles of Confederation or the republican tradition, both of which they thought to be unrealistic? The public choice theorists leave "choices" undefined and uncriticized, and move to "rational behavior" as the means to the ends given to them, however foolish or self-destructive.

Once the ends are given, the theorists take possession of the means with their modeling. A *model* of choice is no longer a choice; it shows how choice must necessarily proceed. Such a model, as Riker says, "permits one to transcend the obstacle of the existence of choice."[55] Choice is an obstacle to reason because there's always the chance, often a good chance, that it will not in fact be exercised according to reason. A "leap over choice"[56] is thus a leap over chance. The rationality of choice is then within the competence of the social scientist and is his to play and romp with (since the habit of abstraction makes social scientists lightheaded) without interference from those who have set the ends to which he will supply the means. The democratism with which the analysis began—all ends are equal—gives way suddenly to the expertise of social science so that Buchanan and Tullock, for example, can make a logical constitution without holding a constitutional convention and a vote of ratification. Their expertise in modeling takes over from the actual consent of the people because they can show what the people, if rational, would have consented to. For actual majority rule, they substitute "conceptual unanimity."

Social scientists occupy an office similar to that of Hobbes's sovereign. Once authorized to find the rational means to the people's ends, they brook no interference from those who might want to specify the means as well as the ends. The people can reset the problem by changing their ends, but they cannot insert their opinion as to which model will best achieve them. The people do not, in effect, have the right "to alter or to abolish it, and to institute new government, laying its foundation on such principles, and organizing its powers in such form, as to them shall seem most likely to effect their safety and happiness." For if they were to have such a right and exercise it, they would not get what they want! Social science with its expertise in modeling can guarantee choice, that is, get the people what they want, only if the people do not exercise their choice of getting what they want in their own way.

Thus we see that the initial aloof objectivity of social science in seeming not to care what the people's wants were and whether they were good was actually the only way of getting them what they want, and also the most effectual way of caring for them. To have offered a frown at the meaner and more bizarre wants of the people would have been attempting to set their reason against their will with no sure prospect of victory for either and the likelihood of a tense debate. The trick, then, is to leave the people their will and take away their reason; then social science can bring its reason to serve their will, showing them their inconsistencies and telling them how to get more of what they want.[57] The value neutrality of social science is the best or only means by which government can bring value to the people. And how do we ensure the loyalty of social scientists to democracy rather than some other model? Pay them more! The most mercenary servant is the most reliable.

Despite their fondness for the word *process* and their reverence for such precursors of public choice as Arthur Bentley (*The Process of Government*, 1908) and David Truman (*The Governmental Process*, 1951), the public choice theorists have no justification for the actual processes of government, in America or elsewhere, except as they approximate the contours of their models.[58] Those models are the contrivance of a scientific or theoretical reason that does not care whether it reaches its destination through human beings who reason; in fact, as we have seen, the way is surer if the model does not depend on them. So the various functions that *The Federalist* expects from appropriate constitutional offices and forms—deliberation from the House of Representatives, experience from the Senate, energy, direction, and duration from the executive, stability from the judiciary, and refinement of popular will through elections—do not appear in public choice models. These functions are nontheoretical helps to reason or aspects of practical reason, which make reason effective in the practical world of politics where it has to contend with unreason, as opposed to the laboratory or library where these nontheoretical aspects are hindrances to reason.

So public choice adopts an attitude of theoretical disdain for both the functions and the men who perform them. it understands the constitutional offices only as negative checks on a majority (as in *Federalist* 51), not as positive contributions to a majority (as in later sections of *The Federalist* on the three branches); for a "qualified" majority means one that is checked, not one that is capable. Deliberation is logrolling and bargaining is "bribery."[59] But according to *Federalist* 51 the defensive strongholds of the separated powers are manned by the ambitious; such people do not exist in theories of public choice (except, once again, for Riker, who makes tenuous allowance for leaders).[60] *Homo politicus*, the rational individual, is a consumer like *homo economicus*,[61] concerned for the costs of decision making. That there might actually be a type of human being called "politician" who likes politics, and that the few of this type might be both useful and dangerous to the many who care less for politics are problems that do not appear or are not themes in theories of public choice. They do speak of the "intensity" of preferences, since they have no other way to speak of what is noble or higher in rank except as multiplication of what is banal or mundane.[62] With this much admired makeshift they run the risk of underestimating the danger (so well appreciated in *Federalist* 10) as well as the contribution of "intensity" to democracy. And most notoriously, those theories cannot explain why people take the trouble to vote.[63]

Social Science Innocence

In sum, public choice and social science in general cannot understand why the Constitution should be an end in itself; they see it only as a means to an end.[64] They do not see anything admirable in *self*-government, that is, good government from reflection and choice rather than from accident and force. Under the name of choice, social science promotes government from reflection and accident, its reflection on what democratic peoples happen to want. If they could get their wants satisfied by other governments, social science would have no objection; and, it would say, if democratic peoples want to insist on self-government, let that be added to their accidental wants.[65] In the argument presented here, social science begins its objection to constitutional forms from the dependence of their working on chance. But at the end of all its ingenious conceits fashioned to overcome this chance, it appears as the servant of a people that, by historical chance, wants to govern itself.

Social scientists are for the most part innocent of philosophy. They have, of course, absorbed the subjectivity of utility, and with it have accepted the necessity that their positivism—the naive alliance of science and human good—become a logical positivism or philosophy of science that promises much less. They have surely heard of Thomas S. Kuhn's *Structure of Scientific Revolutions* (1962), and some of them must have noted, more wryly than gloatingly, the political character of the behavioral revolution since World War II that has transformed political science into social science. But social scientists have not yet penetrated to the Nietzschean critique of science lying behind Kuhn's book; that critique says that science depends on a prescientific insight, hence concludes that science itself is a historical accident. One can say, however, that the materials for the discovery of this critique and for the greater self-understanding to which it would lead lie within social science and are concentrated in its treatment of the Constitution or lack thereof.

I am aware that I have dealt with only a few books in social science and those not the most recent, but I am persuaded that they are neither incidental nor obsolete. Social science is all around us; it is a rubric that covers many diverse individuals and activities. Yet precisely because of this diversity, its general and remarkable inattention to the Constitution cannot be accidental. Those who want to take refuge in the diversity still have to take thought for what they are involved in. If they should come to have doubts, the political science of *The Federalist* beckons as an attractive and impressive alternative.

12

The Media World and Constitutional Democracy

The media are in the middle of something—that is for certain—but of what? They appear at first to be nothing in themselves, merely a facility of communication. They facilitate communication among a people, especially among a large people, and thus make that people more of a people, a whole that is conscious of itself and that, being so, can move together. We call a people of this sort a democratic people, or simply a democracy, implying that the communication among a people that makes possible a whole people is, or substitutes for, a form of government. As the media facilitate communication especially among a large people, they especially facilitate modern democracy, which, as opposed to ancient democracy, is the democracy of a large people.

The media facilitate communication not only among a large people but also among peoples. This they do not so much bilaterally between peoples, as if in the manner of ambassadors with the extended but still specific mission of lying for their country. In an arrest of two American reporters in Moscow a while ago, nothing was more impressive than their greater solidarity with the editors of their newspapers than with the ambassador of their country.[1] The media facilitate communication among peoples generally without limiting themselves to specific purposes or specific audiences. They facilitate communication among a large people only because it is larger than a small people, not because it is in the interest of a people to be large. A large people is preferred because it is closer to humanity itself, and it is for humanity itself that the media wish to facilitate communication. Their wish is not yet accomplished fact, and perhaps never will be. But their wish has accomplished this much: it has overcome every objection to itself in principle. Though there may remain local reactionaries who grumble to their friends about the invasion of the media, all those heard on the media must speak or follow the doctrine of the media and seek to further communication among all peoples. Only through the media can mankind realize itself as the world.

With this observation, the media now appear to be not *a* facility but *the* facility of communication. As *the* facility of communication they do not merely report to a particular community the doing of that community: this is "local news" which is of continuing concern and occasional urgency but always subordinate in importance. More than merely reporting to a given community, the media create a community by catching people's attention and holding it for events that would otherwise have taken place outside their notice. Local news may suddenly be given worldwide significance, and any individual or small group dramatically unfortunate or sufficiently determined to terrorism can be advertised to humanity. It is the media that create the "world" in which we live and are linked to the lives of others who would never have entered our community.

When the discrepancy is seen between the people of a local community and the people of a world that the media have made or would like to make for us, and when the creative or constitutive function of the media is recognized, the dependence of the media on intellectuals can be sensed. Intellectuals provide the ideal conception of the world toward which the media, as they convey to us, convey us. What is this world and how is it governed? If the media are creative and depend on intellectuals for their communication, how can that communication be as democratic as it first appears? To answer these questions it is necessary to return to the communication of the media and to expand on the world of the intellectuals.

We must ask first, what is communicated by the media? The media do not transmit the tradition, customary belief, religion, or moral standards of a community: these are for the most part still spoken face to face by parents, relatives, or friends. They come from an existing community that seeks to maintain that community as it has been. It would be a theoretical affectation to call such customs or mores "communication," because *communication* as opposed to speech implies a transaction that may or may not take place. Aristotle said that human beings were by nature political because they have by nature the power of speech.[2] They cannot help speaking, even in Sparta, and so they must live together chiefly on the basis of their spoken notions. But humans do not communicate by nature: they cannot communicate without the media that Aristotle somehow failed to mention (perhaps because he thought them identical to government or regime).

The Craving for News

The media, then, do not transmit custom or tradition. On the contrary, they transmit *the news*. It is only human, but it is especially modern, to crave what is new. In modern times, *modern* is a term of praise; and as modern means new, modernity has been a movement of endless self-criticism in which any modern practice or institution, established because it was more modern than the custom that preceded it, is criticized, destroyed, and replaced in accordance with its own principle by something else more modern. In keeping with the dynamism of modernity, what is known already, whether for a long time or just yesterday, is vulnerable to the news. And the news can be "scooped" when someone gets ahead of you and leaves you with yesterday's news.

Not everything communicated on the media is news so called, of course, but entertainment and art reflect the same avid desire for the new and exhibit the same self-canceling principle. The latest music easily combines technical virtuosity with a graceless, unsuccessful search for the newest elemental feeling, so that we are easily apprised of the difference between a lower and a deeper feeling. The entertainment does ñot merely entertain, despite the disclaimers of media moguls that they mean only to entertain. Entertainment informs us of the latest trends and thus tells us what we ought to find entertaining. Although the consuming public does not swallow everything new, the skill of media entertainers is exercised to discern the public's latest preoccupation so as to make a place for themselves in it or, better, slightly beyond it. Nonetheless, the popularity of old shows on television (contemptuously called "reruns") should remind us that, though modernity can deal with the passé, it cannot always dispose of reactionaries.

Somehow we moderns believe that the new is both more reliable and more liberating than the old, and we feel obliged to keep up with the news partly because we wish to be guided by the latest events and partly to free ourselves of dependence on yesterday's happenings. Alexander Solzhenitsyn, in his 1978 Harvard commencement speech criticizing the media, spoke of the people's right not to know. Anyone who has listened for a while to one of the radio stations in America now broadcasting continuous news will have an inkling of what he means, but in his formulation the idea is shocking to us.

Solzhenitsyn explains that people have a right not to have their divine souls filled with vain talk.[3] Yet the news is presented as anything but vain talk; it is grave and only occasionally turns to what is called, with due solemnity, "the lighter side." The news focuses on others' troubles, of which we would know nothing or something very late and inadequate but for the media. It requires us to bear the burden of others' troubles, which is often too much for us. When peoples around the world are invited to sympathize with prominent victims such as Nelson Mandela or Andrei Sakharov, they are likely to waste their compassion in helpless partisan indignation; and in less well-known cases of misery and oppression, we sometimes shrug our shoulders.

Thus the news provides the information that "breaks down barriers" between peoples, as it is said, and that makes "a smaller world" for us, a smaller world that is more complex, it is also said. In place of variety in the different peoples living more or less ignorant of one another, the media introduce us to complexity in their interdependence. Each people lives dependent on the fortunes of others, not merely because of commercial dealings or military threats, but also by being informed of others' fortunes. And since each people is absorbed in its interdependence (a more democratic word than "dependence"), it tends to dissolve into its constituent individuals. The media direct their news at individuals rather than peoples and give them information interesting to them as human beings rather than as nationals or citizens. The media communicate in such a way as to increase communicability; they create individuals with a desire for information. They would like, it seems, to create a world of universalized information in which everyone knows the same things and wants and needs to know those things. The isolated individualism that Tocqueville saw and foresaw as the social condition of modern democracy is the ideal toward which the media are conducting us.[4]

The universality of the information provided by the media is not grounded in, or made possible by, anything outside human beings. The media are not in the middle between man and God, and altogether the men and women in the media have nothing angelic about them. In contrast to priests (who are also intermediaries) they do not claim to speak for God. Also, as we have seen, the media do not rest on any natural faculty of speech that would make communication possible. They posit no universal grammar that might promise a common recognition of human concerns in human speech through the variety of languages. Nor do those in the media speak Esperanto or study Latin. Furthermore, they do not argue or even bicker. They step across differences of language with technical terms or brand names known as Americanisms in honor of the country of origin. They speak not to the speech of others but rather to their feelings.

If we ask what would make possible the universal communication of the media, the answer can be found in the insecurity of the human condition, our common mortality. Whatever we find surprising or disturbing is interesting news to us,[5] as opposed to higher concerns of the heart and intellect which can always be postponed. But this insecurity is subject to twofold interpretation. The soft appeal of liberalism is to compassion for the suffering of others in poverty, misery, or disaster; and the commentators speak easily of "tragedy" because it is tragedy without grandeur.

The harsh call of communism is for indignation on behalf of others suffering under the oppression of poverty; here anger becomes routine. Liberalism in its present phase of soft compassion does not worry much over oppression unless it is associated with poverty, and communism is not much concerned with poverty unless it can claim that it is caused by oppression. But both assume that neither God nor nature demands patience or moderation in human beings, a recognition of their own limits, and a resignation to their ordained duties. Both assume that men can overcome their differences and be united by releasing themselves to moral feeling and giving it full scope. Only the hardhearted (the liberals say) or only the softhearted (the Communists say) stand in the way of the unification of mankind. In consequence, media commentators have the choice of shedding crocodile tears or grinding polished teeth in consonance with the appropriate universal feeling. In either case, the usual tendency is toward the Left.

In Western countries, sports news provides the best reminder that mankind is divided and that pity is not the only worthy passion. Even though the results of sporting contests neither help nor hurt one's material interests (when nothing is bet), fans everywhere avidly follow sports news as a sign of local or national superiority. A fan of any sport shows concern for that sport wherever it is played and by whomever. But he is so distinguished from a humanitarian that to him a humanitarian appears, as it were, to be a fan of mankind in general without ever cheering for any particular team or applauding any special feat. It is in the nature of a fan both to cheer for his own side regardless of the quality of play and to applaud good or beautiful play on the other side, for modern men best appreciate in sport what the Greeks knew as noble or beautiful deeds. The media, however, do not permit their sports news to influence their view of politics. They do ensure that athletes are overpaid.

Men can communicate because they ought to communicate; but in the media formulation of the categorical imperative, no moral action is required of us as rational beings. What is communicated through the media, then, is a "news" (something new) interesting to a universal moral feeling, compassion, or indignation that divides men into individuals and then unites them without regard for group or national differences and without reference to any guide or standard outside men.

Effectual Truth

Although the communication of the media is addressed to feeling, we are nonetheless compelled to ask what is the truth of what is communicated. For communication is speech after all, and if nothing true has been spoken, words have been exchanged but nothing has been communicated. The need to ask the question of truth is confirmed by the fact that the rights and privileges of the media are said to rest on "the people's right to know," not on the people's need to feel. The people must be supplied with the *knowledge* they thirst for. But this must not be done in such a way as will interfere with their *judgment*, since the people have, in addition to the right to know, the right to judge. In order to respect both rights, or for some other reason, the media often convey information without accepting responsibility for its truth. They report what is said and pass on every allegation; and given the necessity of editorial selection, they can even be said to amplify human claims and assertions. The media do not respect the dignity of quiet suffering or of tolerant forbearance from claiming one's due; they favor accusers, complainers, and whiners. In "editorials" they advise the people on what is true and how they should judge, but they are careful not to usurp the people's rights. When journalists claim the right to protect their sources, they say in effect that the people's right to know does not extend to a right to know the sources. But withholding the sources is justified as necessary in supplying the people with information, even though it may make such information more difficult to judge.

So the information conveyed by the media is, if not truth, a claim to truth—or perhaps better to say, a claim to be fact. The media do not state principles or develop arguments. Even though most of the news reported by the media tells what is said, the media have a preference for deeds or "events" over speech. Speeches are reported as events, with neglect for the argument and with exclusive attention on the target, the upshot, and the consequences. The media look for the "effectual truth" of a speech in the manner of Machiavelli, though not so acutely. For, unlike Machiavelli, they are uncritical of compassion and justice and they assume that men are free to be as soft as they please and as hard as they will. "What will happen now?" is the question to be answered. The media seek to present facts, and a fact is an event impending on the future. Whether or not facts in themselves exist, the media are concerned only with relevant facts, those relevant to our universal human feelings. The best, most factual facts are those that leave us breathless.

Facts of universal interest relevant to human suffering in poverty bespeak a philosophy of materialism. The suffering we hear of on the media is not that of the highest souls or of the highest in ordinary men; it is the suffering—sometimes loosely called deprivation—of the poor who are poor in the goods of this world and of the body. At the same time, since the suffering is complained of, and its cause found in exploitation, there is nothing of resignation to brute matter in this materialism. The media are inspired, one might say, by an idealism of materialism, by a restless, dissatisfied materialism in which even, or especially, the rich are not happy until everyone is rich—because only the rich are happy. Idealistic materialism depends on an expanding technology to fight the war on poverty and, as regards the media, to make us aware of others' poverty so that we can become unhappy about it and deplore it.

It is obvious that the media could not exist without modern technology. Modern technology makes possible instant communication that is not face to face. Thus it leaps across the natural boundaries of rhetoric in what can be shouted to a certain, definite crowd by an orator who knows his audience. With television, modern technology even makes possible faceless communication with faces, the faces of media people who presume they know their audience from surveys and ratings. On television there is no recognition of individuality, hence no mutual recognition; there is only feedback of information. When materialism is joined to the idea of improvement, the individual matter of anyone's body matters little and enjoyment is postponed to the day when all can share it. The only innocent enjoyment is universal, and though everyone on television is obliged to smile, it is something of a sin to laugh. One cannot laugh at the human condition, although, properly appreciated, this prohibition would not permit any laughter at all. Laughter implies an undercurrent of skepticism about any social system and especially about a technological society that claims to be able to communicate despite all difficulties. Such a society pretends to be not merely not laughable, but beyond the reach of ridicule.

Who Rules?

A third question concerning the media is, who rules? Does government control the media and use it both subtly and blatantly to secure its tyrannical ends? In this case we should worry about governmental interference and try to secure the freedom and independence of the press. Or, to the contrary, is the press too powerful? According to Solzhenitsyn in the same speech at Harvard quoted before, "the press has become the greatest power within the Western countries, more powerful than the legislature, the executive, and the judiciary."[6] From this diagnosis it would follow that the media are too free, or misuse their freedom.

Clearly in the West, the media reinforce the fundamental principle of modern democracy, which Tocqueville long ago discerned, that each is capable of deciding on one's own.[7] According to the media, the people have the rights to know and to judge, but these rights belong not to any definite people deciding together. They are not the rights of a people constituting itself and, as in the American Declaration of Independence, declaring itself independent so as to form a government to secure these rights. With the principle and practice of the media, it is rather that a people, indefinitely large, decides as each individual decides on his own and without reference to any government, informal or formal. The government, if such there be, is merely what results from the addition of all the individual decisions, as happens in an opinion survey or an audience rating. These are decisions rather than deliberations, for, as one could learn from Aristotle (or by experience), deliberation normally requires, and is improved by, the advice of other human beings.

That there need be *no common deliberation* is the most salient political consequence of the media. The media do not encourage deliberation in common; they actually discourage it by passing over every definite political or national boundary that would constitute a people in order to deliberate in common; and they themselves substitute for common deliberation in the "news" they provide to each individual regarding events outside him.[8] Common deliberation is no guarantee of a prudent result; the result will depend on the prudence of those who deliberate, including their persuasiveness. But in discussion or debate, an individual has to advance his cause with reasons and at least wait patiently, if not listen, while others of contrary views advance their reasons. Prejudice must be made vocal in a situation in which it must meet the competition of other voices, and is thus forced to give reasons that may moderate it or take away some of its sting. If prejudice nonetheless triumphs, as it often will, at least there remains the memory of those who opposed, who "told you so," whose remarks might later stir the beginning of repentance. With information supplied by the media, however, individuals do not have to state their opinions, much less defend them. And when something goes wrong, it is easy to change one's opinion as seems necessary and convenient, without any need to explain one's principle, defend one's consistency, or swallow one's words. In deliberation, persuasion is often effected more by the character of the persuader than by the logic of his syllogisms. But known and tested character is a reasonable substitute for reason: *image*, or the projecting of a perception in advance of common experience or without regard for it, is not.

What effect does the lack of common deliberation have on the practices of a modern constitutional democracy? It should be admitted immediately that this lack cannot be blamed solely on the media, for the media merely actualize a principle and culminate a trend that, as we have noted, were observed by Tocqueville. Many other influences are at work, and perhaps ultimately one must trace the principle of each deciding on his own, as does Tocqueville, to modern philosophy.[9] Yet the media have made two effects of this principle especially evident.

First, the principle of each deciding on his own paradoxically strengthens national governments. In America it strengthens the national government as compared with local and state governments, and elsewhere in free countries, not to mention Communist countries, already powerful centralizing tendencies have been intensified. The principle that each is capable of deciding on his own, as Tocqueville again saw, does not guarantee the principle's own success.[10] In fact, each individual is weakened by lack of support from his fellows in the family and in local or occupational associations, or in general in what have been called "mediating structures." Each unsupported individual is therefore sucked into dependence on the one source of authority that remains, the national government and national institutions. In America, radio and television are locally owned and operated, but stations serve as outlets for syndicated programs shown everywhere, and especially for the national institutions beautifully called "networks." The press, less locally owned, operates with comparable national institutions such as the wire services and the press corps in Washington ever ready to think alike if not to deliberate together. Elsewhere in free countries, the media are even more centralized.

Even though, as has been argued above, the media are universal in character, transnational and hence hostile to national authority, they must emanate from somewhere. Wherever the point of emanation—and it will not be a cottage in the country—it will tend to draw the attention of the audience and to have a strong, disproportionate effect on the character of the emanations. Moreover, since local influences tend to be effaced, resistance to the central sources tends to be diminished. Individuals hear little or nothing from respectable sources outside the media, at home, at work, or in politics, to contradict what they receive from the media. Only their own observations, sometimes exchanged with reactionary neighbors, provide them with a just sense of stubborn self-direction. But these are not given currency on the media or they are dismissed and denounced as prejudice. An individual may continue to run his own life on the basis of his own observations, but the limits within which he chooses and the general notions by which he interprets his observations are set by the media. For the most part, the sovereign individual, while never yielding his sovereignty in principle, gives himself up to the voice of the media, and the universality of the media in effect means New York, Washington, and Hollywood.

Thus, to address our question about government control of the media, it is not so much that free governments claim sway over the media as that the media invite government control by drawing attention to themselves and by undermining institutions that might resist central authority through autonomous local control. Seeking independence from the tyranny of benighted local reactionaries, the media demand a national policy and thereby open the door to national control. National authority used as the means of liberation may be turned to the uses of indoctrination and suppression.

Open Government

Yet one should not conclude from the susceptibility of the media to government control that government will be strengthened by controlling the media. Though it is true that government, that is, the central or national government, may collect the actual loyalties left or created by the universalistic pretensions of the media, lending apparent strength to isolated, weakened individuals, the government may come to believe those pretensions and thus fall victim itself to the media. This is the truth in Solzhenitsyn's justifiable exaggeration regarding the power of the media as a whole. Free governments have increasingly adopted the political principle of the media, each deciding for himself on the basis of information made available by the government through the media. In America this is known as "open government."

Open government not only makes its policies clear for all to see—for all governments do so sooner or later—but also makes its policy making clear for all to see. It is like a modern house with glass walls inside and out, including the bedroom and the bathroom. No doubt the conception of open government can be traced to Kant, not a prying man but one who believed that secrecy in government could safely and usefully be abolished. Since evil requires fraud, it begins in secrecy; and Kant wished to deny to evil the dark corners in which its plots are hatched. Today we might regard Kant's confidence in knowing evil and good as naive, but to make up for our superiority, we assume with greater complacency than he that ignorance of evil and good does not matter. It is seemingly sufficient for the people to possess their right to know, even if in fact they cannot enjoy it because they do not or cannot know the crucial things.

In any case, open government goes beyond respecting freedom of the press to making available everything the press would like to find out, thus adopting its principle. No doubt a healthy tension remains in practice between government and the media because no government can satisfy the demand of the media for the secret behind the secret. If news is to be new, it must be a surprise; and if it is news of a policy, the surprise must be the revelation of a secret. Both government and the media have an interest in secrecy, therefore, and the tension between them is shown in a struggle as to who shall reveal the secret first. The struggle over secrecy is a struggle for sovereignty, since the sovereign power in a state is the one that has the right to act in public, shamelessly, on the basis of plans made in private. It has been a sign of the media's subservience in the Soviet Union that "news" is often announced days late, at the convenience of the government. When the media claim the right to conceal their sources from government, they claim in effect the privilege of sovereignty, or at the least, the privilege of thwarting sovereignty. Would the media have the right to penetrate the secrecy of the voting booth where the electorate in a representative democracy exercises its sovereignty? If not, then why do they have the right to expose the secrets of the government elected by the sovereign electorate?

Solzhenitsyn and others have asked by whom the press has been elected, and to whom it is responsible.[11] Clearly the men and women of the media have not been elected and yet they surely claim to represent the people as much as, or more than, their elected representatives. Since the people are sovereign, they have the right to judge their elected representatives. But first they must know what their elected representatives have done or failed to do. To discover this, they must make the media their nonelective representatives armed with the people's right to know. In principle, at least, the right to know is a carte blanche extending into the same illegalities into which the duty to protect "national security" is sometimes supposed to lead the executive. Thus the media's claim to check all elected government carries them above the pretension of the "fourth estate" or even the "fourth branch."[12] Nonelective representation seems to be necessary for elective representation, contrary to the original hopes placed in democratic representation. There is a notion of informal, nonelective representation abroad today that differs significantly from the notion of formal elective representation established in free countries during the eighteenth century.

In ancient democracies the people met together in assemblies to deliberate and decide. But they gave demagogues in those assemblies such sway over their affairs that modern theorists of popular government rejected the example and excluded assemblies of the people from the constitutions of popular governments they proposed. Instead, they adopted the principle of modern democracy, opposed to deliberation in common, that each should decide for himself. But with a view to the advantages of deliberation, they attempted to moderate that principle by instituting constitutional assemblies in which representatives could deliberate away from the people so as not to give opportunity to demagogues. Such assemblies have had a hard job to maintain their independence. Originally their independence was established through forms of election in which the people, while exercising a choice, actually removed themselves from further choice. They chose representatives, whether legislative or executive, to choose for them. Certain forms of indirect choice were devised in which the people chose one representative who chose another, as with executive appointment of the judiciary.

Formless Representation

In time—in America, soon after the Constitution was established—democratic forces eroded the forms of representation that had been constructed to protect deliberation. Extraconstitutional institutions, especially parties, gained power and became dominant, in some countries using the irresistible mass power of the democratic principle against its own formal modifications. But party leaders were elected by the party membership or some portion of it, perhaps quite small. They were not elected by the people, but still they claimed to represent the people, and to represent them more faithfully and effectually than their formal, constitutional representatives. The latter had office with its formal powers, but since nothing could be done in a democracy without the people's consent, or rather, their active cooperation (for in a large country general consent lacks intensity and must be sharpened with the appetite of the interests involved), those who could rally the people—party leaders, leaders of organized interests and of social movements, journalists, and others—could claim to represent them. In Communist countries the doctrine of the Party vanguard, which put the Party representing the people some distance ahead of the people, has flourished.

The media confirm and culminate the trend toward formless non-elective representation in democracies. More than merely checking the elected government, they attempt to bypass representative institutions by providing "news" directly to the people to which the people are expected to give an immediate reaction. No time is given for the people's representatives to deliberate on the news; indeed their immediate reactions may also be part of the news. The news may come with an analysis provided by the media, an "instant analysis" of course, given on television particularly by persons of slick appearance and superficial education. The analysis is directed toward the question "what will happen?"—not to the question of deliberation "what shall we do?" The reaction of the people, reported as part of the news, is similarly undeliberative; the question put to them, in contempt for their right to know, is not "what do you think?" but "how do you feel?" Answers to this question may vary, but the people come to consensus, without deliberating, by means of surveys. Here their responses are added up and put in order not by elected representatives but by clerks, statisticians, public opinion experts, and other weighty but undeliberative analysts.

In bypassing formal representative institutions, the media also tend to replace earlier, informal institutions, such as parties and organized interest groups that also bypassed the formal representative institutions. It may be correct to say that the newest of the media, television, has bypassed the oldest, the press. Though the rights of a free press were first established to promote the deliberation of a free people, they have now been extended to television and increasingly used in practices hostile to deliberation.[13] At the same time newspapers more and more seek to resemble television and to overcome, with "advocacy journalism," "journalese," and populistic moralism, the formal barriers to democratization imposed by the written word.

Much of the self-justification of the media—that they make democracy more open and more democratic—reminds an observer of the self-justification of parties and the press at their inception; and much of the criticism of the media reminds one likewise of early attacks upon parties and the press. The media accuse the other nonelective representative institutions of being unresponsive to the people, and in their way they are right. As democracy becomes more democratic, it becomes more informal. Forms of election, in particular, disappear; for election, as Aristotle noted, is an aristocratic principle.[14] It is also true that one does not get rid of leaders and "elites" simply by attacking, undermining, or ignoring the leaders who have been elected. Informal leaders spring up like weeds to replace the deposed formal leaders, and doubt remains whether democracy can survive if it rushes toward more democracy by neglect of the forms of democracy.

To whom, then, are the informal leaders of the media responsible? They are responsive (informally) but not responsible (formally) to the people. They are not, perhaps, responsible to intellectuals, but they are dependent on them. Precisely because those in the media are persons of slight education, they depend on the intellectuals whom they surpass in beauty and income. They sense that "news" looks to the future but they cannot see with their tongues, as can intellectuals. The meaning of the news escapes them. Since the news communicates everything, and makes everything communicable, the latest trends in thought, in economics, and even in cosmology, which once were held of interest only to philosophers, must be communicated to the people; and only intellectuals can do so without being subjected to derision. Intellectuals must tell us what is behind the latest anti-inflation policy or the space program. Theory has become confused with practice in the realm of technology where theory has practical results and practice changes with new theoretical discoveries. The media people, who live on nothing if not technology, are hardly in a position to boast of their common sense to distinguish themselves from intellectuals. They are city slickers par excellence. If they communicate anything, they must communicate information to the uninformed, that is, sophistication to the unsophisticated. They therefore depend on the sources of sophistication.

Perhaps the best example of this dependence is the media's promotion, apparently against their own interest, of the intellectuals' disdain for technology. The media stop short of endorsing the intellectuals' attacks on themselves. But they go out of their way to report criticism of modern industry, products, and corporations—though not criticism of modern art, music, and books. They share, without understanding, the intellectuals' (not unreasonable) doubt that rational control of the world through technology is possible, or if possible, productive of good for mankind. Dating from Rousseau, this doubt has in time acquired much of the sophistication it was originally directed against, and the doubters now express themselves over the media with media amplification of uncertain but sincere fidelity.

Meanwhile, the intellectuals from their side depend on the media. The world of media communication we have described is in fact the world of the intellectuals. Their world excludes the fundamental principle of the ancient philosophers that thinking requires, and makes possible, detachment from one's "worldly" concerns. The world of the intellectuals is this world, the world of worldly concern; and therefore it contains a place, not too modest, for the intellectuals themselves. They are not above it all; they are no strangers to wealth and fame; they do not lack the desire to rule.

Whether in fact intellectuals rule the world they interpret may well be doubted. Politics has its own imperatives that do not respond to direction from above. Moreover, the world of the intellectuals appears to be divided in contradiction, as we have seen, between the news we are filled with and its meaning, which we are ignorant of, between the right to know and the lack of knowledge. How can intellectuals maintain their status if they admit that information has replaced deliberation and no longer assert that the intellect elevates them above others? To reflect on this question, a philosopher is needed.

13
Tocqueville and the Future of the American Constitution

If ever liberty is lost in America, one will have to lay the blame on the omnipotence of the majority which will have driven minorities to despair and forced them to appeal to material force.

(Tocqueville, *Democracy in America* 1.2.7)

It seems that if despotism came to be established in the democratic nations of our day, it would have different characteristics [from those of violent, arbitrary tyranny]: it would be more widespread and milder, and it would degrade men without tormenting them.

(Tocqueville, *Democracy in America* 2.4.6)

These quite contrary judgments of Tocqueville as to the principal danger to democracy, one taken from the first volume of *Democracy in America* and the other from the second, pose the problem of understanding the future of the American Constitution. Within the five years separating his first volume from the second (1835 to 1840) Tocqueville seems to have changed the object of his anxiety for the future from fear of a people too active to fear of a people too inactive.[1]

The change within Tocqueville's book is well known to his scholars, and I have no new solution to propose. I mention it because it mirrors the change in outlook between the founders of the American Constitution and most Americans today: the founders feared an overbearing majority faction (Madison's famous argument in *Federalist* 10 leaps to mind), but today we fear an apathetic or disabled majority that does not claim its rights or cannot exercise them. Now, the founders' remedy against an overactive people was, to describe it generally, a constitution that put government at a distance from the people. Our question today must be: is such a constitution, resting on the assumption of an active people, now obsolete? What should we think of the remedy in our day called "populism," which, contrary to the intention of the founders, attempts to reduce the distance between government and people?

The Constitution as Form of Government

It is not easy to recover the original understanding of the Constitution because the difference between then and now is largely a matter of the spirit with which the Constitution is regarded and of practices related to that spirit; the document and the formal institutions remain largely the same. Nor was the difference properly appreciated by J. Allen Smith and Charles Beard when they maintained seventy five years ago, Smith more directly than Beard, that the Constitution was originally undemocratic.[2]Beard in particular initiated an attitude of scholarly skepticism as to the democratic character of the Constitution which has survived the demise of his "economic interpretation." For though later research has overturned Beard's conclusions and displayed some embarrassment with his arguments,[3] most scholars today still accept the premise of his work.[4]Quickly stated, his premise was that measures taken to control the people are antidemocratic. But this is precisely the premise on which popular movements of our day, both right and left, act in regard to the Constitution. They regard the Constitution not as a *form of government* but as a *means of getting what they want.*

Some conservatives have a series of constitutional amendments they seem to favor more than the Constitution itself, and the recent advance of "conservative" ideas has not emphasized, sometimes not included, the conservation or restoration of the Constitution from liberal misinterpretation. Instead, these conservatives are eager merely to get their own back by expelling liberals and replacing them with conservatives who also do not respect the Constitution. They push for a conservatism no longer considered a constitutional interpretation but rather a set of salutary ideas unconnected to a form of government. Liberals, for their part, have adopted an openly exploitative attitude toward a "living constitution" that is theirs to use, manipulate, or ignore as they please. Liberals are fearful that if they leave the Constitution as it is, it will become out-of-date—which means, a hindrance to liberals. They seem to have lost any sense that a constitution should embody principles, procedures, and institutions that do not go out-of-date. From both sides, then, the Constitution appears today as an instrument of the people, not as a control on them; it is to be used, not to be lived under; it is to be regarded with a spirit of utilitarian opportunism, not indeed as having a "spirit" of its own by which we must live. The Constitution, we think, is below the people, not above them. Although we sometimes admit—and rarely deny altogether—the need for divine authority, we have forgotten why we need a human authority over the people.

Then what does it mean to consider the Constitution as a form of government? This was the intent of the framers of the Constitution, as set forth most authoritatively in *The Federalist*. There it is explained that the American Constitution establishes a popular government, but of a new kind—it is an "experiment." An experiment is needed because almost all previous popular governments outside America had failed (as we learn from *Federalist* 9, 10, and 14). Instead of appealing to classical republican tradition as one might expect in a country of republican governments that had allied to fight and win a war of independence against a monarchy, Publius attacks that tradition. He expresses "horror and disgust" at the extremes of tyranny and anarchy that are continually to be found in the history of "the petty Republics of Greece and Italy." Their defect—also to be seen in the republican state governments then existing in America—was susceptibility to "majority faction," through which measures were decided "by the superior force of an interested and overbearing majority."

Thus Publius presents the Constitution as mainly addressing the problem of majority faction arising from an overconfident and overzealous republican people. This people does not have to be roused from stupid subservience to the false majesty of monarchy, nor does it need to be taught lessons in how to use the government to get what it wants. Its republican ardor and its pursuit of self-interest are unquestioned, but its justice and its devotion to the public good are in doubt, so much so that "enlightened friends to liberty" would have been obliged to abandon the cause of republicanism if the modern "science of politics" had not been able to suggest improvements in republican government (*Federalist* 9).

The celebrated *Federalist* 10 singles out and presents two such improvements as remedies for the general failure of popular government.[5] These are the principle of representation, by which government is delegated to a small number elected by the rest, and the idea of an extensive republic, in which the imperial size that had previously been thought fatal to a republic is deliberately embraced as a means of its salvation. If you "extend the sphere" or "enlarge the orbit," you include many more "fit characters" to serve as representatives, who are more likely to be elected from large constituencies; and more important, you take in a greater variety of parties and interests less likely to combine in a majority faction than a homogeneous majority would be. These two remedies together constitute a "Republican remedy for the diseases most incident to Republican Government" because they do not qualify the principle that the people should rule but only specify how it should do so. They are not the devices of mixed government which would not be agreeable to the republicanism of the American people. They are, however, remedies that will distinguish the American republic from a democracy (or a "pure democracy") in which the people, necessarily a small number, administer the government in person rather than through representatives.

So political science comes to the rescue of republicanism, first by accepting the principle of republicanism, but second, by also accepting that republican diseases exist and not agreeing that the republican principle by itself produces remedies for them. Political science demonstrates that the qualities of imperial size and remoteness of the government from the people, previously thought to be antirepublican (and still proclaimed so by the Antifederalists), are in fact republican as opposed to democratic. *Federalist* 10 distinguishes republics from democracies but not from their usual enemies, aristocracies and monarchies. In America, republicanism is so strong as to be its own worst enemy when uninstructed by political science. Political science is capable of such instruction, we may note for the attention of political scientists today, not when it is value-free but when its end or guiding "value" is wider than the mere promotion of republicanism or democracy. To adopt such an end may in a sense be undemocratic, since it admits that democracy can go wrong, but since it forces democracy to cure its ills, it is not antidemocratic.

Thus the American Constitution, according to Publius, is "wholly popular government" because in all its parts it is derived from the people. But it is also a wholly representative government because it never allows the people to rule directly; as opposed to pure democracy, or to the idea of mixed government, the people are not a part of the government but rather the source of all government. The reason for the deliberate withdrawal of government from the people and its implications are not made clear in *Federalist* 10, in which it is enough to contend that republicanism has a characteristic problem and the American Constitution a brand-new republican remedy for it. But as Publius proceeds to explain and defend the nature of the Constitution, after proving the need for it (in the first thirty six papers), he discloses less arguably republican aspects. In *Federalist* 49 James Madison as Publius advises against a proposal by his friend Thomas Jefferson for an appeal to a convention of the people whenever breaches of the Constitution might occur. Publius objects that government that has its origin in the people cannot recur to the people if it is to maintain its authority over the people. Although—indeed, *because*—the Constitution must originate in the people, it must be elevated over the people if they are to respect it. Popular government needs not merely legitimacy or credibility, as we would say today to emphasize its closeness to the people, but especially "veneration" and "a reverence for the laws." To recur to the people on the occasion of a breach of the Constitution would invite a partisan quarrel followed by a partisan decision. It would encourage the will or the passion of the people to predominate. But, Publius says, it is the *reason* of the public alone that ought to control and regulate the government. The passions ought to be controlled and regulated *by* the government. Popular government cannot dispense with the necessity of keeping reason paramount over the passions, and to do so, it cannot dispense with a seemingly irrational "veneration" for the Constitution because that makes it possible for the government to keep reason paramount. The framers of the Constitution were neither so foolishly optimistic as to think that a republican people was rational because of its republicanism nor so foolishly sophisticated as to think that its irrationality did not matter.

In the new Constitution, then, were two other innovations besides representation and extensive size. Although we take them for granted today, they were not proclaimed as innovations in *The Federalist* because they were generally thought to be unrepublican or undemocratic. These are a strong executive and judicial review. In considering them, *The Federalist* maintains that each is a way of enabling the reason of the people to prevail over their passions. A strong, energetic executive is needed for sound administration of the government and for developing long-term plans to direct it. The people are not merely to be *led*, as we would say now; they are to be *directed*. "Leader" in *The Federalist* is a pejorative term usually reserved for demagogues who try to ride to power on popular passions.[6] Similarly, judicial review of laws and executive actions that might be breaches of the Constitution is justified because judges will not have "too great a disposition to consult popularity" (*Federalist* 78). Instead, they will consult "the intention of the people" as is revealed in the Constitution and the laws. The people's intention is more settled, thus presumably more reasonable, than their will or "momentary inclination." Judges must have "firmness and independence" to help ensure that popular government is exercised not by popular will alone but through the rule of law.

Even the branch of government closest to the people, the legislative, is presented as effective insofar as it does not merely reflect popular will. In explaining the Senate, Publius takes a stand against the instability of most republican governments and offers that notoriously aristocratic institution as a remedy against the "impulse of sudden and violent passions" to which republican assemblies without a senate are likely to yield. Unstable government, it is pointed out, gives an unreasonable advantage to "the sagacious, the enterprising and the moneyed few"; so an institution of the few is enlisted to hinder the few who prosper unreasonably from the instability of a legislature too republican. And in discussing the popular branch itself, Publius is at pains to refute the opinion that the greater the number of representatives, the safer is government from oligarchy; for in a crowd, the few will prevail either by oratory or by secret machination. Publius, moreover, emphasizes the knowledge and experience necessary for representatives, qualities that lift them above the people they represent. Once again, we are impressed, on the one hand, that nonrepublican qualities and devices are made instrumental to republicanism, but, on the other, that republican government needs such things. When Publius comes to explain the separation of powers to a fellow-founder, he says, in a famous sentence: "You must first enable the government to control the governed; and in the next place, oblige it to control itself" (*Federalist* 51). Clearly the separate institutions of constitutional government, which oblige the government to control itself, also, by being separated from the people, enable the government to control the people. Control the people! What statesman today could speak so frankly of the first necessity of popular government?

In response to this question, however, a statesman or an observer might say that the American people are not sufficiently spirited to *need* control. The problem today, it seems, is not the overbearing majority faction that the founders feared but an apathetic, disabled, dependent majority that does not claim its rights or cannot exercise them. We do not worry about majority tyranny but rather about low voter turnout. We are afraid not so much of demagogues stirring a democratic people into frenzies as of the power of television and popular music to absorb that people's attention in private fantasies. We are concerned not for the envy and hatred of the poor for the rich, but for the welfare and drug dependency by which the poor seem to keep themselves in subjection. How this change came about I cannot explain, but one can see it caused or reflected in the change in our thinking about *rights*, especially *the right of consent*.

The Right of Consent

In considering the Constitution as a form of government we have not yet discussed *rights*; yet surely the Constitution was intended to secure rights. To see how it was intended to do so, one must revert to a distinction well known to the founders that is forgotten, or is not stressed, in current discussion—that between natural and civil rights. *Natural rights* are the rights on which civil society is founded; *civil rights* are the ones it secures. Natural rights belong to natural man, who is understood as having a fixed nature worthy of certain rights; these would be the rights to life, liberty, and the pursuit of happiness, according to the Declaration of Independence. They are the rights for the sake of which we establish a Constitution. But the rights actually secured under this Constitution are civil rights, such as those in the Bill of Rights. They are more specific, but therefore also more limited than natural rights. The hallmark of civil rights is that you cannot be deprived of them without due process of law—but you can be deprived of them. Civil society secures rights precisely by *depriving* of their rights those who violate the rights of others, providing of course that this deprivation occurs by due process of law. You cannot be deprived of your natural rights, but you cannot secure them by yourself without a government either; the "state of nature" in constitutional theory describes a situation in which rights are unlimited but very insecure. So it makes sense to deprive yourself of the exercise of natural rights in order to establish a Constitution that will secure civil rights.

The move from natural to civil rights is accomplished by consent and protected by the right of consent, which means the right of consent to government. The right of consent is derived from the rights to life, liberty, and the pursuit of happiness because those rights cannot be effective without government yet would not be rights unless each person could consent on his own. (If someone else consents for you, then your right depends on him.) The right of consent, therefore, is both natural and civil, and between natural and civil rights; natural insofar as it is prior to civil rights; civil insofar as consent establishes conventional, limited civil rights (including the right to vote, which is the civil version of the right of consent). Consent is the crucial right that joins rights to government and makes it clear that although rights are *secured* by government, they are not *created* by government and do not exist merely at the *convenience* of government. When we consider today whether governments maintain the "human rights" of their peoples, we should be concerned with the right of consent above all others, because governments that create rights without seeking consent can as easily take them away.

At the same time, we should be aware on our own account that rights must be understood as being accompanied by a form of government. That form secures rights by governing under law so that the rule of the majority is the rule of a *constitutional* majority as opposed to a *factious* majority. The form and the working of this government are set down in the body of the Constitution rather than in the Bill of Rights. Hamilton was correct to say that the Constitution itself is a Bill of Rights (*Federalist* 84) even if he was wrong to deny the need for a Bill of Rights. The due process of law mentioned above refers most obviously to procedural rights in trials, to the right of habeas corpus, and to protections against ex post facto laws and bills of attainder. But ultimately due process of law depends on the rule of law that results from the rule of a constitutional majority through our form of government, for no right of due process could withstand a determined majority faction. Since all civil rights depend on the people's right of consent, all civil rights depend on the form of government through which they exercise their consent.

This dependence of rights on our form of government is not denied but forgotten today. We speak constantly of rights and frequently invent new rights that a free of civilized people cannot live without. We also calculate policies to guarantee these rights. But we take for granted the Constitution that secures rights and forms the government that makes policies. We regard the Constitution as instrumental to the policies that are instrumental to our rights. As our instrument, the Constitution is not above us; it is not to be honored, revered, or looked up to. Accordingly, today it is not the object of scholarly study, either in political science or law. Political scientists deplore "systemic" faults in political parties and in the constitutional institutions, but they do not look at the whole Constitution; they never see it as a whole because they are always trying to look underneath or behind it. Legal scholarship on constitutional history hardly exists today, and legal publicists use the Constitution to supply an aura for rights without really believing in its power to do so, often while denying that power. The philosophy professors who elaborated and solemnly discuss rights are oblivious of the Constitution; if it were brought to their attention, they would regard it as an accident not deserving consideration in their arguments.

Such general disregard for the Constitution in the political elite and in intellectual and scholarly establishments can perhaps be explained best by examining the new understanding of rights that has succeeded that of the founders. Todays rights are not distinguished as natural and civil because humans are understood fundamentally as changing, historical beings rather than natural beings with a fixed definition. When rights are defined historically, they are in practice impossible to distinguish from wants (even "needs" come to mean "felt needs"). These wants alternate in status between posited rights whose positing is not necessary but merely asserted (the deontological view) and preferences capable of being "traded off" for one another (the utilitarian view). Their status alternates because in practice proponents find the first view too absolute and the second too relative. They have abandoned the distinction between natural and civil rights by which the absoluteness and the relativity of rights are reconciled through the right of consent, and they have substituted for it two partisan views that cannot be reconciled and hence must be alternated.

Postconstitutional Rights

When rights are defined as wants, government is set the impossible task of guaranteeing those wants that happen to be defined as rights in our time, or in our decade. It cannot justify limiting rights or providing what is practicable in present circumstances since, in the absence of any distinction, every civil right is demanded with the full force of a natural right: justice *now*! And who does the demanding? When rights are wants, those who have the wants are no longer required to claim their rights, to fight for them, and to defend them once gained. Elite groups can make the necessary claims on behalf of those who want, who are regarded as too weak actually to enjoy the rights they have had until now in a merely formal sense. For in the constitutional understanding of rights, a right is a license or permission to be exercised on one's own; and some people by choice or circumstance will always excel others in the exercise of rights, being better speakers of free speech or better enterprisers under free enterprise. But in the new *postconstitutional* understanding, any discrepancy between the formal possession of a right and its actual exercise cannot be tolerated: you do not have a right or a choice unless it is an equal right or choice. If you show by your inactivity that you are too weak to exercise your rights, the government, prompted by elite groups, will step in to guarantee those rights, in effect exercising them better than you do. Guaranteeing rights now means guaranteeing their exercise, not the possibility or free choice of their exercise. To do so, government does not by right have to seek your consent or the consent of your fellow citizens because you may feel too weak to consent and your fellow citizens may be overlooking your wants when they consent.

In the postconstitutional understanding, progress in the attainment of rights consists in exposing and correcting the formal and consensual character of rights hitherto; it consists in denying previous progress toward rights. Indeed, when rights are defined historically, no standard exists by which to judge progress except today's wants, which will be superseded by tomorrow's. A critique of rights because of their unequal exercise implies a definition of rights by their exercise alone. But such "rights" do not have to be exercised by those who are said to have them; they do not require consent and cannot result in progress.

Since these new rights are guaranteed to each individual, and individuals do not have to claim them, individuals do not have to take responsibility for their exercise. In this view you have a right to fair housing, for example, not merely a right to seek housing on your own under fair terms specified by the government. And as your rights do not necessitate that you take responsibility for their exercise, they do not result from any contribution you make or might make to the community, if they were secured to you. Your rights do not flow from strengths—your talents and capacities—but rather from weaknesses—your handicaps and needs. Indeed, you do not "deserve" your rights.[7] Since in the latest conception rights are not rights unless they are equal in exercise or in result, you have rights especially when you do not deserve them, and they must be asserted especially against those who might deserve them and thus exercise them better than yourself. Instead of examining the weak to find their latent strength and then calling forth that strength by securing a right to use it, we seek out weakness itself and finding it mute (since no one boasts of his or her weakness in order to claim rights), we file a suit on its behalf. To be weak is to be "disadvantaged"; we may claim a tort against society to require society to make you whole without any effort of your own. Compassion takes over from justice, even usurping its name; and society discovers its victims but forgets to make them citizens.

In the new version, we have seen, rights are no longer *civil* as distinguished from and related to natural rights. They are human rights, and as such have no necessary relationship to civil society, the Constitution, or the common good. Your right is not qualified by any requirement to contribute to society by improving, maintaining, or defending it. You do not even have to obey its laws; so it has now become more correct to speak of prisoners' rights than of citizens' rights. *Human* rights so understood have both the absoluteness of natural rights and the specificity of civil rights without the insecurity of the former or the limitedness of the latter. They are unembarrassed, unrelenting claims on the public treasury, private compassion, nature, and God to be made whole according to an increasingly costly, if not lofty, definition of what it means to be a whole human being. In our day they are known as *entitlements*, as we have seen. When rights in general are taken as entitlements, even the sky is not the limit, and your rights culminate, not in the right of consent, but in your right to feel dissatisfied. One could sum up entitlements in this way: they have no reference to the common good; they result from no actual or potential contribution by the entitled; they do not have to be individually, much less responsibly, exercised; and they deny past progress in rights while producing a static society of defensive special interests.

Bureaucracy

The new *entitlements* are guaranteed by a government no longer seen as constitutional. Although the American people of course continue to vote, voting is understood more as the registering of wants than as consent to a government under the Constitution, thus over the people. As an instrument to get the people what they want government comes more and more to be regarded as a *bureaucracy*—and not merely in one subordinate part but as a whole. Judged by the instrumental standard, American government proves to be inefficient; precisely the constitutional safeguards make it seem too remote to serve the people faithfully and expeditiously. When judged as a bureaucracy, American government proves to have the faults of bureaucracy. For some reason, these faults, unlike other human faults, have no hidden compensations: for bureaucracy is large but petty, meddlesome but unconcerned, stupid but complex, flighty but insistent, and forgetful but inflexible. Politicians from both parties have in recent times run electoral campaigns successfully against government by equating government with bureaucracy. They and we regard government as unreason with the outward look of reason, as if government were meant to be a rational or efficient instrument of the people that somehow in practice never works properly. That our government was intended through its constitutional processes to *add* reason to the will of the people so as to produce the reasoned "intention" of the people as opposed to their "momentary inclinations" (*Federalist* 78) is now all but forgotten. What the founders praised as constitutional government we now condemn, from both the Left and the Right, as "bureaucracy."

Bureaucracy as it appears in its accusatory usage is an instrument that fails as an instrument because it always tries to be more than an instrument. It should confine itself to rationally effecting the will of the people, but the reason it brings to this task has an ambition of its own that refuses to be so confined. Bureaucracy is unresponsive to the people because it claims to know better than they what is good for them; it tries to correct or "refine" (Publius's word) their will. Bureaucracy, like reason itself, is heavy, cold, and remote. It is too formal and too paternal, like an old-fashioned father who shows his love by making rules. It now seems hardly conceivable that a people, knowing the fallibility of its reason when judging in one's own cause and when ignorant of the circumstances of others, might actually choose—not a father but a constitutional government—over itself.

In our view today the main problem facing government becomes government itself. Nothing the government has to do is more important or even more urgent than overcoming its own bureaucratic nature. To do so, it is thought that government cannot turn to reason, and try to make the reason of the American people control their passions as the framers did. Too much reliance on reason in the sense of either unhurried deliberation or bureaucratic formalism is precisely the problem rather than the solution. The solution, we seem to believe, has to be a new resort to passion so that government can recover its lost connection to the American people.

The passion in question is usually compassion, sometimes anger; both are included in the vogue word *care*. Thus government, it is supposed, can overcome its unfeeling bureaucratic nature by showing that it cares. Showing compassion or anger makes a direct and informal contact with the people that is quite different from the formal connections between government and people established in our constitutional system. It is as if all government can and should behave to the people in the manner of a passerby who sees an accident in the street and rushes to see if he can be of any assistance. Our politicians, when running for office, promise to act not as the deliberative legislator or responsible bureaucrat but as the compassionate passerby.

The institutions closest to the people in our society are believed to be the media; so to get closer to the people, government tries to resemble the media, which relentlessly demand and provide direct contact between the people and their government. The media are not, of course, *institutions* in the sense of associations formally established by consent of the people. They are networks for informing and entertaining the people that con- stitute the indispensable "medium" between people and government in which the right of consent takes effect. They seem to be nothing in themselves, and often say that they merely report what goes on. In truth, they *do* nothing on their own; they act in the manner of a compassionate passerby who sees an accident in the street and rushes to see if someone else can be of any assistance. But the media greatly affect how we regard government. With unfailing emphasis and unremitting insinuation they require the government to be "responsive" and "sensitive" to the people, not to control them, because they find enough morality and wisdom in what the people want or feel.

In order to be responsive and sensitive, government is forced to be "charismatic." *Charisma*, a term to designate irregular authority, is taken from Max Weber's sociology and now moralized and democratized in current usage. Charisma now means popularity that is deserved, yet for no apparent reason. Charisma resembles *leadership*—the term used pe- joratively by Publius that Woodrow Wilson brought into favor as praise— but it is more irrational and it is unconnected to progress. Charisma is an inexplicable, unpredictable gift for knowing what the people want or think right before they know, and it attaches to the person, not the office. All officers in the regular constitutional departments must now reckon with charisma: the president must have it, as must legislators who seek to be president; senators and congressmen must deliberate in the shadow of charisma, aware that undramatic sober prudence is not appreciated; even judges are not immune from charisma's temptations, which many of them regard as innocent. Although each of the branches of government retains the flavor of its constitutional essence, our praise for charisma is a sign that we no longer consider popularity to be an evil, or *the* evil, of popular government.

Popularity and Voluntarism

It would take too long to show how the workings of the constitutional branches today reflect the spirit of charismatic popularity that has originated in our ideas and been spread by the media. But one can mention such well-known features of our politics as our presidential primaries, media-based campaigns, and populistic programs in the executive; loss of leadership, subcommittee proliferation, constituency servicing, and an uncontrolled budget in the Congress; and the complex of intrusions upon the legislature, executive, and state governments known as "judicial activism." And besides the influence of the media and its own workings, government must contend with a plethora of surveys, many originating from the government, which imply that people ought to have what they want, and right away.

Yet somehow the new requirements of exposure do not make government more honest, the new demands for compassion do not make it more popular. The reason is that our capacity to fool ourselves easily surpasses every advance in technology or social science. The more popular government tries to be, the more unpopular it becomes, because popularity is not a standard any government can live by—even, or especially, a popular government. No government can govern without imposing duties and asking for sacrifices, but duty and sacrifice must be called forth by a higher ideal than popularity.

When government seeks popularity, it seeks more than consent. With the right of consent, the people call government to account and give it scope to govern within the limits of the Constitution and constrained by the need to maintain a constitutional majority. To do so, the people put aside their desire to rule directly but retain, through elections, their right of independent judgment. But when government seeks to do what is popular, it must claim to know what people will consent to in advance of elections. Popularity as determined by surveys becomes a substitute for consent in elections, and we face the paradox of a popular government seeking popularity under which many people do not bother to vote. The right of consent to government becomes the right—in the new sense of entitlement—to have the government do popular things.

Our government's eagerness for popularity might make one believe that it is trying to please a people that knows what it wants and is determined to have it. But as we have seen, the American people, no longer so ready to exercise their rights, have been made anxious over their entitlements. And because both people and government are so large, each individual has so small a share in popularity that he has to consider it an outside force to which he must conform rather than a means of self-government. The sovereign people have yielded to a sovereignty of popularity in which the people are like—or are—a weak ruler open to the suggestion and manipulation of dubious advisers, both venal and partisan. Bringing government closer to the people by forcing it to seek popularity has weakened both our government and our people. We seem to have arrived at the *individualism* that Tocqueville feared might become the fate of a democratic people.[8]

In contrast to this gloomy picture, it might be said, is the assertion Americans have made in the 1980s through taxpayers' revolts and by electing President Reagan, to "get the government off our backs." Does not this perky act imply a people not yet lost in dependency? Perhaps it does, but one cannot yet be sure that it signifies more than a desire to be rid of responsibility for oneself and for others. The government's guarantee of entitlements can seem more oppressive to some at some times, for example, when one is young and employed, but the mere act of throwing off that weight, however exhilarating for the moment, does not signify an ability to live without entitlements. With some age or after ill success in an "opportunity" the desire for entitlements may return.

Thus the libertarian impulse that has gained momentum in our time may turn out to be nothing more than an alternative mode of Tocqueville's *individualism*. One mode would be collectivist, as individuals let government run their lives; the other would be individualist, when individuals refuse to pay for the first mode. In both modes people are inactive, either allowing the government to exercise their rights or not understanding the exercise of rights as a responsibility to do something worthwhile—especially, to *govern* oneself. Libertarianism does not admit that the *self* must govern itself in order that self-government may thrive. It is content to let people have what they want, so long as they do not want government, and it suspects, with some reason, that any call to greater responsibility is nothing but the prelude to another expensive and foolish entitlement program. In fact, however, entitlements make people irresponsible, whether they pay or receive. If they pay, they become patrons of a society of clients without realizing the harm they do; if they receive, they envy those who pay—but not for paying. Those who both pay for entitlements and receive them do not get their money's worth, as with social security in America today. It is not possible to protect liberty by disconnecting it from responsibility, and thus from government. For nothing prevents the irresponsible from demanding more government, not even previous experience—since who says I must be responsible for my costs or for my memory?

Libertarianism needs to become reacquainted with constitutionalism and to stop flirting with the populism that undermines constitutional government. The way back to limited government cannot be found by denying or minimizing the need for government or by setting off government against liberty. Rather, limited government is free *government*, in which a people is free because it governs itself freely. Tocqueville reminds us that free government requires both an active people and a government to control it. As against the entitlements of our day, he praises the active voluntary spirit of Americans; but in contrast to those who dissociate liberty from government, he recommends—and provides in his book—both the art and the science of association[9] by which free people are made competent to do what they can and warned against attempting what they cannot. A people cannot be active unless it knows how to associate; but such association requires as its precondition a constitution that allows and encourages it, the mother association that gives birth to free, responsible associations throughout a free society but does not try to rule their activities. So long as they live in the spirit of this constitution, the American people will not give up their rights in exchange for guarantees from government because they will want to continue governing themselves.

What can political science do to help them? Two tasks seem to be defined for a constitutional political science today: first, to explain and defend the forms of constitutions and of our Constitution; second, to show a democratic people how to overcome its dependency on government and recover its sense of capacity and accomplishment. We need to recover both the political science of *The Federalist* (with improvements, if we can) and the active people it wanted to guard against. So stated, these tasks might seem to be in conflict with each other: the first is antipopulist, the second is populist. But in principle they do not conflict; in fact, it may well be that they can only be accomplished together.

The defense of constitutional forms is necessary to any lasting inspiration of activity in a democratic people. Government must withdraw from attempting to guarantee the exercise of rights to a less ambitious and less threatening policy of securing those rights in some formal manner. A formal manner permits and requires people as individuals and in groups to become responsible on their own for exercising rights. *Only the formalism of constitutionalism leaves room for the voluntarism of democracy.* Every attempt to bring government closer to the people so that it can make formal equality actual runs the risk of making the people dependent on government. When this happens, the people lose their vigilance and assertiveness over government as a whole and begin to look after their special interests, each group for its own. An active people needs the limits of a limited government to call forth and sustain its activity. And limited government can be defended on principled grounds only when the limits are embodied in the formal orders and practices of a constitution; otherwise, limited government will come down to less government for you, more for me.

If there is a connection from constitutionalism to voluntarism, there is also one from voluntarism to constitutionalism. If today's liberals need to be restrained from using government to rule people's lives, libertarians need to be taught that mere release from government is not enough to make a people capable of self-government. The people also need a well-made constitution enabling them to elevate their will into an intention and calling forth the virtues necessary to the task. That intention will not take shape or survive if it is confused with popularity and made agreeable to every momentary shift of popular feeling. *Only the formalism of constitutionalism gives effect to the voluntarism of democracy.* Constitutional government must make its people aware of the demands as well as the pleasures of freedom and not leave the impression that, when government is limited, things will take care of themselves. If the American people can be convinced to become active again by claiming for themselves the rights they have left with the government, they must be warned to consider this activity a duty. The independence of a people consists in its public spirit as much as in its private enterprise.

14

The Forms and Formalities of Liberty

Men living in democratic centuries do not readily understand the utility of forms; they feel an instinctive contempt for them. . . . Forms arouse their disdain and often their hatred. As they usually aspire to none but facile and immediate enjoyments, they rush impetuously toward the object of each of their desires, and the least delays exasperate them. This temperament, which they transport into political life, disposes them against the forms which daily hold them up or prevent them in one or another of their designs.

Yet it is this inconvenience, which men of democracies find in forms, that makes them so useful to liberty, their principal merit being to serve as a barrier between the strong and the weak, the government and the governed. Thus democratic peoples naturally have more need of forms than other peoples, and naturally respect them less.

(Tocqueville, *Democracy in America* 2.4.7)

This long statement is dense enough to require explanation and deep enough to reward reflection. Speaking of forms, Tocqueville directs our attention to institutions or practices that are form rather than substance, in which the manner of action is more important than the end achieved.

To understand what these forms are, we may think of manners in society, meaning *society* not in any comprehensive sociological sense but as the place where we are on our best behavior, the parlor or drawing room of human life. Society so understood imposes certain forms of correct behavior on us that are neither moral duties (though manners are obviously somehow related to morals) nor simply cost-efficient methods of attaining our ends.

Indeed, these forms seem designed to *avoid* raising moral questions directly and to prevent us from using the most efficient instrument to gain our desires; they are barriers, as Tocqueville says, in the first instance between ourselves and the objects of our desires, and also between one person and another.

The Wisdom of Miss Manners

That we now say "living room" rather than "parlor" or "drawing room" illustrates the drive toward informality that Tocqueville says is in the nature of democracy, yet, as Tocqueville also indicates, democracy is not always well served by informality. Tocqueville's point was made recently by Judith Martin, who writes a column on etiquette for the *Washington Post* under the name Miss Manners. Miss Manners inveighs against waiters and waitresses who have taken up a new practice of introducing themselves to customers by their first names, as if to put business relationships on the level of friendships. Such a practice, she says, not only perverts friendship by using it for business—suffusing the latter with false warmth—but also hurts business by robbing the working person of his dignity. "If you and I are friends," Miss Manners asks, "how come I have to wait on you? But if I can be on equal terms with friends of my own choosing, it doesn't matter if I perform a service for wages."[1]

With this excellent remark, we have suddenly received a lesson in constitutional democracy more valuable than much academic discussion that is more directly political or economic. We learn, first, the obvious truth that even a democratic society is not a society of friends, or a fraternity, because it must necessarily comprise unequal relationships. How, then, are these inequalities to be made consistent with democratic equality? The answer is that the formalities of unequal relationships can preserve equality by upholding the dignity of inferiors and by restraining the pride of superiors. That customers can order a waiter to do their bidding is disguised and softened by the manner in which they do it. Precisely because the waiter is *not* a friend, customers are limited in what they can command, and the waiter is thereby freed from total submission.

Forms or formalities equalize human relationships while preserving necessary inequalities, by preventing them from being relationships of mere unrestrained power. Freedom is maintained for inferiors because they choose friends outside their jobs with whom to live on an equal basis, and within the necessity of having and keeping a job, they can choose which job to hold. Without the formal demarcations surrounding a job, either jobs would not get done because they would be inconsistent with democratic fraternity, or jobs would be done perforce with no respect for democratic equality and liberty. In the first case, friendship spills over the bounds of choice; in the second, necessity intrudes where it is not needed. In both cases, formality is overcome by informality. As Miss Manners notes, there is something sinister in undiscriminating informality: "If you and I are friends, how come I have to wait on you?" In our democratic age, overflowing informality is a source of tyranny and rebellion.

When we hear of *inequality* we assume that the superiority of a few is meant, and we frown. Living under democracy, we forget that democracy is a form of rule, with superiors and inferiors, in which the many are superior to the few. The example of many customers and few waiters reminds us that democracy has its menials as well as its elites. If democracy is to make use of both while remaining true to its principle, it must find the method for raising up menials and holding down elites while at the same time restraining the truly superior class in a democracy—the majority of the people. The adoption of forms is one such method; it not only retains inequalities necessary to any society larger than a friendship but also equalizes inequalities by confining them to formal relationships. Formal relationships keep society in a safe and free middle ground between friendship and sheer power.

The formality of an action is what can be separated from its end, and this separation is possible because the end can be achieved in more than one way. When one means is absolutely necessary to attain the end, no formality exists; but when a choice of means is required, the one chosen (or developed unconsciously) as "correct" is the formality. *Correct reasoning* is following the single most direct way to the conclusion, but *correct behavior* is following the prescribed mode of several or many possibilities. "There's more than one way to skin a cat" is advice to ignore the prescribed way. This prescribed mode or manner has a certain look or shape that distinguishes it from other modes and makes it recognizable as that formality without having to wait for the action to accomplish its end in order to learn what it is. Unlike correct reasoning, which follows its own logic and, so to speak, does not know where it is going until it gets there, correct behavior is instantly recognizable as such on its face, before the end is attained; we can appreciate polite eating, for example, without knowing or caring whether it leads to efficient digestion. Hence, formalities depend on forms, the *looks* of things and actions as separable from their ends or results.

Could we then recognize democratic equality in the forms or formalities of democracy without having to wait to judge the equality of result? This question, arising from recent American politics, suggests a connection between the formalities of manners in a democratic society and other, political and economic, forms—its constitution and its property. These forms are taken to be more formal than the formalities of manners, since they are the ways prescribed by law as opposed to custom. Law is more formal than custom because the procedure by which a law is made law is publicly visible. To have such a procedure is to have a constitution in some sense, and one can often judge more of the character of a constitution from looking at the way laws are changed than from looking at the laws that remain unchanged, just as one learns most about the state of one's property by trying to change it. Social formalities, then, culminate in forms of constitutions and conventions of property.

Such formalities are always open to challenge from democratic peoples. It is in the nature of democracy to look for results and to regard any deliberate delay in reaching them as undemocratic. To have the object of one's desire is of course a natural human inclination; but people can be finicky and fussy as well as lazy and direct, and it is a difficult question whether human nature is more democratic than aristocratic. We cannot assume that democratic manners, though second nature to us, are more natural in truth.

In our day, however, as Tocqueville might have granted, informality comes from a second source as well. My purpose, after this introduction, is to consider how the informality of our times undermines our Constitution and property. I shall proceed by describing this informality further, in order to show its hostility to democratic constitutionalism; then, to explain our constitutionalism, I shall contrast the Aristotelian conception with the liberal one, which is tied closely to property; and I shall end with a remark on the relationship between human rights and property rights.

Populist Informality

The innocent waiter or waitress who wants to be friendly not only reveals the nature of democracy in general but also reflects in a small way a political movement of the 1970s known as populism. Actually, this populism began in the 1960s, when the movement was angrier, rougher, and narrower—when it promoted "participatory democracy" and was known as the New Left. Its progress has come by dilution and through respectability, just as students who once dressed down to the uniform of the working class now sport designer jeans. Respectability came easily, despite the electoral failures of the New Left and the oblivion of its early leaders, for unlike previous populism in American history, this recent variety began and still thrives among the educated.

Besides making our manners more informal, this movement has attacked our political institutions for serving as barriers between the people's will and their object, that is, for being too formal. President Jimmy Carter, a prime beneficiary and exponent of populism, stated the populist principle in his demand that we make government as good as the people.

Thus, the power of government is to be exercised, not through, but against its formal institutions, and whatever agency is available will be used to effect the people's will (as discerned or presumed by the populists), regardless of the formal character of the agency. Judicial activism was one obvious result—and not because judges were thought wiser, but because their actions could be more direct. Also, the populist complaint against bureaucracy was not that it was too precise or overbearing, but that it stood in the way. Because of the political defeat suffered by this populism in 1980, one is tempted to speak of it in the past tense; but to do so would be too hasty. Some of the victors of 1980, particularly the New Right, have picked up and perfected the techniques of populism; and the *techniques* of populism, not Left or Right, are its essence.

A third target of the educated populists has been private property. Although they have made a point of the right to live as you please (not so much for the pleasure of it as because we all must do our own thing), and have therefore asserted a general right of privacy (again, not so much to have fun in the dark as to defy decorum in public), they have also mounted an attack on private property. That their claims to privacy do not also support private property makes sense if one sees private property as the chief form or formality, after the Constitution, of liberal society.

Property is a legal convention (perhaps based on a natural right) that establishes certain formalities of acquisition, maintenance, and transfer. When these are satisfied, the property is yours to use as you please; thus, the form of property is prescribed, the end is left open. Property thereby constitutes a barrier between people, defined by John Locke as that which cannot be taken from you without your consent (*Two Treatises of Government*, 2:138–40). Property epitomizes the nature of law in liberal society: if you stay within bounds, you can do as you like. One thing you may do is to set up a corporation, a legal or formal person that creates a distance within yourself between your moral and legal duties and also between yourself and others, since your duties to them are reduced to legal correctness. Populists have been particularly hostile to corporate private property because of its impersonality.

For the populists, such freedom is purely formal, that is, meaningless in itself. For them, its meaning depends on being rich or middle class so that one actually has property to use. Since the *meaning* of the right to private property is in its actual effect, the *existence* of the right is judged also by its effect. Since one does not have a right unless it can be exercised, rights are not equal unless they are exercised equally. So government can and should intervene to ensure rights, not as equal opportunities, but rather as equal in exercise. Though, in the populists' view, it may not be necessary to abolish private property, its use by private individuals and corporations must be examined from the standpoint of the public interest, which means the right of others to an equal exercise of their right. Governmental regulation to clean the air and water, supply seat belts, and aid the handicapped has been justified for the purpose of "opening up" society—that is, forcing the barriers of private property and compelling owners to answer for its use. Such regulation goes beyond setting the formal conditions of fair competition, as in minimum wage or antitrust legislation, because it raises the question of whether *any* formal statement of private property can be found. In truth, the populists not only put human rights above property rights, they hardly speak of property rights. To hold property is, in their view, more a liability than an opportunity: you make yourself a target of litigation.

The distinction between formal right and its informal exercise has been most obviously overcome in programs of affirmative action, in which the change from "equality of opportunity" to "equality of result" was explicit and deliberate. Affirmative action arose from the idea of abolishing de facto (informal) segregation of blacks. According to this idea, the government must not merely take care that the law does not discriminate against blacks, but must also use the law to eradicate nonlegal (informal) sources of discrimination. The policy goes far, and the principle goes further: for example, what in principle is to prevent governmental policies requiring affirmative action in interracial dating and marriage? Certainly reluctance to intermarry is racial discrimination, and in no small matter.

More important yet is reinterpretation of voting rights in recent cases and in the renewal of the Voting Rights Act in 1982 which tends toward a governmental guarantee of minority representation.[2] The most fundamental right in liberal society, the right of consent to government, has become open to inspection by the very government that claims consent, in order to ensure that the right to vote is the right to an effective vote. This challenge to elected governments is derived from earlier reapportionment cases on "one person, one vote," by which the test of legitimacy was whether each individual, urban or rural, had the same power with his or her vote as every other individual.[3] The right to vote, in this populist view, is the right to a vote that is equal in effect. What of the right of free speech? Is it merely the right to whistle in the wind, or is it not the right to be listened to, equally with others; hence, the "right to reply" and to be replied to? And is the right to life not then an equal right to an effective, expansive, flourishing life?

The equality of exercise of rights or, to speak more plainly, the equality of power, comes from the idea of self-expression developed by the New Left out of a strange combination of Marx and Nietzsche that would be remarkable in the natural history of hybrids if it were not also destined for a prominent place in American political history. To constitute the idea of self-expression, Marx's critique of bourgeois formalism was the first ingredient. In that critique, which is most evident in his early writing *On the Jewish Question* (1843), the "rights of man" proclaimed by the liberal philosophers are shown to be, in effect, merely the rights of bourgeois man. Then, rejecting Marx's economic determinism, the New Left turned to Nietzsche's account of how the self produced itself in history by stages of *consciousness* (still a Marxist term) in which the self had motive power of its own. But then, rejecting Nietzsche's call for sacrifice and aristocracy so that the self can rescue itself from nihilism, the New Left turned back to Marx's early notion of *species-being*, which promised effortless fulfillment for all selves.

Essential to the idea of self-expression, and common to both Marx and Nietzsche, is the belief that the self is totally produced, not at all given or fixed. Men do not have the defined self that is required for the liberal right of self-preservation: by nature, we lack any "sense of identity," and so we must seek it out in our experience of life and in magazines. Lacking definition, the self must assert itself (for assertion is the effectual truth of "expression"), and in its self-assertion it has no reason to respect the self-assertion of others. Others would deserve respect if they had rights, but rights attach only to selves that can be defined. If the self has no fixity, no definition even in its potentiality, then the self can be only what it becomes by its act of assertion. Its "right" is as much or as little as it can exercise; the distinction between a right and its exercise is overridden.

From the lack of a fixed *self*, in the liberal sense of self-preservation or self-government, it follows that liberal equality of opportunity is meaningless. An authentic equality of opportunity assumes the possibility of a fresh start, regardless of one's past history. If the artificial restraints of social convention are removed, it is supposed, one's natural talents will be permitted to flourish, and each person will progress as far as his or her nature and effort allow. But if there is no fixed self, then one has no nature, no "God-given talent," to resort to; and the self must be what it has been and what it might become. In effect the self must be what it has been, if one's will is weak; or the self will be what it can become, if one's will is strong. The strength of one's expression or assertion begins to replace the language of rights (e.g., black *power* as opposed to civil *rights*), since the distinction between right and exercise has been overcome.

That self-assertion necessarily reveals and promotes the difference between the strong and the weak has not, however, been an embarrassment to the democratic feeling of the New Left and its populist cousins. The weak can join their wills together to become strong, forgetting liberal individuality; and when united, they can use the power of government to equalize wills, or to ensure that the exercise of liberal rights does not result in inequality. Besides, it is advantageous for these educated populists to be able to stress the weakness of human will when they want to blame the past and the strength of human will when they want to incite change.

The populism I have described as aggressive informality is fundamentally opposed to constitutionalism, which promotes respect for forms above all. Governing in a constitutional manner is governing regularly, that is, formally. Locke said that the "form of government" (which we may take to be the constitution) depends on where the legislative power is placed; and the legislative power must be supreme, so that government can be by "settled, standing laws" and "stated rules" (*Two Treatises*, 2:132, 137). Such government is opposed to the rule by the arbitrary will of one, few, or many because it appears, at least in our constitutionalism today, to elevate the form of government over the end. Locke, to be sure, announces the end of the legislative power in the same place that he insists on its formal character; the laws must aim at the "public good," which is the "preservation" of the society (*Two Treatises*, 2:134, 135, 142). But this end is also described as the "preservation of property" (2:138–39), and property (as we have seen, and shall see in Locke) as a formality.

As we have been taught to understand constitutional government, it is governing by due process, by forms, and even by technicalities, in which the form or manner of an action is raised above its end; the means are more important than the end. For example, respecting the rights of criminals is more important than convicting them. Those conservatives who might contest the current application of this principle would not want, we may assume, to set up lynch law, in which the end is raised above the means so that the end justifies any efficient means. In its emphasis on forms and formalities, constitutionalism, both ancient and modern, is above all opposed to Machiavellism. Yet within constitutionalism there is a critical difference between Aristotle and Locke in regard to form and end, which we need to appreciate. Locke's modification of Aristotle's constitutionalism set the terms of the problem of constitutional formalism as we see it and opened the way for the challenge to constitutionalism today.

Aristotle's Constitutionalism

Aristotle's constitutionalism is easy to locate, in Book 3 of the *Politics*, but it is not easy to explain. Some discussion of his text will be necessary.[4] Aristotle begins Book 3 by asking the question "What is the city, anyway?" He answers it, and introduces his notion of constitution, by investigating what a citizen is, since citizens are parts of the city, which is a whole. The citizen is not a part from which the city grows, such as the family, but a part, created by the city, that presupposes the city. Yet the citizen also speaks for the city; he is a part created by the whole that speaks for the whole. In speaking, the citizen asserts what a citizen should be—typically whether citizenship should be confined to a few, as in an oligarchy, or extended to the many, as in a democracy. Aristotle begins his discussion of citizenship by reminding us that the definition of citizen is a matter of political dispute, so that someone who would be a citizen in a democracy would not be a citizen under an oligarchy.

Aristotle proceeds with a presentation of the citizen's perspective on citizenship. Apparently he gives the floor first to a democratic citizen, who begins by saying what a citizen is not. Being a citizen is not merely living or working in the city, nor is it possessing legal rights, for resident aliens have these characteristics and slaves live and work in the city. Children may be born to citizenship, but they, as well as the aged, are only incomplete citizens, because citizenship is participation in ruling. We can see a difficulty in this democratic definition that should still puzzle defenders of modern democracies. Children are excluded from citizenship because they are immature, but some mature persons are excluded because they are not free born (in modern democracies, native-born). An unresolved tension between being able to be a citizen and being born a citizen remains in the definition.

Someone then objects from an oligarchical standpoint that this definition is too democratic (*Politics* 1275b6). Being able to rule requires skill, for ruling means ruling well and to the proper end; thus, only those who rule well are truly citizens. The democratic and the oligarchical citizens agree that the citizen is born a citizen and is able to share in rule, but they are divided over how seriously to take the ability needed to rule, and in any case the incoherence between ability and birth remains. To consider these difficulties in the citizen's perspective, Aristotle resorts to the philosopher's perspective (*Politics* 1275b27). He relates a pun made by the sophist Gorgias about Larissa, a city where a kind of pot called a *larissa* was made. In Larissa, Gorgias said, "perhaps in doubt and also ironically," the magistrates make Larissaeans. With this pun Gorgias exposes the fact, overlooked in the citizen's perspective, that if one looks back far enough, one sees that citizens were once made, not born. In the same way, Americans were made citizens by the Constitution of 1787, by an act of legislation; only thereafter could they be born into citizenship. The first citizen, the artisan who fashioned all the other citizens as if he were making pots (*demiourgos*, the word for "magistrate" in Larissa, also means maker or first maker), was not made. He made himself a citizen;

like George Washington, he was the father of his country. But was the first maker—the founder or the founding generation—the best artisan or merely the first maker who happens to be our ancestor? Gorgias's pun makes us doubt whether the citizenship we were born with is the best or merely our conventional definition.

By sending us back to the origins of our citizenship and making us see that we have been made and not born citizens, Gorgias brings to light the latent incoherence between ability and birth in the citizen's definition. The ability of a citizen comes from his nature, and his citizen birth is in fact his inheritance of an original convention by which he was made a citizen. In the philosopher's perspective of citizenship, nature and convention are distinguished, if not seen altogether as contraries. But in the citizen's perspective they are confused. The citizen thinks that his world, the world of his city or society, is *the* world. Still today we speak of "natural-born" citizens, and we say that a person who has been made a citizen has been "naturalized," as if the born citizen were prior. But in fact, contrary to the citizen's way of thinking and to immigration laws that reflect such thinking, before any citizen could be born, citizens had to be made. No one is a citizen, therefore, merely by being born a human being; some act of legislation is always necessary in order to produce a citizen.

After telling us Gorgias's pun, Aristotle then deflects the inquiry into the origins of citizenship that it implies (and that is so uncomfortable for citizens) by raising the question of justice. He mentions a democratic revolution in Athens made by Cleisthenes, when, after the overthrow of a tyranny, citizenship was extended to many who had been foreigners or slaves. Clearly, citizens had been made, but had they been made justly (*Politics* 1275b38–39)? One might ask further, says Aristotle, whether a person unjustly made a citizen is truly a citizen, since unjustly has the same effect as falsely. *Justice* is equivalent to *truth* for a citizen, because when he thinks about the city and deliberates about what is good for it, doing justice requires him to consider the whole of the city, and thus its end. If the citizen were merely a pot maker, as in Gorgias's pun, he would not worry about the use to which the pot would be put; he would not need to know the whole and its end or ends, because to him the city would merely be the means to an end that is beyond his ken as a citizen. But to think of justice, he must try or claim to know the whole. The whole includes things not made by men—for example, goods or ends that they may have by nature, as well as conventions or artifices they have made. The citizen's confusion of nature and convention, his tendency to look on his city as something natural or unmade, allows him to think more (if with confusion) than do traveling sophisticates such as Gorgias. Citizens are made, as Gorgias suggests, but how does one make them justly?

This large topic becomes a matter for public deliberation when the regime changes—say, from tyranny to democracy—and the question arises whether the new regime should be responsible for the debts of the old regime, debts that it had not incurred. Those who want to repudiate the debts argue that the money was borrowed, not by the city, but by a tyrant. Akin to this question, Aristotle says, is the question of what makes the city the same city as before; for one must know what defines the city in order to decide whether it has debts. We now approach the notion of constitution.

In considering what makes a city the same and not different, Aristotle rejects the superficial answer that the city is the same when the inhabitants and the place are the same, because one cannot make a city by enclosing a certain place (for example, the Peloponnesus) with a wall. Instead, Aristotle defines two possibilities for us. The first is that the city is the same if, in the same population and place, the race is the same, even though some are always dying and others are being born, just as we speak of a river or spring as the same, even though water is always being taken away and added. The second possibility is that although the human beings may remain the same, the city is different from them (*Politics* 1276a34–1276b31).

These two possible ways in which a city remains the same seem to correspond to two philosophical positions and to two political opinions. The first, with its example of the river or spring, reminds us of Heraclitus, according to whom one cannot step into the same river twice: all is flow or flux, nothing is fixed or distinct. One might say that the river is always different, or one might also say with equal reason that it is always the same, since nothing fixed changes. This possibility would suggest that cities and citizens are only temporarily and arbitrarily distinguishable in their kinds; fundamentally, in their matter, they are all the same. It is as if all things were watery bodies, with the shape of their temporary containers, like the river bank that itself winds and changes. This is a *democratic* view of nature, if democracy is carried to its logical extreme in which all distinctions and distinctiveness are abolished.

The other, opposite, possibility, in which the city is utterly distinct from the human beings or matter composing it, is harder to identify. No analogy or example is offered. One might hazard a guess, however, that Plato's scheme or something like it is intended for consideration; for if the city is altogether distinct from the human beings composing it, then some distinctive element within human beings—their reason—must appear to enable them to rise above their material needs. This position would seem to be *oligarchy* carried to its logical extreme in which men form a city only on the basis of the reason that distinguishes them from the rest of nature. In this city, if such a city were possible, the skill element in citizenship would be all important, just as human birth, or indeed any continuity with nature, would alone suffice in the logical extreme of democracy.

The solution Aristotle chooses, or asserts, is between these two possibilities, but not in the middle; it is closer to the second. He introduces the notion of constitution or regime (*politeia*), which he had mentioned at the very beginning of Book 3, and he brings up the distinction between form and matter (though without mentioning *matter*) that is featured in his metaphysics. He says that if the city is a kind of community, and a community of citizens is a regime, then when the regime changes in form, it seems necessary that the city is not the same, just as we assert that a chorus is different if it plays a comedy one time and a tragedy another even though the human beings composing it are the same. Similarly, Aristotle continues (in a remark that goes beyond politics), we say of any community and synthetic whole that it is different if the form is different; so clearly we must speak of the city as the same city especially with regard to its constitution or regime.

The regime, then, is the form, and the city is especially (note: not *only*) its form. Thus, the city is not like a river that has no form except as a container that has a changing form, as in the first possibility. Citizens are citizens of a regime; they do not merely rule—they rule in a certain way according to a certain order in institutions that make the order of the regime visible. When the order of the regime visibly changes, when the regime takes on a new shape, then the city is no longer the same. But the form is not *above* the matter, or above human beings, as in the second possibility; it is *in* them. Human beings, having a political nature, are capable of receiving a political form. Indeed, one never sees men who do not possess some political inclination, typically either democratic or oligarchic; men are never unformed, like pure matter, nor unformable, like water. Therefore, the power of convention or of making in politics is the power to *change* the form, not a power to make out of malleable matter, as the artisan who makes a pot. A political founder can only make in another form what has already been made in one form. The initial making does not define the city forever, as does the artisan's making of a pot; hence, the interesting question is not whether citizens are made (they have indeed been made but are always capable of being remade), but how they are made and for what end.

Political science does not fully endorse the citizen's obliviousness of the origins of his citizenship, because in forgetting that citizenship is made, the citizen may unduly narrow his range of choice and give away too much to the power of custom. But when political science investigates the founding of a city, it is to see the intent of the founders as made visible in the form of the constitution or regime they founded. It is not to suppose that founders are omnipotent artisans of the whole who confer all meaning on the communities they found. Thus, political science enlarges the citizen's perspective without attempting to change the end he has in view, which is the good of the whole community.

In Aristotle's constitutionalism, form is more important than matter, but the form is united with the end because it reveals the end.[5] Respecting the forms of a constitution is respecting its character, and respecting its character is living according to that constitution when it is most itself, at its best. The reality of a constitution, therefore, is not opposed to its form, as if its form were a "mere formality," as we say; on the contrary, the reality of a city, Aristotle said, is especially its constitution or regime. Our liberal democracy is a certain form but also has a certain end, and in Aristotle's view its end is identical with itself as a form. Its end as a liberal democracy is to live by the forms of liberal democracy; if it did not live by those forms it would not be behaving as a liberal democracy, as itself, and so could not achieve its end.

The difficulty in Aristotle's conception is evident: it provides no clear standard by which to judge among constitutions. What is the true end of a constitution, and which is its correct form? Aristotle seems to run the risk of relativism. Since each constitution has its own end in its own form, each appears to have its own reality. Aristotle is surely aware of this difficulty. He immediately turns to a discussion of the good man, who is not relative to his constitution, and the good citizen, who is (*Politics* 1276b16–1277b33); indeed, he devotes the rest of Book 3 to a consideration of this difficulty. But Aristotle himself does not claim to solve it,[6] and the tendency of his discussion toward the absolute monarchy of the good man was unsatisfactory to Locke and to modern constitutionalism generally.

Locke's Constitutionalism

Modern constitutionalism appears to take the Heraclitean choice in the alternative Aristotle posed; it appears to say that the constitution or regime does not determine the city or country, but the matter does. The matter is human nature, especially the passions, and the task of the constitution maker is to invent institutions that will direct the passions into useful or acceptable channels. Any more ambitious conception of founding that endows the constitution maker with formative power to make men good according to an exacting definition will not work: it will make them zealous for good, rather than good. Thus, in *Federalist* 10 the "latent causes of faction" are said to be "sown in the nature of man"; and the cure is, not to try to improve human nature, but to "involve the spirit of party and faction in the necessary and ordinary operations of government." It is easy to exaggerate the mechanical character of the "institutional political science" that generated and supports modern constitutionalism, and one can insist too much on the high-mindedness of Aristotle,[7] but the contrast between ancient forming and modern channeling remains sound.

Yet the human nature that modern constitutions channel cannot be considered mere matter. Human beings are not a formless sea of humanity; they are not body but bodies, and each body has a form and an end that, though common to other bodies, distinguish it from other bodies: the self and its preservation. Men are not unformed; the form is given by nature—in the state of nature, according to Locke. This form is arranged and managed in the constitution of civil society, but is not itself changed by the constitution maker. Rather than being a Heraclitean, then, Locke is indebted to Aristotle; he accepts Aristotle's solution to the problem raised by Gorgias. His constitutionalism is not merely materialistic, for it does respect the form of man in the state of nature. It is based on an original, perfect democracy of men equal in the state of nature (*Two Treatises*, 2:132); this is the natural form or constitution that may proceed to establish itself or any other form in civil society.

Civil constitutions exist to serve and protect the form and end that men have in the state of nature, the rights of *man*, not of citizens. If there are rights of citizens only—and the trend in American constitutional law has been to expand the rights of citizens to all persons—that is because the rights of man are best protected in independent communities that are obliged to prefer, as they enlist, their own citizens. It is not that the rights of man have ceased to become relevant as the standard of constitutions. Man-made constitutions are conceived to secure natural rights: the man-made form is for the protection of the natural form and end.

Modern constitutionalism, therefore, has a great advantage over Aristotle's constitutionalism. Unlike Aristotle's, it has a clear standard by which to judge regimes: do they respect the rights of man? Despite all the difficulties of applying this standard—for example, in recent American foreign policy—no one has found or even sought a clearer one. Or do those difficulties reveal that the standard is not so clear as it seems? For we do not know whether to uphold the sanctity of constitutionalism or to secure the protection of life, to focus on the form or the end, and in a pinch we sacrifice the form to the end; we find that nonconstitutional regimes must be tolerated because they better serve our end or even the end of their own peoples. In recent American foreign policy liberals have found excuses for the nonconstitutional Sandinista regime in Nicaragua; conservatives preferred to forgive the trespasses of the nonconstitutional Pinochet regime in Chile. Both parties can bear witness to the unclarity of human rights as a standard for policy.

The trouble with modern constitutionalism is that civil liberties and man-made constitutional forms are made subordinate to the natural end that comprises life, liberty, and the pursuit of happiness. They are *means* to that end, not united with it; the form is not united with the end, as in Aristotle's constitutionalism. Hence, we are willing to jettison our liberal constitutional forms if they do not achieve their end. Indeed, all respect for rights remain exposed to a similar judgment, whether it is exercised constitutionally by an executive in an emergency when there is no time for due process, or legitimately by a people that is fed up with tyranny, or illegitimately by citizens who, as Tocqueville said, "rush impetuously toward the object of each of their desires." Although we know that respect for rights requires us to put the form or due process ahead of the end, we are always tempted by the liberal argument itself to a Machiavellian decision to treat the form as means to the end.[8] So the status of constitutional forms is in doubt under modern constitutionalism. Precisely because the standard for judging forms appears to be so clear and unforgiving, the standard tends to undermine them. Despite its nonliberal sources, the populist perversion of liberal constitutionalism is the realization of an inherent liability within liberal constitutionalism.

No better illustration of this problem could be found than in property. According to Locke, the end of government is the protection of property. By *property* he usually means external goods in the ordinary sense, but he also uses the term in an enlarged sense that includes "Life, Liberty and Estate" (*Two Treatises*, 2:87, 123, 173). What justifies the enlarged sense? Property in its ordinary sense supplies the needs of life, but in its enlarged sense it protects both liberty and life. If your property is secure, your liberty is secure; and if your liberty is secure, your life is secure (*Two Treatises*, 2:17, 174, 193–94). It is not that property in the narrow sense is more valuable than liberty and life. Rather, property is a convention or form enlarged out of its matter so that it becomes an end in itself. We know, then, that if anyone's property is insecure, everyone's is insecure. Property is a whole that includes all members of society as well as all the objects of their desires. It includes them formally or conventionally, not only because property is defined by laws in civil society (*Two Treatises*, 2:50, 138), but also because property is here considered as a formality without regard to whether it is equal or enough. However rich or poor anyone may be, all profit from having a right to property; and in a sense, because liberty and life are good without regard to how they are used, all profit equally. The equality of the property right is shown in the connection or identification between property and consent. Since property is what cannot be taken from you without your consent (that is, the consent of a majority; *Two Treatises*, 2:138–40), the right to property becomes the visible, formal protection of the right of consent. This is the connection, so often hastily dismissed today, between property rights and human rights.[9]

Yet of course it is not wrong to question whether property rights protect human rights. Suppose indeed that property rights are exercised so unequally that the many live in misery at the mercy of a few; what then? To meet this objection, Locke does not leave his argument at the formal enlargement of property; he also promises material increase. Unequal property for some will bring more property for all. In his famous phrase, a savage king in America "feeds, lodges and is clad worse than a day laborer in England" (*Two Treatises*, 2:41). Through material increase of property all profit, though some profit more. Here Locke introduces a reference to the end, to a standard of performance: Are you better off? Even if the answer is yes (for now), this question is not the same as asking whether your rights are being respected. At the least, the first question ensures that liberal societies will be infested with economists as well as lawyers. At worst, we may believe it compels us to sacrifice our rights in a futile attempt to force the equal exercising of them.

15
Constitutional Government: The Soul of Modern Democracy

Although modern democracy is unhappy with the word *soul*, it has one nonetheless; and its soul is not healthy today. The disease is widely known as *dependency*, the popular disposition, denounced mainly by conservatives, to depend on others, especially government, to secure one's well-being. This disease extends beyond welfare dependency in the narrow sense to include all who depend on their entitlements in a society that no longer requires or encourages (and often does not permit) free choice. The liberal version of dependency, heard a generation ago, was *apathy* toward social problems; and the radical or neo-Marxist term has been *false consciousness* distracting the people from revolution.

Clearly a similar concern exists in diverse quarters, but is defined diversely in partisan modes. One might be tempted to object that the complaints cancel each other out because each is aimed at the others. One might add that to be concerned with one's health is a sign of health rather than of dependency, apathy, or false consciousness. But these objections to the diagnosis are complacent. If nothing else, the authority of Tocqueville, whose word is worth far more than our perceptions (because it is based on his), should prompt us to fear the onset of *individualism*, as he called the disease.[1] The similarity in the complaints we hear today suggests that each may have told of an important truth in its own way, though not necessarily with equal discernment. And the healthiness of concern for one's health depends on the cure one chooses.

To understand this disease of modern democracy, we should begin by comparing it to the evil that the American founders feared from popular government when they made the Constitution. We see quickly that, whereas we fear a people with too little spirit and activity, they feared one with too much spirit and aggressiveness. Whereas we fear an apathetic or dependent majority that does not know how to claim its rights or to exercise them, they feared an overbearing majority faction—Madison's famous argument in *Federalist* 10 leaps to mind. The founders' remedy against an overactive people was a constitution that puts government at a distance from the people. By contrast to previous republics outside America, this one was entirely representative; the people could not act themselves but could only elect others to act in their place. These representatives (in the federal government) had longer terms of office than were usual even in the American states. And since within the government the founders were most wary of "legislative usurpation" from the branch closest to the people, they built a strong executive and an independent judiciary to stand up against the people. These two branches were said to be *derived* from the people and to be acting in the *interest* of the people, but their strength, it was thought, would not be exercised at the *behest* of the people. On the contrary, these two essentially nonrepublican institutions, whose democratic legitimacy we now take for granted, were originally intended to oppose the momentary inclinations of the people. This popular government would not *lead* the people ("leadership" is, as mentioned, used pejoratively in *The Federalist*) so much as *control* it. Imagine an official today who offered his excellent control of the people as an inducement to his reelection. And yet, when one reflects on it, what is so wrong with a people controlling itself through its government? In the choice between government leadership and government control, we note that a people or an individual may achieve *self*-control, but can only *be led* by someone else.

Or must we accept that leadership and control are necessarily in conflict? According to the argument so far, the Constitution would seem to be precisely a combination of the two in which the people governs itself by electing leaders to control it. The Constitution established a limited government not only in the sense that the people set limits to its scope, but also because, in establishing it, the people set limits on itself. Ratifying the Constitution was a choice of the people to set limits on its choice. For if the American people had merely wanted a government to serve it as an instrument, it could have done without a constitution and have set up a system of mandates and commissions. But the essential character of the American Constitution is that, whereas all its parts are *derived* from the people, none of them *is* the people. Indeed, the people that ratified the Constitution in 1787–88, the sovereign people, has disappeared from view except for an occasional appearance to make an amendment (which is not a fully sovereign act because amendments are made under the procedures of the Constitution). The sovereign people has been replaced by the constitutional people, the highest authority to be sure, but highest *under the Constitution*. This "constitutional people" is self-controlled; in its ordinary feelings, it does not want to govern more or otherwise than by electing officials who will govern it.

It appears, then, that the American people, as sovereign, transformed itself with the leadership of the founders into a constitutional people. While retaining its sovereign right under the Declaration of Independence to alter or abolish a defective government and set up a new one, it would do any of these things with the same intent of controlling itself. This intent is stated best in *The Federalist*, the most authoritative, yet unofficial, commentary on the Constitution. Its authors assume that any American government will be popular; therefore, the fundamental distinction to be established is between the two forms of popular governments: republic (good) and democracy (bad).

Republican Governments Old and New

A republic is based on the presumption that *the* problem of popular government comes from within the regime—from factions and tyrannical majorities. So it provides a constitution through which the people chooses to limit itself not by preventing the majority from ruling as in oligarchy, or by retaining a privileged class to rule with the majority as in "mixed government," but by constructing the majority so that it will not be factious and tyrannical. This new kind of republic is contrasted (*Federalist* 9, 10, and 14) to the old kind found in the republican tradition, which is given the pejorative label *democracy*. In democracy, the presumption is that the danger comes from outside the regime—from monarchy and oligarchy. So the popular spirit must be aroused and kept in a state of vigilance against its enemies; and instead of a constitution providing self-chosen limited government, the main requirement is to cultivate this vigilant spirit in republican virtue. Republican virtue, in turn, requires a homogeneous people and a small territory so that citizens can know and trust one another. The Antifederalist opponents of the Constitution promoted this combination in what has been called the "small-republic argument," a considerably modified version of classical republicanism.

Both kinds of popular government are by choice, it was thought. For whatever may be said in favor of the rule of the wise or of the few most virtuous, monarchy and oligarchy in practice come down to hereditary rule. The alternative, then, appeared to be between government the people choose and government imposed by chance through heredity: To be republican was to opt for choice. Since choice is a certain activity of the soul, republicanism was the choice to establish and protect that activity in the soul. Its claim was not to make a people richer or more secure but to make it free—and free not in the sense of more mobile or more capricious, but in the sense of free to choose.

Yet how free to choose can a people be? This was the issue between *The Federalist* and the Antifederalists. A people would not choose to limit itself in a constitution if there were no difficulties in its choosing. Classical or primitive republicanism, with its dependence on a small territory, homogeneous people, and cultivated virtues, exaggerates the extent of human choice. But the new constitutional republicanism takes account of things in nature and by chance that cannot be chosen and joins them to things that can be chosen. A republic might prefer to live by itself, under a homogeneous majority, and with virtues to keep it moderate. But a regard to the necessities of international relations and of human nature will reveal that these desirable things are beyond the power of human choice. Taught by the new political science of *The Federalist*, a republic will not choose what is, abstractly, most choice-worthy, but will be content with, or indeed make the best of, a large territory, a diverse people, and a spirit of interest and ambition.

It is characteristic of the American Constitution, by contrast with republican tradition, to *constitutionalize* necessities. Those necessities limiting our choice, which we would like to wish away, are brought into the Constitution so that the people, through its government, can choose how to deal with them after having anticipated the necessity of dealing with them. The difference between republic and democracy—or in our terms, between constitutional democracy and pure democracy (or classical republicanism)—is made by a constitution that constitutionalizes the necessities limiting political choice. Whereas a pure democracy is small, homogeneous, and (it hopes) virtuous, a constitutional democracy is large, diverse, and ambitious, and represents those necessities in its constitution.

Necessities represented in the Constitution must also be represented in the souls of American citizens. The warmth of their republican genius must somehow be cooled; the confidence in their own sovereignty, which is responsible for the factiousness of democratic majorities, must be restrained. The Constitution is designed to make reason paramount over the passions: It is "the reason, alone, of the public that ought to control and regulate the government. The passions ought to be controlled and regulated by the government" (*Federalist* 49). Control of the people by government must be control of the passions by reason, by the *public*'s reason since this government is not an aristocracy of the wise. The "cool and deliberate sense of the community" must be found (*Federalist* 63). This is the job of the Constitution, which has been made with the aid of a new political science. The new political science, based on constitutionalists such as Locke, Hume, and Montesquieu, but more republican than they, will teach republicans to put government at arm's length, out of immediate control, instead of within their grasp, as in classical republicanism. The public's reason will then be enabled to rise above the passion or interest of a temporary majority, and the horrifying alternation between anarchy and tyranny that has characterized heretofore the histories of republics will be avoided.

The Scientific Concept of *Interest*

It has become quite usual, on the Right as well as the Left, to misunderstand the cooling or sobering effect of the Constitution as an innovation that makes it unnecessary to worry about souls. It is believed that the framers meant to replace the difficult and disputable notion of soul with a scientific concept of *interest*. Woodrow Wilson, the first president to criticize the Constitution as a whole, blamed it for being based on an obsolete eighteenth-century version of Newtonian mechanics. Others in our day have praised it for anticipating the magic of cybernetics, for being "the machine that would work of itself." One prominent conservative, George Will, has denied that the Constitution is an exercise in "soulcraft." Behind these views is the opinion that the *limits* to choice introduced by the Constitution to cool the republican consciousness extend to the *elimination* of choice, insofar as possible.

When choice has been eliminated, human behavior becomes predictable with exactness, not merely as a trend or a tendency. In this condition, it does not matter what citizens have in their souls that may prompt them to act constitutionally, or in such manner as to make the Constitution work properly. Instead of looking into their souls—surely a difficult and dubious enterprise—one may simply consult their self-interest. Any departure from self-interest becomes quickly or visibly evident to an observer, and, except in the case of stupidity or stubbornness, also to the person concerned. The Constitution so understood works automatically. It may have flaws because the interactions of self-interest have been miscalculated, but these can be corrected by knowledgeable, state-of-the-art political scientists. These political scientists may disagree in their diagnoses, but only temporarily, for their studies will accumulate and converge on an ascertainable standard, the self-interest of a rational actor. If one adds the intention of the framers to this convergence, then the machine has an identifiable manufacturer.

As between those who approve of such a system and those who deplore it, it is hard not to side with the latter. They are correct to say that the Constitution so understood bears a strong resemblance to the disease of the soul from which we began—the dependency discerned variously by

Tocqueville and critics today. A system of interests, indeed, is nothing other than the rigorous definition of a nation of dependents. To be independent, one must choose; but it is often expensive to choose and easier—less costly, annoying, or dangerous—to let someone else choose for you. *Interest* is the concept that allows someone else to choose for you because you do not choose your interest, and it can be imputed to you as a "rational actor." In the literature of rational actors, it is notorious that no justification can be found for the act of voting. Since your absence at the polls will not be noticed, it is rational for you to stay home and be a "free rider." Here is the fundamental act of constitutional sovereignty found foolish, and the come-to-me apathy of the consumer in a service economy and entitlements polity pronounced reasonable. A system of interests wants to know for sure how you will behave. It cannot tolerate the indeterminacy of hoping for the chance that you may act according to the virtue in your soul. So it proceeds as if that virtue were unnecessary and, in doing so, *makes* it unnecessary. Citizens have nothing to live up to, nothing to sacrifice for, no sense of honor, no pride. All they have is their interest, rather, their separate interests, to which their freedom is a hindrance and the state of their souls an irrelevance.

Fortunately, it seems clear that the founders did not foist such a system of interests on us. The description of the Constitution in *The Federalist* does not sustain this interpretation, not even the analyses in *Federalist* 10 and 51, which are the main reliances of the automatic or mechanical view. In *Federalist* 10, one does not indeed find an argument for representative as opposed to direct popular government, and for an extensive rather than a small republic; and to control majority faction, it is said, an increased variety of parties and sects will succeed when moral and religious motives alone will not. But citizens are expected to desire liberty as well as to promote their interests, to form parties to advance their opinions as well as to protect their property, and to elect "fit characters" as well as to check the sinister influence of dominant majorities.

Not only the people but also those who run for office are expected to be virtuous. The famous phrase in *Federalist* 51 "Ambition must be made to counteract ambition" is often cited as proof of the self-interested character of the Constitution. But the "rational actor," we have seen, is more likely to be a free rider than an ambitious man. He will let someone else do the work, take the risk, and suffer the indignity of running for office. And, in fact, if the system of ambition counteracting itself works, no personal gains in office can be hoped for. The ambition allowed, even encouraged, in the working of the Constitution is surely a departure from the suspicion of one-man rule characteristic of republics previous to this one. It is a sober accommodation to the desire for self-promotion in human nature. But it does not forget the pride in achievement also to be found in human nature.

Adam Smith distinguished between the "sober undertaking" characteristic of the self-interested and the "spirited undertaking" in which a glory-seeker will waste his substance. But the framers of the Constitution, with better understanding of politics, hence of human nature, recognized that it was sobriety to take care of the spirited desire to choose, in the people, and to succeed, in the ambitious. Instead of establishing a government that requires and cultivates republican virtue, the Constitution calls it forth. The virtue called forth in our constitutional republic is less martial and less egalitarian than in the direct democracies and mixed republics that *Federalist* 10 blames for "instability, injustice and confusion." But since sobriety and love of honor are not automatically produced, they remain virtues. If they are consistent with each other and with human nature, and so altogether more reliable as republican virtue than the classical version, this does not make them dispensable or detract from them as virtues.

Virtue and Interest

Still, one might object: How can a constitution that says nothing of education be concerned with souls? The answer is, indirectly. The Constitution, by implication, leaves education to the states. But it does so, not out of unconcern, but to encourage local communities in the states to provide education. The new federalism (as it was then) of the Constitution allows the people to use government without being awed by its size, and so to organize a common life without becoming prisoners of organization. And in the federal government, separation of powers has a similar effect and intent, as we have seen in Chapters 9 and 11. The formal characteristics of the three branches of government (term, mode of appointment, powers) imply appropriate virtues in officeholders if the job is to be done well. But such specifications, because they are formal, do not expressly call for virtue. To do so would suggest the natural superiority of a virtuous, or in practice, propertied elite contrary to the republican principle of election.

The Constitution cannot guarantee success in the discovery and election of persons with the requisite qualities to take advantage of the opportunities of these offices for the exercise of virtue. To provide such a guarantee, even if it were somehow possible, would detract from the voluntariness of choosing to seek office and of electing. Virtue cannot be guaranteed without losing its character as virtue. But the Constitution can improve the chances for virtue; it can set up a tendency to responsible government. Responsible government is responsive to the people, but it also takes responsibility out of the hands of the people on their behalf.

The Federalist's interpretation of the Constitution stresses the voluntary rather than the habitual or cultivated side of virtue. A certain understatement may be more effective and appropriate than exhortation. Virtue may go under the modest name of *interest*, as when the long term of a president is said to create his "interest" in avoiding "servile pliancy" to a prevailing current either in the people or in the legislature (*Federalist* 71). Interest in the office is a republican concealment of virtue. This is the "interest" of the kind of person who cannot live by his interest in the more usual, confined sense of the word, but insists instead on taking the risks necessary to be known as an energetic president. (And *energy* is another term, introduced by *The Federalist* and now ever so American, by which we mean virtue and say less.) In the same spirit of constitutionalized democracy, Americans today use a distinction between short-term and long-term interest to hide their virtue. *Short-term* interest is really your interest, and *long-term* interest is really your duty; but the choice between them sounds more voluntary, less demanded, if both options are kinds of interest. A respectable journal would hesitate to use the name *Public Virtue*, but this does not mean that every consideration of interest belongs in the *Journal of Sordid Calculation*.[2]

It is of course important that, under the influence of our political science, the word *virtue* has largely been replaced by *interest*; but this usage does not imply that the qualities once designated as virtues or helpers of virtue are such no longer. They remain virtues, and (in a sense I have been arguing) all the more so for lacking the praise and splendor usually accorded the virtues. The vital question, however, is whether we continue to think, with the founders, that virtue must be *self*-generated, or now believe that virtue will be *automatically* generated. The latter is destructive of virtue as voluntary, hence destructive of the independence of citizens. It seems that, by the realism of not exhorting to virtue, we are attempting to add voluntariness to it because virtue not required is freer and even nobler. But virtue not required is also the essence of the permissiveness we deplore today, for the worst thing about permissiveness is not that everything is permitted, but that, given this condition, *nothing interesting happens*.

The Realm of the Soul

How did it come about that virtue is not required but somehow expected under our Constitution? To explain our embarrassment with the notion of *virtue*, we must see why modern democracy is unhappy with the word *soul*. For virtue was once thought to be the virtue of a soul directed or inclined to an end that is beyond the satisfaction of mere bodily appetites. What is this higher end? The classical political philosophers such as Plato and Aristotle tried to define it, but in practice, in politics, the higher end was defined by religion, and by each religion in an exclusive and contentious recipe for saving one's soul. The constitutionalist philosophers, above all John Locke, decided that this issue—the religious issue—could be solved if the human desire for seeking higher ends could be contained. Locke attempted to do so by establishing a distinction that is the basis of modern constitutionalism.

Modern constitutional government is limited government, as we have seen; and the limitation on government is expressed in the distinction between *state* and *society*. Difficulties arise for the constitutional distinction between state and society, and for limited government, when (or because) the soul is not content with ruling itself but tries to rule other souls. It was to prevent such abuse in the form of religious intolerance that the constitutional distinction was established. When the soul seeks a higher principle than self-preservation, it is sure to find one that justifies rule of others besides yourself. Self-preservation as an end may be universal, but it is also quite personal to your own body and does not justify interference with others (this individuality was its advantage to Locke). But salvation and virtue prompt devotion and sacrifice. And if these ends hurt me, why not you too? A higher principle that asks much of oneself may reasonably, must rationally, make demands on others. If others cannot or will not comply, they deserve compulsion or contempt, not tolerance.

Therefore, to contain the soul, one must diminish it. To keep one person's soul from claiming jurisdiction over others' souls so as to tell others what to do and how to live, it is necessary to reduce his capacity for ruling himself. To keep one person (or an aristocratic few) from choosing for others and becoming responsible for them, it is necessary to limit the scope of his choice and responsibility for himself. That is why, in the psychology of Locke and the thinkers who followed him, the notion of necessity begins to replace choice, and interest begins to replace virtue. If you *have* to act as you do because it is your necessity or your interest, you cannot blame others, and claim to *rule* them, because they do the same. Paradoxically, liberty can be advanced and secured to a degree never before seen in the world if only individuals can be convinced that each is less free to choose than it had previously been acceptable to believe.

Ruling Oneself—and Others

Constitutionalism then faces a dilemma that helps to explain the condition of democratic souls today. On the one hand, limited, constitutional government requires that the people and society be independent and distrustful of the state. For how can the state serve society if society craves the state? If government is to remain limited, individuals must be able to stand on their own feet and rule themselves, to a considerable extent at least. They must be able to feel that they control government rather than the reverse. But on the other hand, if the people feel themselves independent and capable of ruling themselves, what prevents them from extending their sense of responsibility, not merely to the behavior, but to the souls of others? From the example used in Chapter 8 of the abortion debate, we recall that the pro-choice party chooses for others just as much, though in a contrary direction, as the pro-life party. From this one can infer that the desire to rule others derives from the desire to rule oneself, so that there is something dangerous to liberty in the responsible individual. It is better, as we have seen, that he should stick to his interest and forget about his soul. But then, as we have also seen, your interest can make you the servant of whoever serves your interest, leaving you dependent and apathetic and suffering under the false consciousness that being a free rider is the same as being free. Constitutionalism demands a people that is independent, but not so much as to think itself capable of governing without a constitution; it needs a sense of responsibility that is aware of the limits to responsibility.

Modern constitutionalism began with a defense of the independence of the human soul against the claims of divine right. But the very measures taken to protect the soul have reduced its independence so that we are embarrassed to use the word. For us, to speak of *soul* smacks of religion, yet we cannot help feeling that the *self* is something much less noble than the soul, and when used (as it often is) in the sense of automatic, much less free too. We should not be surprised, then, even from the standpoint of constitutionalism, let alone that of religion, that the demon of divine right still needs to be exorcised, and that the "lost soul" of Puritan America reappears in a revival of fundamentalist religion. For the fundamentalists are no more wrong than was Nietzsche to protest the flatness of our democratic souls.

For the most part, however, religion under our constitutionalism takes the form of religiosity, which is religion of the self rather than the soul, more concerned with being religious than with God. Religiosity can be associated with either one of two rival conceptions in our day that attempt to inspire independence in the souls of citizens: on the Right, the *work ethic*; on the Left, the *doctrine of the creative self*. Though the work ethic is much to be preferred, both conceptions are defective in what they attempt. The doctrine of creativity does not distinguish valuing from worth, does not identify the truly creative, and ends in flattering democratic vanity. The work ethic is superior because it asks for effort from citizens and requires them to stand up to be judged instead of merely confirming them in their dependence. But the work ethic does not clarify the relationship between the individual responsibility that brings success and the collective responsibility of self-government. Its proponents want to minimize or privatize the public, and they forget that, although the public can be put on a regimen and a diet, it cannot be done away with. For the public comes from our desire to rule, a desire that can be ennobled or perverted but cannot be evaded or extinguished. The spirit of liberty that forms democratic souls must find ways of choosing together as well as protect our choosing apart. Combining them so as to do justice to both is the work of our Constitution.

Notes

Chapter 1   Introduction: Political Science and the Constitution

1. See the recent "new institutionalism" of public choice theorists described by James G. March and Johan P. Olsen, *Rediscovering Institutions: The Organizational Basis of Politics* (New York: Free Press, 1989), esp. ch. 1. On the public or rational choice school see chapter 11 below.

2. Soterios A. Barber ably argues an "aspirational" view of the Constitution; *On What the Constitution Means* (Baltimore: Johns Hopkins University Press, 1984), chs. 2, 4. But, as he knows, it is also necessary to maintain constitutional checks on our aspirations.

Chapter 2   The 1980 Election: Toward Constitutional Democracy?

1. See Richard Rose, ed., *Electoral Participation: A Comparative Analysis* (Beverly Hills: Sage Publications, 1980).

2. See especially Austin Ranney, "The Political Parties: Reform and Decline," and Jeane J. Kirkpatrick, "Changing Patterns of Electoral Competition," in Anthony King, ed., *The New American Political System* (Washington, D.C., American Enterprise Institute, 1978), pp. 213–48, 249–86.

3. James W. Ceaser, *Presidential Selection: Theory and Development* (Princeton: Princeton University Press, 1979), ch. 3.

4. Hugh Heclo, "Issue Networks and the Executive Establishment," in King, *The New American Political System*, pp. 87–124.

5. Abraham Lincoln, "On the Perpetuation of Our Political Institutions," 27 January 1838, in Roy P. Basler, ed., *The Collected Works of Abraham Lincoln*, 9 vols. (New Brunswick, N.J.: Rutgers University Press, 1953), 1:108–15.

Chapter 4   The 1984 Election: Entitlements versus Opportunity

1. Reagan did give two notable speeches earlier in the year on the American soldiers who died in Normandy in 1944 and in Lebanon in 1983.

Chapter 5   The 1988 Election: Another Reagan Triumph

1. This current Americanism identifies, with mock superstition, a word that is needed but is bad luck (or obscene) to pronounce.

2. Jeffrey Tulis, *The Rhetorical Presidency* (Princeton: Princeton University Press, 1987).

3. See Mark Blitz, "The Character of Executive and Legislative Action in a Country Based on Natural Rights," in James W. Muller, ed., *The Revival of Constitutionalism* (Lincoln: University of Nebraska Press, 1988), p. 209.

Chapter 11   Social Science and the Constitution

1. Robert A. Dahl, *A Preface to Democratic Theory* (Chicago: University of Chicago Press, 1956), pp. 149–51.

2. Ibid., p. 135.

3. See Bernard Crick, *The American Science of Politics* (Berkeley: University of California Press, 1959).

4. Jeffrey T. Bergner, *The Origin of Formalism in Social Science* (Chicago: University of Chicago Press, 1981).

5. *The Federalist*, ed. Clinton Rossiter (New York: New American Library, 1961), 6, p. 89; 10, p. 81; 15, p. 106; 36, p. 224; 55, pp. 345–46; 57, pp. 350, 353. See David F. Epstein, *The Political Theory of "The Federalist"* (Chicago: University of Chicago Press, 1984), Intro.; and *The Federalist Concordance*, ed. T. S. Engeman, E. J. Erler, and T. B. Hofeller (Middletown, Conn.: Wesleyan University Press, 1980).

6. *Federalist* 51, p. 324; Epstein, *The Political Theory of "The Federalist,"* pp. 144–46.

7. Compare Plato *Laws* 650b; Aristotle, *Nicomachean Ethics* 1102a8–17.

8. *Federalist* 9, pp. 72–73; 10, p. 77; 14, pp. 100–101. Probably the authors mean Locke, Montesquieu, Hume, and others who took the British Constitution for their model of political liberty.

9. *Federalist* 14, p. 104; 39, p. 240. Useful inheritances are of course acknowledged by *The Federalist*, and *experiment* is not always used in a good sense; see *Federalist* 49, p. 315.

10. See Jack N. Racoue, *The Beginnings of National Politics* (Baltimore: Johns Hopkins University Press, 1982), p. 388.

11. On the first page of *The Federalist* Publius speaks of the danger of a "wrong election" by Americans as to the proposed Constitution.

12. See Epstein, *The Political Theory of "The Federalist,"* pp. 118–25.

13. Note the references to "a handful of tyrannical nobles" within a republic, in *Federalist* 39, p. 241, and to the "hereditary or self-appointed authority" that is rejected in *Federalist* 51, p. 324.

14. See the argument by which Montesquieu progressively exposes these defects of the virtuous ancient republics; *Spirit of the Laws* 4.7, 8; 5.6; 6.9; 7.10; 8.2; 9.1; 11.4.

15. For the notion of constitutionalizing I am indebted to Herbert J. Storing, and also to Gerald Stourzh; see the latter's "Fundamental Laws and Individual Rights in the Eighteenth Century Constitution," Claremont Bicentennial Essay, no. 5 (1984), pp. 14–15.

16. "When a majority is included in a faction, the form of popular government . . . enables it to sacrifice to its ruling passion or interest both the public good and the rights of other citizens," *Federalist* 10, p. 80.

17. "You must first enable the government to control the governed," *Federalist* 51, p. 322.

18. When social scientists question the rationality of voting, they point out

that it is in your interest to take a "free ride," that is, to let someone else exercise your freedom.

19. Epstein's book makes a theme of this "honorable determination," as opposed to the one-sided interpretation of *The Federalist*, based on a quick reading of *Federalist* 10 and 51, as promoting self-interest only; *The Political Theory of "The Federalist,"* Intro. and ch. 4.

20. *Federalist* 43, p. 279; also 28, p. 180; 40, p. 254; 45, p. 289; 51, p. 325.

21. Epstein, *The Political Theory of "The Federalist,"* pp. 40–44, 59–85, 162–55.

22. Ibid., pp. 85, 163.

23. Ibid., p. 165; cf. Gerald Stourzh, *Alexander Hamilton and the Idea of Republican Government* (Stanford: Stanford University Press, 1970), p. 83.

24. For the presidency, see *Federalist* 68, p. 414.

25. Epstein, *The Political Theory of "The Federalist,"* p. 166.

26. Ibid., pp. 179–84; see *Federalist* 70, p. 424.

27. Dahl, *A Preface to Democratic Theory*, p. 21. Great Britain does indeed have a separation of powers: the judiciary is separate, and Members of Parliament who are in the cabinet and those who are outside it have very different functions and powers. So I dispute this "fact" of Dahl's. See also Robert A. Dahl, *Dilemmas of Pluralist Democracy* (New Haven: Yale University Press, 1982), pp. 28, 65–66.

28. Yet in a joint work Dahl and Lindblom describe the "First Problem of Politics" as enabling citizens to "keep their rulers from becoming tyrants." When it comes to facing facts, they can recognize tyranny, the enemy of polyarchy; they have more difficulty in understanding faction, the disease of polyarchy. Robert A. Dahl and Charles E. Lindblom, *Politics, Economics and Welfare*, 2d ed. (Chicago: University of Chicago Press, 1976), pp. 273, 295–97. For them the disease of polyarchy is nothing but its imperfection, which results from concessions to inequality or tyranny.

29. This consequence of the first rule is counteracted, as will be seen in regard to *utility*, by the social science relativism that accepts wishful, boastful *preferences* in the place of solid *interests*. But the reason for this acceptance is that interests, which were originally discovered so as to avoid argument, have been found to be arguable after all. In the current phrase *revealed preferences*, *revealed* represents the behavioral element, the *preferences* one acts upon; but preference in its ordinary sense is so flabby and concessive that social scientists still speak of interest (for example, the national interest) in contexts in which some insistence is likely.

30. Behavioralizing the formal, formalizing the behavioral is but a restatement of Galileo's resolutive-compositive method. See Thomas Hobbes, *De Cive*, preface.

31. See Douglass Adair, *Fame and the Founding Fathers*, ed. T. Colbourn (New York: W. W. Norton, 1974); *Federalist* 72, p. 437.

32. Robert A. Dahl, *Polyarchy: Participation and Opposition* (New Haven: Yale University Press, 1971), p. 203. Dahl and Lindblom seem ready to promote the cause of polyarchy, but then their recommendation is lost in the elaboration

of the "necessary conditions" of polyarchy which make recommendation superfluous; Dahl and Lindblom, *Politics, Economics, and Welfare*, pp. 275–323.

33. Robert A. Dahl, *Pluralist Democracy in the United States* (Chicago: Rand McNally, 1967), ch. 2; *A Preface to Democratic Theory*, p. 150.

34. Calvin C. Jillson, "Constitution-Making: Alignment and Re-Alignment in the Federal Convention of 1787," *American Political Science Review* 75 (1982): 598.

35. William H. Riker, "The Heresthetics of Constitution-Making: The Presidency in 1787, with Comments on Determinism and Rational Choice," *American Political Science Review* 78 (1984): 1–16. Despite Riker's insistence (or is it merely a preference?) the role for choice is not "fully preserved" in his heresthetics; see Aristotle, *Nicomachean Ethics* 1112a13–1112b12, 1140a32–1140b2.

36. In *Polyarchy* Dahl speaks of a hypothetical innovator who might wish to establish a polyarchy; he is prudently advised to consult the familiar experience of "the most durable representative democracies"! *Polyarchy*, pp. 215, 227.

37. Dahl, *A Preface to Democratic Theory*, p. 150.

38. Ibid., p. 143.

39. See Robert A. Dahl, "On Removing Certain Impediments to Democracy in the United States" and the critique by James W. Ceaser, "In Defense of Republican Constitutionalism: A Reply to Dahl," in Robert H. Horwitz, ed., *The Moral Foundations of the American Republic*, 3d ed. (Charlottesville: University Press of Virginia, 1986). Also, Robert A. Dahl, "Procedural Democracy," in P. Laslett and J. Fishkin, eds., *Philosophy, Politics and Society*, 5th ser. (New Haven: Yale University Press, 1979), pp. 97–133; Dahl, *Who Governs?* (New Haven: Yale University Press, 1961), pp. 1–4; Dahl, *Dilemmas of Pluralist Democracy*, ch. 5.

40. Dahl, *A Preface to Democratic Theory*, p. 133. In regard to majority rule, Dahl and others take note of Kenneth J. Arrow's voters' paradox, which argues that imprecision in determining a majority denies it reality; Dahl, *Dilemmas of Pluralist Democracy*, p. 139. William H. Riker, *Liberalism against Populism* (San Francisco: W. H. Freeman, 1982), pp. 236–38.

41. Dahl, *A Preface to Democratic Theory*, pp. 54, 124, 132.

42. Perhaps even by Dahl's definition, ibid, p. 135. See Anthony Downs's phrase "duly constituted election," *An Economic Theory of Democracy* (New York: Harper, 1957), p. 25.

43. Aristotle, *Politics* 1294b8; see Julien Freund, *L'Essence du Politique* (Paris: Sirey, 1951), p. 329.

44. Dahl, *A Preface to Democratic Theory*, pp. 133, 143. Slavery, needless to say, is a political question. See also Dahl, *Dilemmas of Pluralist Democracy*, pp. 91–93.

45. James M. Buchanan and Gordon Tullock, *The Calculus of Consent: Logical Foundations of Constitutional Democracy* (Ann Arbor: University of Michigan Press, 1962). This model does not presuppose any difference between a constitutional intention and an ordinary political one, and it does not claim that ordinary politics would be affected by the actual making of its merely logical constitution.

46. John von Neumann and Oskar Morganstern, *The Theory of Games and Economic Behavior* (Princeton: Princeton University Press, 1944, 2d ed. 1947).

47. William Riker, *The Theory of Political Coalitions* (New Haven: Yale University Press, 1962), pp. 22, 30.

48. Downs, *An Economic Theory of Democracy*, pp. 11, 74; Buchanan and Tullock, *The Calculus of Consent*, pp. 23–24.

49. Riker, *The Theory of Political Coalitions*, pp. 31, 210. Buchanan refers to Spinoza as a precursor, but Spinoza, who was not an economist, believed in the natural right of big fish to swallow little fish; Buchanan and Tullock, *The Calculus of Consent*, pp. 312–13.

50. Aristotle, *Physics* 197a7–8.

51. Buchanan and Tullock, *The Calculus of Consent*, p. 5 and subtitle *Logical Foundations of Constitutional Democracy*.

52. Downs, *An Economic Theory of Democracy*, p. 3.

53. Riker, *The Theory of Political Coalitions*, p. 8.

54. In Hume, utility promotes solid *social virtues* over dubious *eminent qualities*; *An Enquiry Concerning the Principles of Morals*, sec. 2, 5. In Bentham, utility is contrasted to *sentiment* or *caprice*; *An Introduction to the Principles of Morals and Legislation*, ch. 1. And even J. S. Mill, who greatly expands *utility*, recommends it in contrast to transcendental theories; *Utilitarianism*, ch. 3.

55. Riker, *The Theory of Political Coalitions*, p. 8.

56. Ibid., p. 15.

57. Ibid., p. 33.

58. Buchanan and Tullock, *The Calculus of Consent*, pp. 286, 301; Dahl, *A Preface to Democratic Theory*, p. 151; Riker, *The Theory of Political Coalitions*, p. 243 (end).

59. Buchanan and Tullock, *The Calculus of Consent*, p. 191; Dahl, *A Preface to Democratic Theory*, p. 68.

60. Riker, *The Theory of Political Coalitions*, chs. 5, 9.

61. Downs, *An Economic Theory of Democracy*, p. 7. Edward C. Banfield, in reproof of Downs, defines *homo economicus* the old-fashioned way, as one who seeks to make money; *Here the People Rule: Selected Essays* (New York: Plenum Press, 1985), ch. 20.

62. Lindblom distinguishes *volitions* from preferences as having been influenced or determined by the attempt to persuade. But which—influenced or determined? As merely influenced, they are beyond the reach of social science; as determined, they are no more than different preferences. Charles E. Lindblom, *Politics and Markets* (New York: Basic Books, 1977), pp. 134–43.

63. Downs, *An Economic Theory of Democracy*, ch. 14; Buchanan and Tullock, *The Calculus of Consent*, p. 133. Howard Margolis has remarked on this anomaly; *Selfishness, Altruism and Rationality* (Cambridge: Cambridge University Press, 1982). He is an excellent critic of public choice from within; Steven E. Rhoads is the same from outside; *The Economist's View of the World* (Cambridge: Cambridge University Press, 1985).

64. See Buchanan and Tullock, *The Calculus of Consent*, pp. 283, 285, for a failed attempt to understand a constitution as an end in itself.

65. See Buchanan and Tullock, *The Calculus of Consent*, p. 11, in which it is unclear whether the rational individual is truly a human possibility or merely a postulate of "Western philosophical tradition."

Chapter 12   The Media World and Constitutional Democracy

1. *New York Times*, 19–20 July 1978.
2. Aristotle, *Politics* 1253a2–18.
3. Alexander Solzhenitsyn, "The Exhausted West," *Harvard Magazine* 80 (July–August 1978): 23.
4. Tocqueville, *Democracy in America*, trans. George Lawrence (New York: Doubleday, 1969), 2.2.2–3, pp. 506–9.
5. I am indebted to Bernard Cazes for this observation.
6. Solzhenitsyn. *"The Exhausted West,"* p. 23.
7. Tocqueville, *Democracy in America*, 1.1.5, p. 66 and 1.2.10, p. 397.
8. Paul H. Weaver, in George F. Will, ed., *Press, Politics and Popular Government* (Washington, D.C.: American Enterprise Institute Press, 1972), p. 38; and George Anastaplo, "Self-Government and the Mass Media: A Practical Man's Guide," in ibid., pp. 193, 197, 217.
9. Tocqueville, *Democracy in America*, 2.1.1, pp. 429–33.
10. Ibid., 1.2.5, pp. 198, 229; 2.1.2, pp. 198, 229; 2.1.2, pp. 434–35.
11. Solzhenitsyn, "The Exhausted West," p. 23; Walter Berns, "The Constitution and Responsible Press," in Harry M. Clor, ed., *The Mass Media and Modern Democracy* (Chicago: Rand McNally, 1974), p. 130.
12. Douglass Cater, *The Fourth Branch of Government* (Boston: Houghton Mifflin, 1959); Marshall McLuhan, *Understanding Media* (New York: McGraw-Hill, 1964), p. 213.
13. Anastaplo, *Press, Politics and Popular Government*, p. 195; McLuhan, *Understanding Media*, chs. 21. 31.
14. Aristotle, *Politics* 1273a27, 1294b9.

Chapter 13   Tocqueville and the Future of the American Constitution

1. Alexis de Tocqueville, *Democracy in America*, trans. George Lawrence (New York: Doubleday, 1969), 2.4.6, p. 690.
2. Charles A. Beard, *An Economic Interpretation of the Constitution of the United States* (New York: Macmillan, 1913), ch. 6; J. Allen Smith, *The Spirit of American Government* (New York: Macmillan, 1907), ch. 3; Richard Hofstadter, *The Progressive Historians* (New York: Knopf, 1968), p. 247.
3. Robert E. Brown, *Charles Beard and the Constitution* (Princeton: Princeton University Press, 1956); Forrest McDonald, *We the People: The Economic Origins of the Constitution* (Chicago: University of Chicago Press, 1958); Lee Benson, *Turner and Beard* (Glencoe, Ill.: Free Press, 1960).
4. Gordon S. Wood, for example, while ignoring Beard, does finally seem to say in his own name that the Constitution is not consistent with the democratic principles of 1776; *Creation of the American Republic, 1776–1787* (Chapel Hill:

University of North Carolina Press, 1969), pp. 294n, 524, 562, 606. Martin Diamond, "Democracy and *The Federalist*," *American Political Science Review* 53 (1959): 52–68.

5. *Federalist* 10 has never been better analyzed than in David Epstein's recent book, *The Political Theory of "The Federalist"* (Chicago: University of Chicago Press, 1984), ch. 3.

6. See the excellent *Federalist Concordance*, ed. Thomas S. Engeman, Edward J. Erler, and Thomas B. Hofeller (Middletown, Conn.: Wesleyan University Press, 1980).

7. " . . . what [persons and groups] are entitled to is not proportional to nor dependent upon their intrinsic worth." John Rawls, *A Theory of Justice* (Cambridge: Harvard University Press, 1971), p. 311.

8. Tocqueville, *Democracy in America* 2.2.3–5.

9. Tocqueville calls the science of association the "mother science" (2.2.5), and then, referring back to this statement, calls the art of association the "mother art" (2.2.7).

Chapter 14   The Forms and Formalities of Liberty

1. *Washington Post*, 30 November 1980. Alexis de Tocqueville, *Democracy in America*, trans. Henry Reeve (New York: Vintage Books, 1945), 2.2.18, pp. 161–62, 2.3.5, 187–95.

2. See the "Statement of Edward J. Erler on the Voting Rights Act for the Senate Committee on the Judiciary, Subcommittee on the Constitution," (Washington, D.C., Government Printing Office, 1982) 28 January 1982; Abigail M. Thernstrom, *Whose Votes Count: Affirmative Action and Minority Voting Rights* (Cambridge: Harvard University Press, 1987); Walter Berns, "Voting Rights and Wrongs," *Commentary* 81 (March 1982): 31–36.

3. Especially *Reynolds v. Sims*, 377 U.S. 533 (1964).

4. For the argument that follows, I have relied on Leo Strauss, *The City and Man* (Chicago: Rand McNally, 1964), ch. 1; Harry V. Jaffa, "Aristotle" in *A History of Political Philosophy*, 2d ed., ed. Leo Strauss and Joseph Cropsey (Chicago: Rand McNally, 1972), pp. 94–100; and Delba Winthrop, "Aristotle and Political Responsibility," *Political Theory* 3 (1975): 406–22, and "Aristotle on Participatory Democracy," *Polity* 2 (1978): 151–71.

5. Aristotle, *Politics* 1276b29–31, 1280b40, 1282b8–13, 1289a13–15.

6. At the end of Book 3 (*Politics* 1288b1), Aristotle admits that the education and habits of a serious man and of a capable citizen are only *almost* the same.

7. In Books 4–6 of the *Politics* Aristotle shows his own deference to the "spirit of party and faction," but always with a view to improvement.

8. Liberal political philosophy today is characterized by an inability to decide between *rights-based* arguments and utilitarian or *consequentialist* arguments; it has lost the ambition of the founders of liberalism to combine them.

9. James Madison: "As a man is said to have a right to his property, he may be equally said to have a property in his rights" (*The Writings of James Madison*, ed. G. Hunt [New York: Putnam's, 1900], 6:101). Daniel Webster: "We have no

experience that teaches us that any other rights are safe where property is not safe" (*The Writings and Speeches of Daniel Webster*, ed. J. McIntyre [Boston: Little, Brown, 1904], 8:170).

Chapter 15   Constitutional Government: The Soul of Modern Democracy

1. "Individualism is a calm and considered feeling which disposes each citizen to isolate himself from the mass of his fellows and withdraw into the circle of family and friends; with this little society formed to his taste, he gladly leaves the greater society to look after itself." Tocqueville, *Democracy in America*, trans. George Lawrence (New York: Doubleday, 1969), 2.2.2, p. 506.

2. This chapter was originally published in the *Public Interest*.

Index

Abortion, 23, 29–30, 59, 79, 103, 218
Absolute, 195; suppression of prejudice as an, 89, 95; Hobbes's sovereign as, 107–8, 111, 116, 118, 141; power, 122, 141; ends as, 145; rights as, 184, 186; monarchy, 205
Accident, 3, 15, 24, 79, 184, 188; vs. intention, in forming institutions, 9, 140–41, 153, 161; natural, Rawls's abstraction from, 130; and social scientists, 150, 161–62. *See also* Arbitrariness; Chance
ACLU, 65
Adams, John, 121
Affirmative action, 23; and Democratic National Party rules, 28; vs. liberalism's forms, 32, 198; Ferraro as, 53–54; vs. Jews, 54; as entitlement, 57; pride and justice in, x, 84–97
AFL-CIO, 53
Ambition: of behavioralists, 4; and interest and virtue, 14, 81, 83, 142, 145, 212, 214–15; of modern political science, 15; and separation of powers, 122–26, 161; of social scientists, 153; and bureaucracy, 187; limits of, 191, 205–6
Anderson, John, 22, 28
Angels: men not, 16, 144; media not, 166
Anger, 24; moralism as cause of, 96; as apathetic individualism, 103; choice not, 129; vs. interest, 152; of communism, 167; to make government caring, 188; of New Left, 196
Antifederalists, 121, 123, 124, 143, 180, 211–12
Aquinas, Thomas, Saint, 129
Arbitrariness, 203; of people and kings, 36; of bureaucracy and judiciary, 97; of "elites," 155–56; of tyranny, 177; vs. formalism, 200
Aristocracy: presidency as, 13; founders reject, 16; founders adopt advantages of, 132, 142, 152, 156, 175, 180–81; as salvation from nihilism, 199; of the wise, 212
Aristocratic: disregarding of interest as, 75, 82; claims, not in state of nature, 106; minority, not main danger to re-

publics, 143; human nature as, 196; few, control of, 217
Aristotle: and best regime, 15; and *ad hominem* rhetoric, 65; and mixed regime, 104–6, 115; and separation of powers, 122–24; and choice, 129, 133; and elections, 156, 175; and speech, 164; and deliberation, 170; and constitutionalism, 196, 200–207; and end of soul, 217
Artificial, the, 6, 33, 199; Hobbes's sovereign as, 107, 110, 116; in modern science, 132; in ancient science, 202
Artisan, 201–2, 204–5
Assertion, 75, 184, 190, 201, 204; values as mere, 13, 64, 149; of the majority's right to rule, 24–25, 54; of the self, 32–33, 199; of republicanism, for republican form, 143; and media's amplification of, 168; of rights, 184, 186, 197; the people's lack of, 192
Atheism, 23, 79
Authority: vs. private sphere, 41, 102; and Hobbes's critique of all previous, 106; as divine, 111, 144, 179; of judges, 126; Constitution as, 144, 179–80, 210; dependence on national, 171–72; charisma as irregular, 188; Tocqueville as, 209

Bakke case, 85
Beard, Charles, 6, 155, 178
Beginning, the, 170, 204; of Constitution, 6, 128; institutionalists' view of, 8; Rawls's view of, 33; of Glazer, 94; Hobbes's view of, 107, 117; of Spinoza, 110; Filmer's view of, 111; Locke's view of, 112, 117; liberalism's view of, 139; of Dahl, 149
Behavior: 27, 32, 79, 218; formal, 9–13, 193, 195; Reagan as cause of, 39; examined by economists, 43; extra-constitutional causes of, 137; examined by *The Federalist*, 143–45, 147; examined by social scientists, 153, 157–59; and interest, 213
Behavioralists, 1–5, 8, 12–13, 16, 26, 139, 147, 149–52, 162
Bentley, Arthur F., 138, 160

Designed by Glen Burris
Set in Sabon text and Galliard display by Ampersand Publisher Services, Inc.
Printed on 50-lb. Booktext Natural and bound in Holliston Roxite cloth by Bookcrafters